Office 2000

for Busy People

Make Your Work Go Faster with These Speed Techniques

Jump from place to place in a Word 2000 document by clicking headings on the document map, which is a convenient roadmap to all the major headings in a document. (page 73).

Click a shortcut icon to go straight to where you want to go—a file, an Office program, even a site on the Internet. (pages 8-12)

Open files quickly by taking advantage of the tools and buttons in the Open dialog box. (pages 7-8)

Create a file from a template and you get a preformatted file. The layout work is done automatically; all you have to do is enter the text. (page 23)

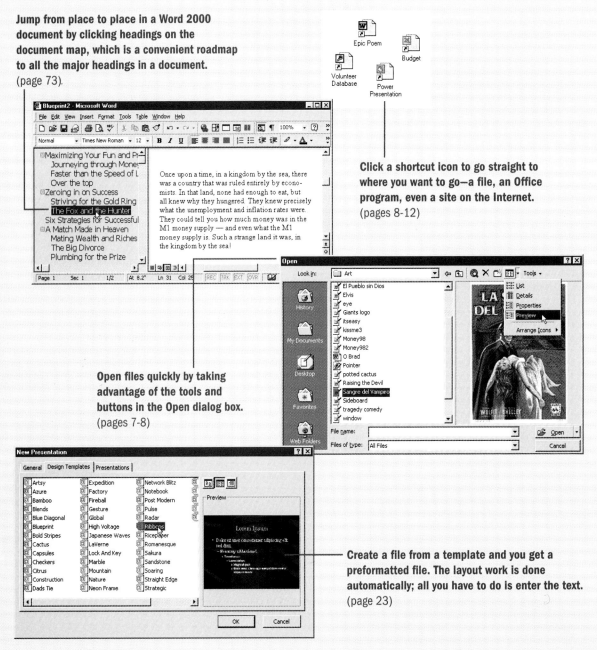

Take Advantage of the Tools and Techniques
That Work Throughout Office 2000

Embellish files with clip art. Office 2000 comes with more than 300 clip art images—and scavenging clip art from Microsoft's Web site is easy
(pages 38-41)

Put some zing in your headings by choosing fonts that will attract your readers' attention. You can also change the color of your text.
(pages 24-26)

Move or change the size of so-called objects—clip art images, text boxes, lines, and shapes. And for a truly elegant effect, make objects overlap on the page.
(pages 41-44)

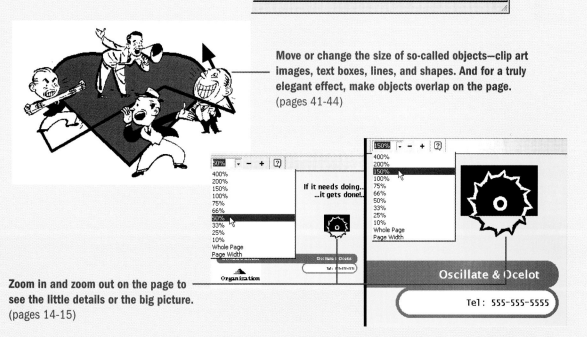

Zoom in and zoom out on the page to see the little details or the big picture.
(pages 14-15)

Express Yourself with Word 2000

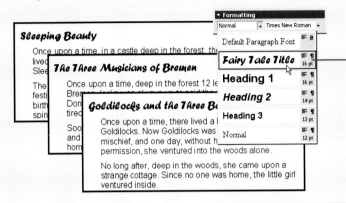

Use styles to ensure that your headings are consistent from page to page. Styles give your documents a professional look. (pages 82-89)

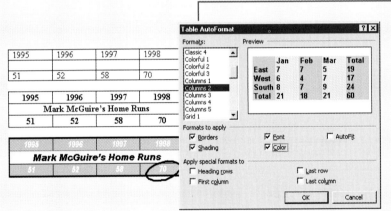

Construct the perfect table by taking advantage of the many commands on the Table menu—or go to the Table AutoFormat dialog box and have Word decorate your table. (pages 89-99)

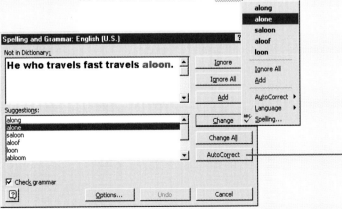

Fear not! Spelling errors in Word 2000 documents are easy to correct. You can even tell Word to "autocorrect" mistakes that you make out of habit. (pages 28-29, 34-35)

Crunch the Numbers with Excel 2000

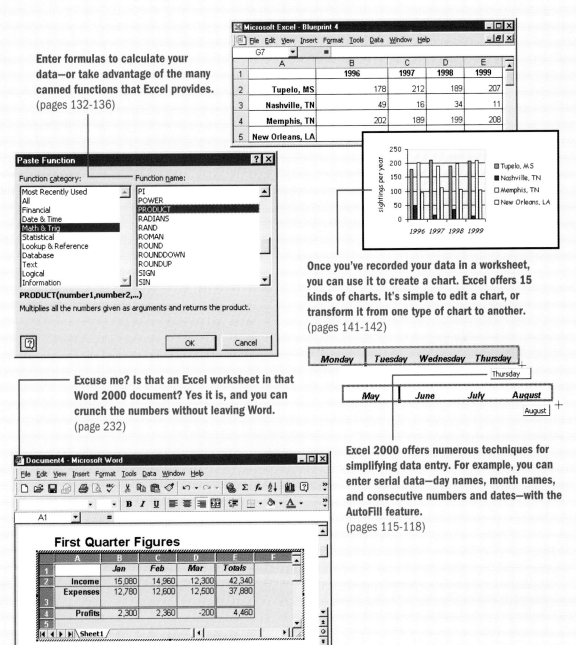

Enter formulas to calculate your data—or take advantage of the many canned functions that Excel provides.
(pages 132-136)

Once you've recorded your data in a worksheet, you can use it to create a chart. Excel offers 15 kinds of charts. It's simple to edit a chart, or transform it from one type of chart to another.
(pages 141-142)

Excuse me? Is that an Excel worksheet in that Word 2000 document? Yes it is, and you can crunch the numbers without leaving Word.
(page 232)

Excel 2000 offers numerous techniques for simplifying data entry. For example, you can enter serial data—day names, month names, and consecutive numbers and dates—with the AutoFill feature.
(pages 115-118)

Organize Your Life with Outlook 2000

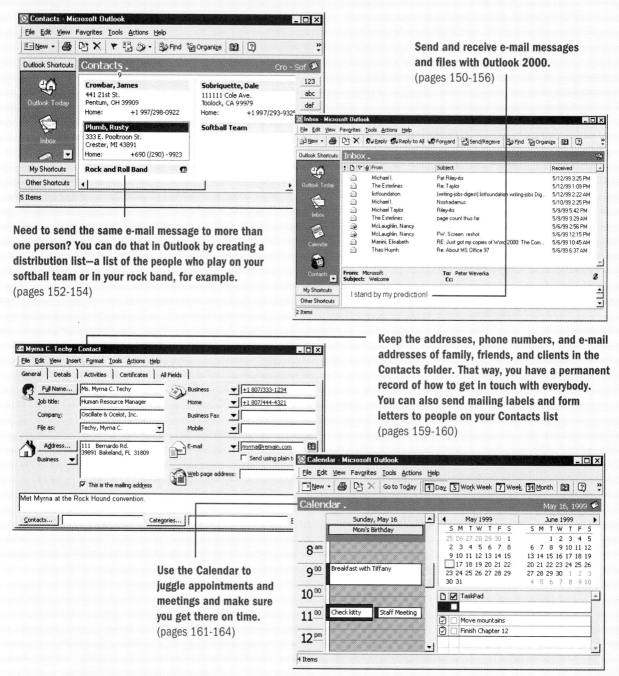

Send and receive e-mail messages and files with Outlook 2000.
(pages 150-156)

Need to send the same e-mail message to more than one person? You can do that in Outlook by creating a distribution list—a list of the people who play on your softball team or in your rock band, for example.
(pages 152-154)

Keep the addresses, phone numbers, and e-mail addresses of family, friends, and clients in the Contacts folder. That way, you have a permanent record of how to get in touch with everybody. You can also send mailing labels and form letters to people on your Contacts list
(pages 159-160)

Use the Calendar to juggle appointments and meetings and make sure you get there on time.
(pages 161-164)

Design Winning Presentations with PowerPoint 2000

You get lots of opportunities to experiment with appearances as you develop a PowerPoint 2000 presentation. To change the look of your slides, simply choose another design template.
(pages 178-180)

The easiest way to impress others with your decorating skills is to plop a WordArt image into an Office file. WordArt looks especially good on PowerPoint slides.
(pages 38-41)

Instead of laboriously entering the text for a slide presentation, get the text from a Word 2000 document. If the presentation is based on a report or white paper that was written in Word, you've got it made.
(pages 233-234)

Keep Track of Important Data with Access 2000

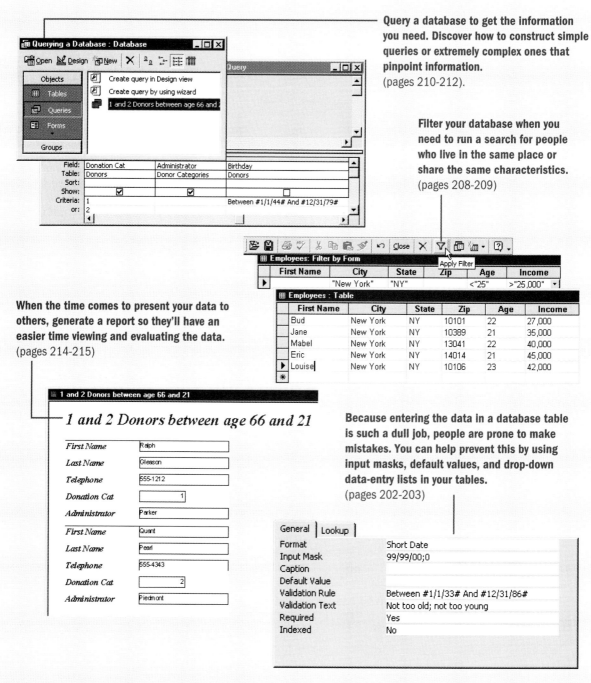

Query a database to get the information you need. Discover how to construct simple queries or extremely complex ones that pinpoint information.
(pages 210-212).

Filter your database when you need to run a search for people who live in the same place or share the same characteristics.
(pages 208-209)

When the time comes to present your data to others, generate a report so they'll have an easier time viewing and evaluating the data.
(pages 214-215)

Because entering the data in a database table is such a dull job, people are prone to make mistakes. You can help prevent this by using input masks, default values, and drop-down data-entry lists in your tables.
(pages 202-203)

1 and 2 Donors between age 66 and 21

First Name	Ralph
Last Name	Gleason
Telephone	555-1212
Donation Cat	1
Administrator	Parker

First Name	Quant
Last Name	Pearl
Telephone	555-4343
Donation Cat	2
Administrator	Piedmont

General | Lookup

Format	Short Date
Input Mask	99/99/00;0
Caption	
Default Value	
Validation Rule	Between #1/1/33# And #12/31/86#
Validation Text	Not too old; not too young
Required	Yes
Indexed	No

Cruise the Internet with Internet Explorer 5

Don't waste time when you're searching for stuff on the Web. Learn how to surf quickly and productively.
(pages 245-249)

Bookmark your favorite Web sites so you can revisit them quickly.
(pages 250-253)

Lost on the Internet? Return to a site you visited before by clicking the Back or History button.
(pages 249-250)

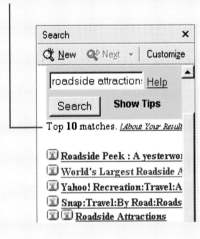

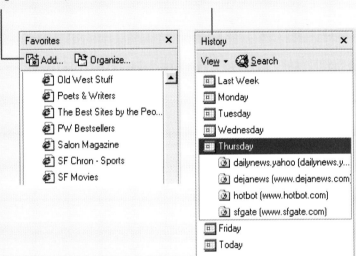

The Internet is a jungle, and sometimes finding your way around is hard. Take advantage of this book's techniques for getting around on the Web with Internet Explorer 5.
(pages 244-256)

It's easy to copy pictures, photos, and text from the Internet.
(pages 258-259)

Create Professional-Looking Publications with Publisher 2000

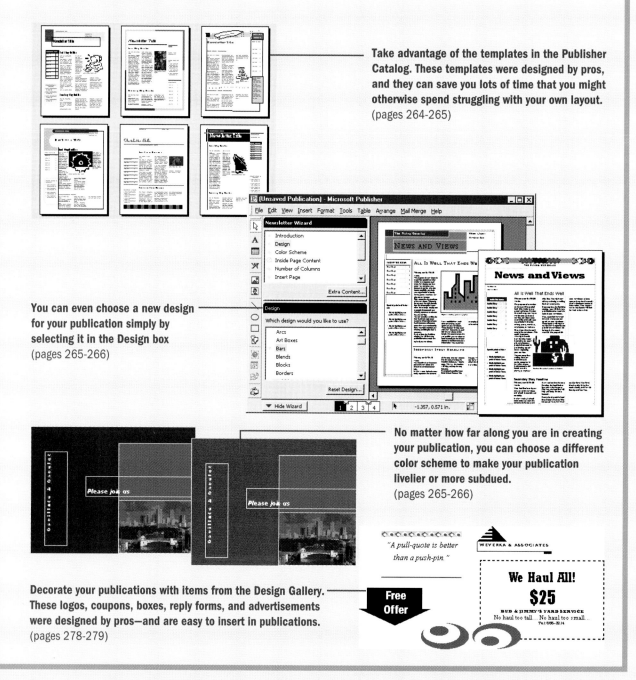

Take advantage of the templates in the Publisher Catalog. These templates were designed by pros, and they can save you lots of time that you might otherwise spend struggling with your own layout. (pages 264-265)

You can even choose a new design for your publication simply by selecting it in the Design box (pages 265-266)

No matter how far along you are in creating your publication, you can choose a different color scheme to make your publication livelier or more subdued. (pages 265-266)

Decorate your publications with items from the Design Gallery. These logos, coupons, boxes, reply forms, and advertisements were designed by pros—and are easy to insert in publications. (pages 278-279)

Office2000

for Busy People

The Book to Use When There's No Time to Lose!

Peter Weverka

OSBORNE

Osborne/**McGraw-Hill**

Berkeley / New York / St. Louis / San Francisco / Auckland / Bogotá
Hamburg / London / Madrid / Mexico City / Milan / Montreal / New Delhi
Panama City / Paris / São Paulo / Singapore / Sydney / Tokyo / Toronto

A Division of The **McGraw·Hill** *Companies*

Osborne/**McGraw-Hill**
2600 Tenth Street
Berkeley, California 94710
U.S.A.

For information on translations or book distributors outside the U.S.A., or to arrange bulk purchase discounts for sales promotions, premiums, or fund-raisers, please contact Osborne/**McGraw-Hill** at the above address.

Office 2000 for Busy People

234567890 DOC DOC 90198765432109

ISBN 0-07-211857-1

Publisher   Brandon A. Nordin
Associate Publisher, Editor-in-Chief   Scott Rogers
Acquisitions Editor   Joanne Cuthbertson
Project Editor   Nancy McLaughlin
Editorial Assistant   Stephane Thomas
Technical Editor   Eric Ray
Copy Editor   Rebecca Pepper
Proofreader, Indexer   Valerie Perry
Graphic Artists   Brian Wells, Beth Young, Robert Hansen
Computer Designers   Gary Corrigan, Roberta Steele
Series Designer   Jil Weil
Cover Design   Damore Johann Design, Inc.
Cover Illustration/Chapter Opening Illustrations   Robert deMichiell

This book was published with Corel VENTURA.

This book is dedicated affectionately to 24th Street between Capp and the St. Francis Fountain & Candy Store.

About the Author . . .

Peter Weverka is the author of *Windows 98 for Busy People, Second Edition, Quicken 99 for Busy People,* and *Word 2000: The Complete Reference.* He has edited 80 computer books on topics ranging from word processing to databases to the Internet. Peter's humorous articles and stories have appeared in *Harper's* and *Exquisite Corpse.*

CONTENTS AT A GLANCE

CONTENTS

Acknowledgments

I am very grateful to everyone at Osborne/McGraw-Hill for their excellent work on this book.

Thanks go especially to acquisitions editor Joanne Cuthbertson, who labored so hard to redesign the Busy People series, and to project editor Nancy McLaughlin, who kept this book in line with the new design specifications. Of course, I would also like to thank Stephane Thomas for making sure that everyone danced in step.

Copy editor Rebecca Pepper scoured the manuscript with aplomb. Technical editor Eric Ray doggedly checked all the instructions for accuracy. Valerie Perry lent her expertise to the index, and she and Patty Mon handled the proofreading with lightning speed and unwavering good humor.

Osborne's Production Department is truly the best in the business, and—as always—they went the extra mile for this book. I am grateful to all of them: designers Jean Butterfield, Gary Corrigan, and Roberta Steele, and illustrators Brian Wells, Beth Young, and Robert Hansen.

I inherited this book from Stephen Nelson, my friend and sometimes co-author. I want to thank Steve for launching me with this book and for writing many helpful instructions on its pages.

Finally, thanks go to my family—Sofia, Henry, and Addie—for accommodating my vampire-like work habits and eerie demeanor at daybreak.

Peter Weverka
San Francisco
July, 1999

Introduction

The book you are holding in your hands is about Office 2000, the most sophisticated grab bag of software programs ever assembled by man or beast. It explains everything that a busy person needs to know to confidently use the programs: Word 2000, Excel 2000, PowerPoint 2000, Outlook 2000, Access 2000, Publisher 2000, and Internet Explorer 5.

Everything that is essential and helpful in Office, everything that might be of use to a busy person, is explained in this book—and explained in such a way that you'll quickly understand how to make Office work at its peak. I don't simply describe here how to use the various features of Office 2000—I tell you how to crack the whip and make Office serve you.

How This Book Differs from Other Books About Office 2000

This book is designed to make learning Office 2000 as easy and comfortable as possible. It is decidedly different from other books about Office, in numerous ways:

SHORTCUT

In Office, there are often two ways to do things—the fast but dicey way and the slow, thorough way. I explain fast-but-dicey techniques in Shortcuts, like this one, which pop up all through the margins of this book.

A TASK-ORIENTED APPROACH Whereas most computer books describe how to use the software, this book explains how to complete a variety of tasks. I assume you've purchased this book because you want to know how to *do* things—set up a worksheet for doing calculations, print form letters, send an e-mail message to a group of people, and/or give a PowerPoint 2000 presentation that runs itself. You've come to the right place. The information here is presented by topic, not according to which menu it is found on. I assume that

TIP

Look for Tips in the margins. They appear throughout the book to offer handy bits of advice that will make you a more effective user of Office 2000.

everyone who reads this book is working under a deadline. In that spirit, the book explains how to get things done, not just what features are available in the Office programs.

INFORMATION THAT'S EASY TO LOOK UP   The editors and I took great pains to make sure that the material in this book is well organized and easy to access. You are invited to turn to a chapter, thumb through the pages, and find out by reading the headings which strategies are available for completing a given task. The descriptive headings help you find information quickly. The bulleted and numbered lists make it simple to follow instructions. The tables make options easier to understand. I want you to be able to look down the pages and quickly find the topics that concern you. You don't have to slog through a morass of commentary to find the information you need in this book.

FAST FORWARDS   Each chapter begins with a handful of Fast Forwards, which are step-by-step, abbreviated instructions for doing things that are explained more fully later on. Each Fast Forward is cross-referenced to pages in the chapter that you can turn to for all the details—but actually, sometimes you might not need the details. For certain topics, the Fast Forwards might teach you all you need to know.

ANNOTATED FIGURES   Most of the figures (not the illustrations) in this book are annotated. They are thoroughly annotated, in fact. A shrewd Office user can simply look at the figures to find out how to complete tasks.

EXPERT ADVICE

Where you see an Expert Advice pointer like this one, be sure to read attentively, because these small boxes offer the kind of advanced tips and techniques that will help you become a savvy, super-productive Office user.

SCREEN SHOTS THAT ARE EASY TO UNDERSTAND   Look closely at the screen shots in this book and you will see that all of them show only what you need to see to understand an Office feature. When instructions refer to one part of the screen, only that part of the screen is shown. In most computer books, you see the entire screen whether you need to see the whole screen or a corner of it. I took great care to make sure that the figures and illustrations in this book serve to help you understand Office and know how to make the best use of the programs and features.

CROSS-REFERENCES   Microsoft has made it easier than ever to trade data across Office programs; most features are linked to other features. In order to complete one task, therefore, you often have to know how to perform another. For that reason, this book is filled to the brim with cross-references. When you need background instructions for a certain task, I refer you by chapter number and heading to the place in the book where you can go to get the information.

Throughout the book, you'll see cross-references in the margins, where it is easy to see and read them.

BLUEPRINTS   The Blueprints at the very front of this book are like previews of coming attractions. While you are waiting for the movie to begin, look at the blueprints. The page numbers tell you where to turn in this book to learn more about a topic that has aroused your curiosity.

A Word About This Book and What It Covers

Thousand-page books have been written about Office 2000. For that matter, thousand-page books have been written about Word 2000, Excel 2000, Outlook 2000, PowerPoint 2000, Access 2000, and Publisher 2000. I've even written one of them: *Word 2000: The Complete Reference* (Osborne McGraw-Hill, 1998). Given that the

DEFINITION
To help you understand Office terminology, Definitions of important terms sometimes appear in the margins of this book.

Office programs are so complex, you may well ask how a single book can cover them completely in only 336 pages.

This book is by no means comprehensive. It does, however, describe all the fundamentals and give you enough instruction so that you can get going on even the complicated things. What's more, many of the techniques presented here are useful no matter which Office program you are working in. Chapters 1 and 2 describe the techniques you can use in all the Office programs. Be sure to read those chapters—you'll find them valuable no matter where you go in Office.

Besides the fundamentals, this book explains all the tasks that I consider especially useful in Office. And it presents all the shortcuts and tricks that I've learned during my many years of daring experimentation. You are hereby invited to skim the table of contents or simply page through the book—you'll almost certainly find instructions for doing things that you didn't know you could do with Office. With a little imagination (and a small amount of courage), you can find many uses for Office; it's a very powerful program. And don't be afraid to venture into Access, Publisher, or one of the other little-used Office programs. As you'll soon find out, those programs aren't as complicated as many people think.

CAUTION

When I describe a task that you might regret doing later—or even one that you should think carefully about before actually doing, I do so in a Caution.

I Wouldn't Mind Hearing from You!

If you have a comment about this book—or a question about Office—please write me an e-mail message! I am currently being held hostage at **Peter_Weverka@msn.com**. I do ask that you put the words "Office 2000 Busy People" in the subject line of the message so I know what the message is about. I will do my best to reply—notwithstanding my busy schedule and natural inclination to be lazy.

CHAPTER 1

Stuff to Do Once to Make Your Life Easier

INCLUDES

- Devising strategies for storing your work on disk
- Using the tools in the Open and Save As dialog boxes
- Opening files quickly
- Creating shortcuts so you can open Office 2000 programs and files quickly
- Manipulating the toolbars
- Minimizing, maximizing, and changing the size of windows
- Splitting windows and opening a second window on a file
- Choosing default font and margin settings in Word 2000

Take Advantage of the Tools in the Open Dialog Box ➡ pp. 5–7

- Use the drop-down Look In menu to look for folders or documents on a different drive or disk.
- Click the Up One Level button to see the contents of the folder one level above the one you are looking at.
- Use the drop-down Views menu to display folder contents differently.
- Double-click a folder to see its contents.
- Click the Favorites button to see the contents of the Favorites folder.

Open Files Quickly ➡ pp. 7–8

- Click the Start button, choose Documents, and click the name of one of the last 15 files you opened to open it again.
- Click the Start button, choose Favorites, and click a folder name to see the folder's contents. Then double-click a file to open it.
- Open the File menu and click a filename at the bottom of the menu to open the file.

Create Shortcut Icons for the Files You Use Most Often ➡ pp. 8–12

- In the Open dialog box, find the folder or file for which you want to create a shortcut. Then click the Tools button and choose Add to Favorites to put a shortcut to the folder or file in the Favorites folder.
- In the Open dialog box, right-click the file, choose Send To from the shortcut menu, and choose Desktop As Shortcut from the submenu.

Hide or Display a Toolbar ➡ p. 13

- Choose View | Toolbars and click the name of the toolbar you want to hide or display.
- Right-click a toolbar or the menu bar and click the name of the toolbar you want to hide or display.

Zoom In and Zoom Out ➥ pp. 14–15

- Click in the Zoom box, enter a percentage, and press the ENTER key.
- Click the Zoom down arrow next to the Zoom box and choose a percentage setting from the Zoom menu.

Move and Resize Windows Onscreen ➥ pp.15–17

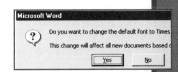

- Click the Minimize button to collapse the window and make it disappear.
- Click the Restore button to shrink the window and the Maximize button to make it fill the screen.
- Drag a window's title bar to move it around on the screen.
- Move the mouse pointer over a border of a window and start dragging to change the window's size.

Split a Document Window
So You Can Be Two Places at Once ➥ p. 17

- Choose Window | Split and click in the middle of the screen.
- Move the mouse pointer to the top of the vertical scroll bar. When you see the pointer change into a two-headed arrow, click and drag downward.

Choose a Default Font
for Your Word Documents ➥ p. 18

1. Choose Format | Font to open the Font dialog box.
2. In the Font list, choose the font that you use most often.
3. In the Size list, choose a font size you prefer to work in.
4. Click the Default button and click Yes when Word asks if you really want to change default fonts.

In every computer program, you can put your best foot forward by learning to do three or four important things right from the start. Because Office 2000 comprises several programs, you can get off to a good start by learning a dozen or so things, not three or four. This chapter explains the dozen things you can do and learn in Office to make the hours you spend in front of your computer more rewarding and enjoyable. You'll learn strategies for storing your work on disk, how to find your way around the Open and Save As dialog boxes, and how to create shortcuts so you can open Office programs and files quickly. This chapter explains how to handle toolbars and zoom in and out to spare your eyes from getting overworked. You will also find advice here for choosing default fonts and page layouts in Word 2000.

Stay Organized: Create Folders for Your Files

Many people mistakenly believe that files created with a program have to be stored on disk deep in the folder hierarchy where the program is located. Nothing could be further from the truth. You can store the files that you create yourself anywhere you want on your computer. And you should store them in a convenient place where you can find them easily.

EXPERT ADVICE

Create new folders with either of these Windows utility programs: Windows Explorer or My Computer. In those programs, click the drive or folder in which the new folder will be located, and choose File | New | Folder. Then type a name and press ENTER. (See *Windows 98 for Busy People, Second Edition* (Osborne McGraw-Hill, 1999) for more information about creating and managing folders.)

This user keeps all her documents in a folder at the top of the C drive called "AAA My Work":

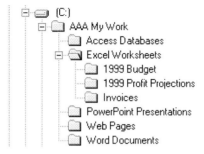

The letters *AAA* ensure that the folder will be the first on the C drive and, therefore, will be easy to find. Devise a strategy like this one for storing your work on disk so you can find files quickly when you want to open, move, copy, or delete them.

When you begin a new project, create a folder or perhaps a folder and subfolders to store the files you will create. While you're at it, name the folder after the project. By keeping files that pertain to the same project in the same place, you make it easier to find and open files.

Learn How to Get Around in the Open and Save As Dialog Boxes

When you choose File | Open, press CTRL-O, or click the Open button to open a file, you see the dialog box shown in Figure 1.1. This dialog box offers many tools for locating a file you want to open. By learning to use the tools, you can save a lot of time opening files—and also storing files when you save them for the first time. The tools in the Open dialog box are also found in the Save As dialog box that appears the first time you save a file.

See "Saving and Naming Files" in Chapter 2 to learn the specifics of saving a new file.

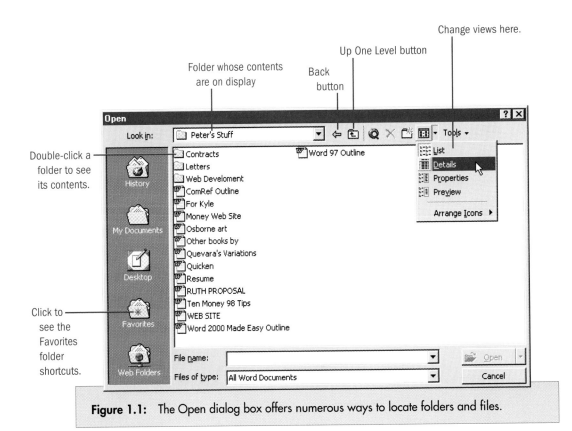

Figure 1.1:   The Open dialog box offers numerous ways to locate folders and files.

The next part of this chapter, "Learn Techniques for Opening Files Quickly," explains how to open a file without visiting the Open dialog box.

Use these tools in the Open and Save As dialog boxes to locate folders and files:

- **Look In menu**   Open this menu to look for folders on a different drive or disk (3½ Floppy [A:] or [C:], for example).
- **Back button**   Click this button to revisit folders you saw before in the course of your search. In other words, click this button to backtrack.
- **Up One Level button**   Click this button to move up the folder hierarchy and see the contents of the folder one level above the one you are looking at.

- **Views menu**   Click this button when you want to display folder contents differently in the Open dialog box. Click the down arrow and select a new view (see Figure 1.1).
- **Folders**   Double-click a folder to see its contents in the Open dialog box. For example, double-clicking the Contracts folder in Figure 1.1 displays the subfolders and files in that folder.
- **History button**   Click this button to see an exhaustive list of the last hundred or so files you opened with Office programs. Double-click a file to open it.
- **My Documents button**   Click this button to see the contents of the My Documents folder, the default folder for storing files. Double-click a file to open it.
- **Favorites**   Click this button to see the shortcuts in the Shortcuts folder. By double-clicking a shortcut, you can open a folder or file directly. (See "Create the Office Shortcut Icons You Need" later in this chapter.)

TIP
Details view shows when each file was last saved; Preview view shows a thumbnail picture of what is in the file.

Learn Techniques for Opening Files Quickly

The preceding section of this chapter explained how to open files from the Open dialog box, but if you can use one of these techniques to open a file without fooling with the Open dialog box, go for it!

EXPERT ADVICE

One way to open files quickly is to keep the documents on which you are currently working in the My Documents folder. That way, all you have to do to open a document is choose File | Open, click the My Documents button in the Open dialog box to see the contents of the My Documents folder, and double-click a document name. When you finish with a document and don't need to open it often, move it from the My Documents folder to a permanent home.

Here are the fast ways to open a file:

- **Windows Documents menu**   The Windows Documents menu lists the last 15 files you opened. If the file you want to open is one of the lucky 15, click the Start button, choose Documents, and click the name of the file to open it.

- **Favorites folder**   Put shortcuts to the files and folders you use often in the Favorites folder. That way, you can get to your favorite files and folders quickly by clicking the Start button, choosing Favorites, and choosing a folder or file from the Favorites menu. If you choose a folder, you see its contents in a My Computer window. From there, you can double-click a file to open it. (See "Create the Office Shortcut Icons You Need," the next part of this chapter, to learn how to create a shortcut to a folder or file.)

- **File menu**   No matter which Office program you are working in, the names of the last four files you opened are listed on the bottom of the File menu. Perhaps the file you want to open is listed there. To find out, open the File menu. Then click a filename if indeed you see the file you want to open.

```
1 View Data.xls
2 Tour.xls
3 \Zudstuff\Office for...\Editing a Chart.xls
4 \Zudstuff\Office f...\Elvis Worksheet.xls
5 \Zudstuff\Offi...\1Speed Techniques.xls
6 \Zudstuff\Office fo...\Elvis Sightings.xls
```

You can make more than four filenames appear at the bottom of the File menu. To do so, choose Tools | Options and click the General tab in the Options dialog box. Then enter a number larger than 4 in the Recently Used File List text box.

Create the Office Shortcut Icons You Need

Word

The fastest way to open a file or an Office 2000 program is to double-click its *shortcut icon*. Shortcut icons save you the trouble of negotiating the Open dialog box to open a file or fooling with menus to start a program. One or two shortcut icons are probably on your desktop already. To find one, look for an icon with an arrow in the lower-left corner. These pages explain how to put a shortcut to an Office program on the desktop, and how to put a shortcut to a file on the desktop or in the Favorites folder.

Creating Shortcut Icons for the Windows Desktop

Put a shortcut icon on the desktop for the Office programs you use often. That way, you can simply double-click the shortcut icon to start your favorite program. Users running Windows 98 can create a shortcut icon simply by right-clicking a program name on a menu; users of Windows 95 have to burrow into the files on their computers to create a shortcut icon. Read on.

DEFINITION

Desktop: Catch-all name for the part of the screen where all the work is done. The desktop is the first thing you see when you start your computer. When you open a new program, it appears in a window on the desktop.

Word Outlook Excel PowerPoint Access

Creating Shortcut Icons for Programs in Windows 98

Figure 1.2 shows you how to create a shortcut icon for your favorite Office program in Windows 98.

EXPERT ADVICE

If you are especially fond of a program, you can put its shortcut icon on the Quick Launch toolbar (see Figure 1.2). To do so, hold down the CTRL key and drag the shortcut icon onto the Quick Launch toolbar to copy it there. Wherever your work takes you, you can see the Quick Launch toolbar and click its shortcut icons to open programs.

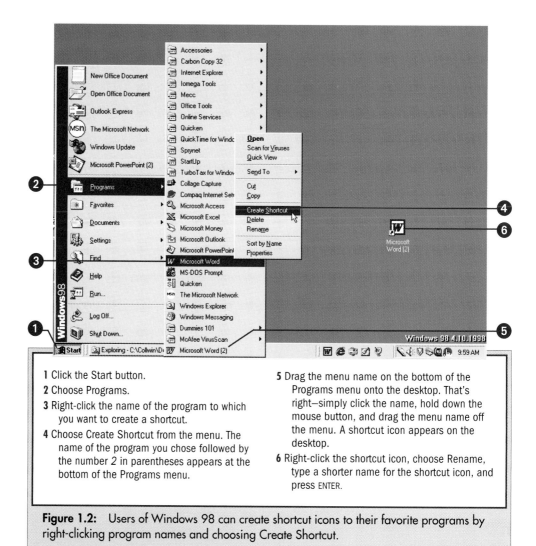

1 Click the Start button.

2 Choose Programs.

3 Right-click the name of the program to which you want to create a shortcut.

4 Choose Create Shortcut from the menu. The name of the program you chose followed by the number *2* in parentheses appears at the bottom of the Programs menu.

5 Drag the menu name on the bottom of the Programs menu onto the desktop. That's right—simply click the name, hold down the mouse button, and drag the menu name off the menu. A shortcut icon appears on the desktop.

6 Right-click the shortcut icon, choose Rename, type a shorter name for the shortcut icon, and press ENTER.

Figure 1.2: Users of Windows 98 can create shortcut icons to their favorite programs by right-clicking program names and choosing Create Shortcut.

Creating Shortcut Icons for Programs in Windows 95

Follow these steps to create a shortcut icon for an Office program if your machine runs Windows 95:

1. Start Windows Explorer or My Computer, and open the C:\Program Files\Microsoft Office\Office folder.

2. Choose View | Details to switch to Details view.

3. Find the program file of the program to which you want to create a shortcut. The program filenames are as follows: msaccess (Access), excel (Excel), outlook (Outlook), powerpnt (PowerPoint), and winword (Word). Filenames are in alphabetical order.

   Make sure you locate the application file, not another file by the same name. For example, there are two winword files in the Office folder, but only one is an application file. In Details view, you can tell which is which by glancing at the Type column, which lists file types.

4. Right-click the program file and choose Create Shortcut. A shortcut icon and the words "Shortcut to *program filename*" appear at the end of the file list. Scroll to the end of the file list to see it, if necessary

5. Drag the shortcut icon out of the window and onto the desktop. If necessary, click the Restore button in the upper-right corner of the window to shrink the Windows Explorer or My Computer window onscreen before you start dragging.

6. Right-click the shortcut icon, choose Rename, type a descriptive name, and press the ENTER key.

Creating Shortcut Icons for Files and Folders

As I explained earlier in this chapter, you can save a lot of time opening files by putting shortcuts to folders and files in the Favorites folder. All you have to do to see the contents of the Favorites folder is click the Favorites button in the Open dialog box (see Figure 1.1) or click the Start button and choose Favorites. These pages explain how to drop a shortcut icon into the Favorites folder and also how to put shortcut icons to oft-used files on the Windows desktop.

CAUTION

Unless a file is extremely important, don't put a shortcut to it in the Favorites folder. Instead, create a shortcut to the folder in which the file is located. If you load up the Favorites folder with shortcuts to files, you will soon have trouble finding anything in it, files or otherwise, because the Favorites folder will get too crowded.

TIP

To remove a shortcut from the Favorites folder, right-click it and choose Delete.

Creating Shortcuts for the Favorites Folder

The Open dialog box offers a special command for creating Favorites folder shortcuts. Follow the steps in Figure 1.3 to put a shortcut to a folder or document in the Favorites folder.

Putting Shortcuts to Files on the Desktop

You can create shortcuts to especially important files and place the shortcuts on the desktop. That way, all you have to do is double-click an icon to open a file and get down to work. To create a shortcut icon for the desktop, choose File | Open and find the file you want to create a shortcut to in the Open dialog box. Then right-click the file, choose Send To from the shortcut menu, and choose Desktop As Shortcut from the submenu. Click Cancel to close the Open dialog box.

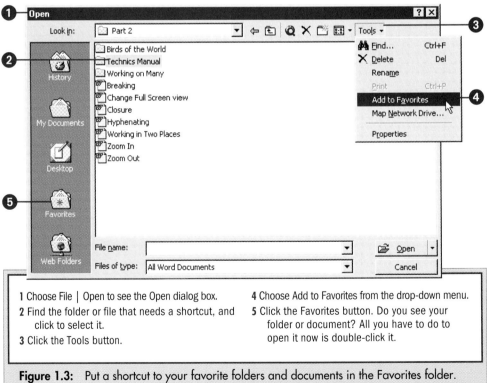

1 Choose File | Open to see the Open dialog box.
2 Find the folder or file that needs a shortcut, and click to select it.
3 Click the Tools button.
4 Choose Add to Favorites from the drop-down menu.
5 Click the Favorites button. Do you see your folder or document? All you have to do to open it now is double-click it.

Figure 1.3: Put a shortcut to your favorite folders and documents in the Favorites folder. That way, you can open a document or see the contents of a folder merely by clicking the Favorites button in the Open dialog box and double-clicking a shortcut icon.

Learn How to Handle the Toolbars

A *toolbar* is an assortment of buttons for performing tasks. Most Office 2000 programs offer a Standard toolbar, a Formatting toolbar, and many other toolbars besides. Perhaps more important than knowing what all the toolbars are, however, is knowing how to display and remove them. Toolbars take up valuable space onscreen. To display or hide a toolbar:

- Choose View | Toolbars and click the name of the toolbar on the submenu.
- Right-click a toolbar or the menu bar and select the name of the toolbar from the shortcut menu, as shown in Figure 1.4.

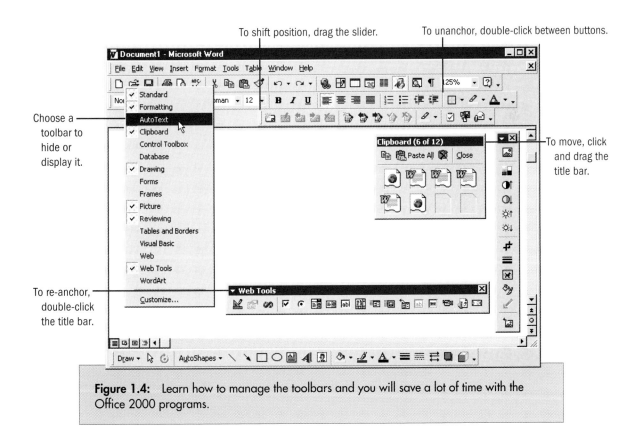

Figure 1.4: Learn how to manage the toolbars and you will save a lot of time with the Office 2000 programs.

EXPERT ADVICE

To find out what a button on a toolbar does, gently slide the mouse pointer over the button. You see the button's name, which gives some idea of its purpose. You can also press SHIFT-F1 (or choose Help | What's This?) and click a button to see the button's name and a description of what it does.

Toolbars are "anchored" to the top or bottom of the screen when you display them. However, as Figure 1.4 shows, you can move a toolbar away from the top or bottom of the screen. You can change its shape, too. If you want to move a toolbar out of the way, but still be able to click its buttons, simply tuck it into a corner of the screen. Here are instructions for manipulating toolbars:

- **Unanchoring**   To move a toolbar away from its home port at the top or bottom of the screen, carefully move the pointer over a line between two buttons and double-click. The toolbar appears in the middle of the screen and you can see its *title bar,* which is the stripe along the top that shows you the toolbar's name.

- **Shifting**   On the left side of every toolbar is a slider. Drag the slider to move an anchored toolbar from side to side.

- **Moving**   Drag the title bar to move a toolbar around onscreen.

- **Changing shape**   Gently move the mouse pointer over the perimeter of the toolbar. When you see the double arrow, click and drag.

- **Re-anchoring**   Double-click the title bar to move a toolbar back to its home port at the top or bottom of the screen.

Learn to Zoom In and Zoom Out

The eye as nature made it is not meant to stare at a computer screen all day. To make the screen easier to look at, get in the habit of zooming. By *zooming,* you can make the screen look larger when you want to do precision work or smaller when you want to see the big

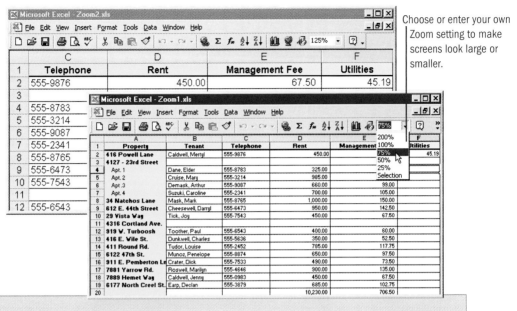

Choose or enter your own Zoom setting to make screens look large or smaller.

Figure 1.5: Depending on the kind of work you want to do, zooming in or zooming out can help you do it faster and better.

picture. As shown in Figure 1.5, the Office 2000 programs offer a special box on the Standard toolbar for zooming. To zoom in or out:

- Click the down arrow next to the Zoom box to open the Zoom menu, and then choose a percentage setting.
- Click in the Zoom box, enter a percentage of your own, and press the ENTER key.

Learn How to Handle Windows

Windows are so important that Microsoft named an operating system after them. If you can learn to take advantage of the commands that pertain to windows, you can make your work go much, much faster. These pages explain how to minimize and maximize windows, arrange windows onscreen, move windows, change the size of windows, split a window, and open a second window on the same file. Take a deep breath and read on.

Minimizing, Maximizing, and Closing Windows

When you open a program, it appears in its own window. Usually the window fills the entire screen, but you can change that by *minimizing* the window. And when you want the window to fill the screen again, you can *maximize* the window. This magic is accomplished with the three square buttons in the upper-right corner of every window—the Minimize, Restore (or Maximize), and Close buttons. Clicking these buttons is the cleanest and surest way to change the size of or close a window:

- **Minimize button**   Collapses the window and makes it disappear. Clicking this button by no means closes the program. To see a program window after it has been minimized, click its button on the Taskbar.

- **Restore button**   Shrinks a window to the size it was before you maximized it last time. After you click the Restore button, its name (and its appearance) changes, and it becomes the Maximize button. You can also double-click the title bar to restore a window.

- **Maximize button**   Enlarges a window to full-screen size. After you click the Maximize button, its name (and appearance) changes, and it becomes the Restore button. You can also double-click the title bar to maximize a window.

- **Close button**   Exits the program.

TIP
Drag a corner of a window to change its size but keep its proportions the same.

Changing the Size and Location of a Window

Sometimes minimizing and maximizing windows is not enough, and you have to change a window's size and position on your own. Use these techniques to move and change the size of windows:

- **Changing a window's size**   Move the mouse pointer over a border of the window and start dragging when the pointer changes into a double-headed arrow. The bare outlines of a new window show how large the window will be when you release the mouse button.

- **Moving a window**   Click the window's title bar and start dragging. The bare outlines of a window appear. When the window outline is where you want the window to be, release the mouse button.

Splitting a Document Window to Work in Two Sections at Once

As Figure 1.6 shows, you can work in two parts of the same file at the same time by splitting a window. To split a window, either choose Window | Split and click in the middle of the screen or gently move the mouse pointer to the top of the vertical scroll bar, click when you see the double-headed arrow, and drag downward. Scroll bars appear in both halves of the screen so you can move around in the bottom or top half.

When you no longer need the split-window arrangement, either double-click the division mark between the two window halves or choose Window | Remove Split to unsplit the screen.

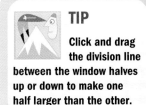

TIP

Click and drag the division line between the window halves up or down to make one half larger than the other.

	A	B	C	D	E	F
1	**Tenant**	**Telephone**	**Amount**	**Premium**	**Acct**	**Deductible**
2	Caldwell, Jenny	555-9876	450.00	67.50	1	100
3	Caldwell, Mertyl	555-1913	350.00	47.19	3	250
4	Cheesewell, Darryl	555-8783	325.00	48.75	2	150
5	Crater, Dick	555-3214	985.00	147.75	2	200
35	Munoz, Penelope	555-6543	400.00	60.00	2	100
36	Roswell, Marilyn	555-5636	350.00	52.50	3	300
37	Suzuki, Caroline	555-2452	785.00	117.75	1	200
38	Tick, Joy	555-8874	650.00	97.50	3	100
39	Toother, Paul	555-7533	490.00	73.50	1	300
40	Tudor, Louise	555-4646	900.00	135.00	2	100

Microsoft Excel - Splitting window.xls

File Edit View Insert Format Tools Data Window Help

Figure 1.6: Choose Window | Split to split a window in half and work in two different parts of the same file.

CAUTION

The Close Window button is located below the Close button. Make sure you don't click the Close button, as doing so closes the program, not the second window.

Opening a Second Window on the File You're Working With

Another way to be in two (or three or four) places at once in a file is to choose Window | New Window. A second window opens; it will be named after the first, but with a *2* after its name. You can move wherever you please in the second window—and you can create several new windows, if you need them. To move from one window to another, open the Window menu and choose from among their names, which will be listed at the bottom. Editorial changes made in any of the windows you create are made to the file; keep in mind that you're working on one file, not two, although it might not seem so. To close either window, click its Close Window button (the × in the upper-right corner).

Choose Your Default Font and Margin Settings

In Chapter 2, "Changing Fonts, Font Sizes, and Text Color" explains what fonts are. See "Opening a New File" in the same chapter to learn the difference between the Normal template and the other templates.

What's your favorite font? What are your favorite margin settings? Instead of choosing your favorites whenever you open a new Word 2000 document, you can make your favorite font and margin settings part of the Normal template, the one that is in effect when you press CTRL-N or click the New Blank Document button to create a new document. That way, your settings are in effect from the get-go and you don't have to change them when you start a new document.

Follow these steps to choose a default font and default margin settings for Word documents:

Default...

- **Font** Choose Format | Font and choose your favorite font and font size in the Font dialog box. Then click the Default button. A dialog box asks whether you really want to make the change. Click Yes.

- **Margin settings** Choose File | Page Setup and, if necessary, click the Margins tab in the Page Setup dialog box. Change the margin measurements (see "Setting the Margins" in Chapter 2 if you need help), and click the Default button. Then click Yes in the dialog box that asks if you really want to change the margin settings.

Tools You Can Use Throughout Office

INCLUDES

- Creating and saving files
- Changing the appearance of text and data
- Techniques for editing faster
- Copying and moving data
- Laying out pages
- Spell-checking your work
- Finding and replacing data
- Decorating files with clip art and WordArt
- Changing the size, shape, and location of objects
- Printing your work

Change the Appearance of Text ➡ pp. 24–26

- Click the Bold, Italic, or Underline button (or press CTRL-B, CTRL-I, or CTRL-U) to boldface, italicize, or underline text.
- Click the down arrow to open the drop-down Font menu and choose a new font; click the down arrow to open the Font Size menu and choose a point size for text.
- Click the down arrow to open the drop-down Font Color menu, and click a color to change the color of text.

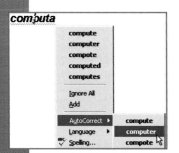

Take Advantage of These Editing Commands ➡ pp. 27–29

- Click the Undo button to correct editing mistakes.
- Press F4 or choose Edit | Repeat to repeat the most recent command you gave.
- Right-click a word you misspell often, choose AutoCorrect from the shortcut menu, and choose the correct spelling of the word to tell Office to correct the word automatically.

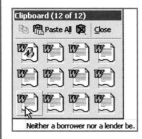

Copy or Move Data from One Place to Another ➡ pp. 29–32

1. Select the data you want to move or copy.
2. To move the data, choose Edit | Cut (or press CTRL-X); to copy the data, choose Edit | Copy (or press CTRL-C).
3. Click where you want to move or copy the data, and either choose Edit | Paste (or press CTRL-V), or display the Clipboard toolbar and click the item you want to paste.

Choose Margin Settings and Page Layouts ➡ pp.32–34

1. Choose File | Page Setup to open the Page Setup dialog box.
2. On the Margins tab, set the margins.
3. On the Page (or Paper Size) tab, choose the Portrait or Landscape option and choose a paper size.

Spell-Check Your Work ➥ pp. 34–35

- Right-click a misspelled word and choose its correct spelling from the shortcut menu.
- Press F7 or choose Tools | Spelling. In the Spelling dialog box, click the correct spelling and then click the Change button.

Find Stray Data in a File ➥ pp. 36–37

1. Press CTRL-F or choose Edit | Find to open the Find dialog box.
2. In the Find What text box, enter the data you want to find.
3. Click the Find Next button.

Insert a Clip Art Image into a File ➥ pp. 38–41

1. Choose Insert | Picture | Clip Art to open the Insert ClipArt dialog box.
2. Either type a search word and press ENTER or click a category name.
3. Select an image and click the Insert Clip button.

Print Your Work ➥ p. 45

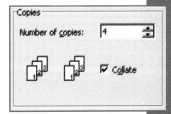

- Click the Print button to print the entire file.
- Choose File | Print (or press CTRL-P) to open the Print dialog box; under Print Range, choose which part of the file to print; in the Number of Copies text box, enter the number of copies to print; click OK.

Welcome to the longest chapter in this book—but don't be discouraged. It's long because it describes the many tools that you can use throughout Office 2000. Learn to use the tools described here and you will feel right at home no matter where you go in Office—to Word 2000, Excel 2000, Outlook 2000, PowerPoint 2000, Access 2000, or Publisher 2000.

This chapter explains how to save, name, and open files, as well as create a file with a template or wizard. You'll learn how to enter and format text, copy and move data, and lay out pages. This chapter also presents some tried-and-true techniques for doing repetitive tasks quickly. You'll find out how to include clip art in your work, check your spelling, print your work, and find and replace text. Better fasten your seatbelt before you undertake this chapter.

Opening a New File

When you want to start a new file in an Office 2000 program, you can either create a generic file or create the file from a template. A *template* is a set of formats. When you create a file with a template, your file is laid out and decorated for you. All you have to do is enter the text or data. Following are instructions for creating a new file from scratch and creating a new file from a template.

Creating a new database file in Access is more complicated than simply choosing File | New. See "Creating a New Database File" in Chapter 9.

Creating a Generic File

A *generic file* is a bare-bones file with hardly any formatting. Generic files are usually easier to work with than files made from templates. To create a generic file:

- Click the New button, the leftmost button on the Standard toolbar.
- Press CTRL-N.

Creating a File from a Template

To create a preformatted file from a template, follow the steps in
Figure 2.1.

Some template files come with representative text that you have to
replace with text of your own. Word offers a peculiar kind of template
called a *wizard*. A wizard is similar to a template in that you also get a
laid-out, formatted document. To create a document with a wizard,
however, you answer questions in dialog boxes about how you want to
lay out the document before Word creates it.

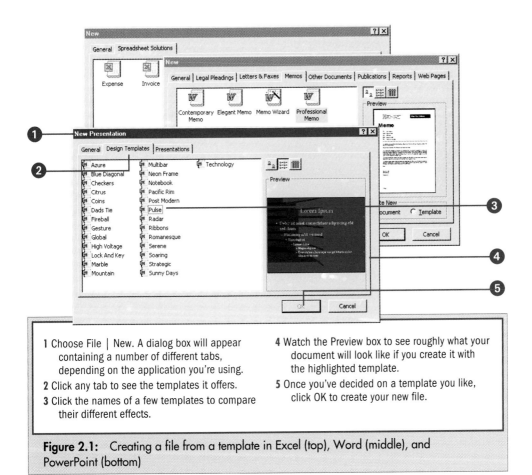

1 Choose File | New. A dialog box will appear
  containing a number of different tabs,
  depending on the application you're using.

2 Click any tab to see the templates it offers.

3 Click the names of a few templates to compare
  their different effects.

4 Watch the Preview box to see roughly what your
  document will look like if you create it with
  the highlighted template.

5 Once you've decided on a template you like,
  click OK to create your new file.

Figure 2.1: Creating a file from a template in Excel (top), Word (middle), and
PowerPoint (bottom)

Saving and Naming Files

When you work on a file, save it from time to time. To save a file, click the Save button, press CTRL-S, or choose File | Save. Until you save a file, the work you did since the last time you saved it is stored in your computer's memory, not on the hard disk. But when you save a file the work is transferred to the hard disk and stored safely. Get in the habit of saving files every few minutes so you don't lose your work if your computer fails or the power goes out.

In Chapter 1, "Learn How to Get Around in the Open and Save As Dialog Boxes" explains how to locate a folder in the Save As dialog box.

The first time you save a file, you see the Save As dialog box. This dialog box asks which folder to store the file in and what to name it. Make sure that the name of the folder you want to store your file in appears in the Save In text box. Enter a name for your file in the File Name text box. Filenames can be 255 characters long and can include blank spaces and all characters and numbers except these punctuation symbols: / ? : * " < > |.

Entering and Formatting Text

To enter text, wiggle your fingers over the keyboard. You can press the DELETE key to erase characters to the right of the cursor and the BACKSPACE key to erase characters to the cursor's left. You probably knew that already. Read on to find out how to boldface, italicize, and underline text, change fonts, and change the color of text. You will also find instructions here for aligning text.

Boldfacing, Italicizing, and Underlining Text

B
I
<u>U</u>

Wherever you travel in Office 2000, you will find three buttons on the Formatting toolbar for boldfacing, italicizing, and underlining text. Click the Bold, Italic, or Underline button (or press CTRL-B, CTRL-I, or CTRL-U) and start typing to do the following to text:

- **Boldface it: Boldface text to make it stand out on the page.**
- *Italicize it: Italics show emphasis and are also used on foreign words such as voilà.*
- <u>Underline it: Underlines highlight important words and text.</u>

To boldface, italicize, and underline text that you have already typed, click and drag over the text to select it and then click a button or press a keyboard shortcut. By the way, you can boldface, italicize, and underline text by clicking a combination of buttons. Word offers many more text effects, including shadow, small caps, and shading. Choose Format | Font to try them out.

Changing Fonts, Font Sizes, and Text Color

Also on the Formatting toolbar in all the Office programs are the drop-down Font and Font Size menus. A *font* is a typeface design. Use the Font and Font Size menus to change the appearance and size of text. Font sizes are measured in *points*; a point is 1/72 of an inch. The larger the point size, the larger the letters. You can change the color of text by opening the drop-down Font Color menu, which is also located on the Formatting toolbar. (See Figure 2.2.)

Select the text or place the cursor where you want the font, font size, or color of text to change, and follow these steps:

- **Change the font**   Click the down arrow to open the drop-down Font menu and choose a new font, as shown in

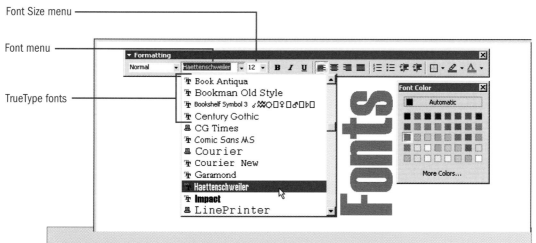

Figure 2.2:   The Formatting toolbar offers commands for changing the fonts, type sizes, and color of your text.

Figure 2.2. Font names on the menu show what the fonts look like. You may have to scroll to the bottom of the menu to find a font.

- **Change the font size** Either click the down arrow to open the Font Size menu and choose a point size, or click in the Font Size box, enter a point size, and press the ENTER key.

- **Change the color of text** Click the down arrow to open the drop-down Font Color menu, and click a color to select it, as shown in Figure 2.2. Choose Automatic to remove color from text.

Aligning and Justifying Text

To change the alignment of text in a paragraph, worksheet cell, database cell, or PowerPoint slide, select the text and click a button on the Formatting toolbar. Table 2.1 shows you the buttons and explains how each one aligns text.

Button	Name	Keyboard Shortcut	How Text Is Aligned
≣	Align Left	CTRL-L	Lined up against the left margin or the left side of the cell.
≣	Center	CTRL-E	Centered between the margins or in the middle of the cell.
≣	Align Right	CTRL-R	Lined up against the right margin or the right side of the cell.
≣	Justify*	CTRL-J	Stretched so it lines up against both margins.

*In Word 2000 only

Table 2.1: Buttons for Aligning Text in Office Programs

Tools for Editing Faster

Throughout the Office 2000 programs you will find the same tools for editing faster: the Undo command, the Repeat command, and the AutoCorrect mechanism. Learn to use these tools and you will be able to finish your work faster, leave the office early, and take the slow, scenic route home instead of the frenzied, unpleasant route.

The Undo Command for Fixing Errors

Suppose you make a mistake and notice it right away. To fix the mistake, all you have to do is click the Undo button on the Standard toolbar (or choose Edit | Undo). What's more, the Undo command "remembers" the last 99 editorial changes you made. To undo an error you made some time ago, click the down arrow to open the Undo menu, scroll through the menu, and click the command or text entry you regret making. Be careful, however, because undoing an error you made some time ago also undoes the actions on the Undo menu above the action you want to undo.

Next to the Undo button is a button called Redo. Click it to reverse your most recent Undo command. The Redo menu also offers a drop-down menu. Click the Redo button or make a choice from its menu to redo your undos, if you get my drift.

The Repeat Command for Doing It Faster

My favorite command in all the Office programs is the Repeat command. The Repeat command repeats the last command you gave, whatever it happened to be. Use this command creatively and you can save yourself a lot of trouble. For example, to insert several columns in an Excel worksheet, insert one column and then give the Repeat command several times. To change the font of several different paragraphs in a Word document, select a paragraph and change its font. Then, one at a time, select (or click) different paragraphs and

SHORTCUT The fastest way to add a misspelled word to the AutoCorrect list is to right-click it, choose AutoCorrect from the shortcut menu, and choose the correct spelling of the word. "Spell-Checking Your Work" later in this chapter explains spell-checking in greater detail.

give the Repeat command after you select each one. (Selecting does not count as a command.)

To give the Repeat command:

- Press F4.
- Choose Edit | Repeat.
- Press CTRL-Y.

Correcting Typos with AutoCorrect

To keep spelling and typing errors to a minimum, you can tell Office to "autocorrect" them. The program already corrects commonly misspelled words. Try typing "consonent"(instead of "consonant") or "pleasent" (instead of "pleasant") to see what I mean—the invisible hand of Office corrects these spelling errors. Office maintains a list of the items it corrects automatically; if you'd like to add words to the list, take a look at Figure 2.3.

EXPERT ADVICE

With a little cunning, you can use the AutoCorrect command to quickly enter hard-to-type scientific names, long company names, and even, in Word, letterhead addresses and clip art images. To do so, select whatever it is you want to enter quickly and choose Tools | AutoCorrect. The AutoCorrect dialog box appears and you see the stuff you selected in the With box. (If you're in Word, click the Formatted Text option button to enter formatted text or clip art.) In the Replace box, enter a couple of letters and maybe a punctuation mark that you would never, never, never really enter (/abc **or** /lehead, **for** example). Then click Add and OK. Type your Replace text and press the SPACEBAR to see how your new AutoCorrect entry works.

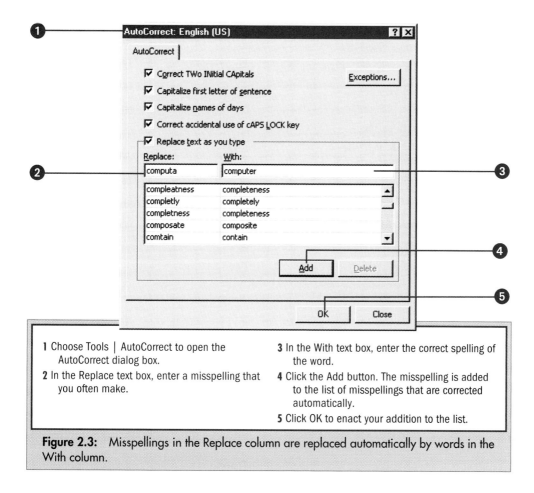

1 Choose Tools | AutoCorrect to open the AutoCorrect dialog box.

2 In the Replace text box, enter a misspelling that you often make.

3 In the With text box, enter the correct spelling of the word.

4 Click the Add button. The misspelling is added to the list of misspellings that are corrected automatically.

5 Click OK to enact your addition to the list.

Figure 2.3: Misspellings in the Replace column are replaced automatically by words in the With column.

Copying and Moving Data

One of the best things going in Office 2000 is being able to copy and move data. A paragraph from the company report, with a few changes,

In Chapter 10, "OLE for Sharing Data Between Programs" explains how to copy or move data from one Office program to another.

can be included in a letter. Data that's been mistakenly entered in one database table can be moved to another. To copy and move data, you can either drag and drop it or paste it from the Clipboard. Both techniques are described here.

Copying and Moving Data with the Clipboard

Copy and move data with the Clipboard when you want to copy or move it long distances or copy or move it to other files. The *Clipboard* is a sort of electronic holding tank for storing data. The last twelve items you cut or copied are stored on the Clipboard. Follow these steps to move or copy data with the Clipboard:

1. Select the data you want to move or copy.

2. Move or copy the data to the Clipboard:
   - **Moving** Choose Edit | Cut, press CTRL-X, click the Cut button, or right-click the text and choose Cut from the shortcut menu. The text is removed from the file.
   - **Copying** Choose Edit | Copy, press CTRL-C, click the Copy button, or right-click and choose Copy. You can also click the Copy button on the Clipboard toolbar.

3. Open a second file, if necessary, and click where you want to move or copy the data.

4. Paste the text into your document:
   - **The item you just cut or copied** Choose Edit | Paste, press CTRL-V, click the Paste button, or right-click and choose Paste.
   - **An item you cut or copied earlier** Display the Clipboard toolbar if it isn't already onscreen by right-clicking a toolbar and choosing Clipboard from the shortcut menu. Then slide the pointer over the scraps to read the first few words of each one, find the item you want to paste, and click it:

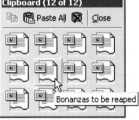

Copying and Moving Data
Short Distances with Drag-and-Drop

The most convenient way to move or copy data short distances is to use the drag-and-drop method. By "short distance," I mean the distance between any two places that are both visible onscreen. You can also drag data from one open window to another. Follow these steps to copy or move data with the drag-and-drop method:

1. Make sure that the data you want to copy or move and the place to which you will copy or move it both appear onscreen.

2. Select the data.

3. Either copy or move the data:

   • **Copying** Hold down the CTRL key as you drag the data where you want to copy it.

   • **Moving** Drag the data where you want to move it.

   As you drag, a box or vertical line shows where the data will go when you release the mouse button. If you are copying the data, a small cross appears beside the pointer.

TIP

In Excel or Access, wait until you see the pointer before you try to drag and drop your selection.

Elvis Sightings by Country - Europe					
	1996	1997	1998	1999	Average\Year
England	178	212	189	207	
France	561	928	317	402	
TOTALS					
Germany	89	47	13		Still the King!

B7:F7

Laying Out the Page

One of the first things you should do when you open a new file is set the margins. Especially in a Word 2000 file, margin settings determine where text lands on the page and whether you have enough room for tables and other things that fall in the "wide load" category. And if you want to change the orientation of the file from portrait to landscape or print on unusual-size paper, do that that from the start, too. These pages explain how to set the margins and change page layout settings.

Setting the Margins

In Chapter 3, "Putting Headers and Footers on Pages" explains how to create headers and footers.

Figure 2.4 shows you how to use Page Setup options to adjust the margins in your document. Notice that the process is basically the same whether you're using Word or Excel.

In Word, the Page Setup dialog box offers the following settings as well:

- **Gutter**   Allows extra space for the inside margins in documents that will be bound. Click the up arrow and watch the binding eat into the sample page.
- **Mirror Margins**   Click this checkbox if you intend to print on both sides of the paper. When you click this box, the labels on the Left and Right margin boxes change to Inside and Outside.
- **2 Pages per Sheet**   Click this checkbox if you intend to print chapbooks or other documents at a smaller size.

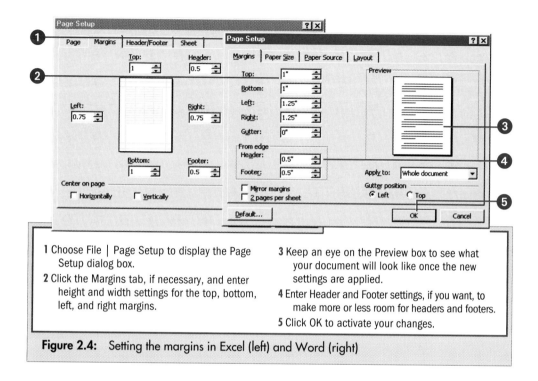

1 Choose File | Page Setup to display the Page Setup dialog box.

2 Click the Margins tab, if necessary, and enter height and width settings for the top, bottom, left, and right margins.

3 Keep an eye on the Preview box to see what your document will look like once the new settings are applied.

4 Enter Header and Footer settings, if you want, to make more or less room for headers and footers.

5 Click OK to activate your changes.

Figure 2.4: Setting the margins in Excel (left) and Word (right)

- **Apply To**   Choose This Section to make your margin settings apply to a section, not the entire document.
- **Gutter Position**   If you intend to bind your document, you can do so at the top instead of the left by clicking the Top option button.

Choosing a Paper Size and Orientation

To print on unusual-size paper or change the page orientation, choose File | Page Setup and click the Page tab in the Page Setup dialog box (click the Paper Size tab in Word). From the drop-down Paper Size menu, choose a new page size (make sure your printer can handle the size you choose). Under Orientation, click Landscape to print a landscape page or Portrait to print a portrait page. A *landscape page* is

In Chapter 3, "Dividing a Document into Sections" explains what sections are.

EXPERT ADVICE

Printing landscape pages can be a great solution when you're having trouble fitting all your text on a page. An Excel worksheet, Access database table, or Word table that is many columns wide can often be made to fit across a single landscape page, which is wider than it is tall.

wider than it is tall, like a landscape painting. Here is a snowman on a landscape page and on a portrait page:

Landscape

Portrait

Spell-Checking Your Work

mispelling

In Word 2000 and PowerPoint 2000, red wiggly lines appear below misspelled words. (If you don't see the red lines and you'd like to, choose Tools | Options, click the Spelling tab in the Options dialog box, and click the Check Spelling As You Type checkbox.) To correct a redlined word, right-click it and choose the correct spelling from the drop-down menu.

So much for the one-at-a-time method of spell-checking. To spell-check an entire file, press F7 or choose Tools | Spelling (the option is called Spelling and Grammar in Word). The Spelling and Grammar dialog box appears, as shown in Figure 2.5, and you see the first misspelling in the Not in Dictionary box.

One at a time, as the program you are working in encounters misspellings, click these buttons in the Spelling dialog box:

- **Ignore**   Click to ignore the misspelling but stop on it again if the same misspelling appears in the file.

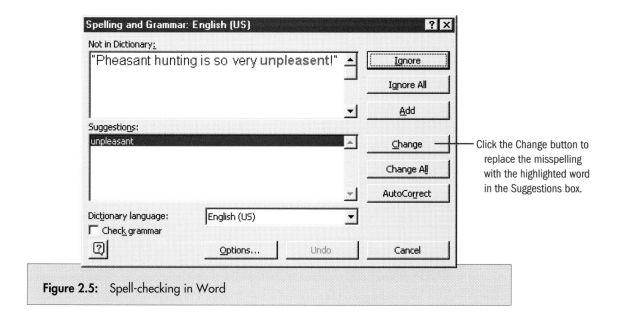

Click the Change button to replace the misspelling with the highlighted word in the Suggestions box.

Figure 2.5: Spell-checking in Word

- **Ignore All** Click to ignore all instances of the misspelling throughout the file.

- **Add** Click if the word is spelled correctly and you want to add it to the Dictionary so that the program never stops on it again.

- **Suggestions** Click a word in the Suggestions box if you want it to replace the misspelling.

- **Change** Click to replace the misspelled word with the highlighted word in the Suggestions box.

- **Change All** Click to use the highlighted word in the Suggestions box not only for this misspelling, but for all identical misspellings in the file.

- **AutoCorrect** Click to add the suggested spelling correction to the list of words that are corrected automatically.

Earlier in this chapter, "Correcting Typos with AutoCorrect" explains how the AutoCorrect Feature works.

Finding (and Replacing) Data

SHORTCUT

If you wish to replace every instance of the text that you're searching for, you can click the Replace All button to make the replacements all at once, throughout your document. Keep in mind, however, that Replace All does not allow you to check every replacement before it's made; this is what makes it so fast. Unless you're sure that a global replacement will cause no unexpected results, it's probably a good idea to make your replacements one at a time so you can confirm that each one is appropriate.

All the Office 2000 programs offer commands for finding data and for replacing it, if you wish, once you have found it. Follow these steps to find data and perhaps replace it:

1. Press CTRL-F or choose Edit | Find to display the Find and Replace dialog box.

   If you wish to replace the text you locate, click the Replace button to display the Replace With text box, shown in Figure 2.6.

2. In the Find What text box, enter the data that you want to find.

   If you'll be replacing the data, enter your preferred text in the Replace With text box.

3. Click the Find Next button. If the program can find what you are looking for, it is highlighted onscreen where it appears in your document.

   If your goal is to replace the highlighted text, simply click the Replace button. The old text is overwritten with the new text you entered.

   To repeat your search, click Find Next again to locate the next instance of the word or phrase you're looking for.

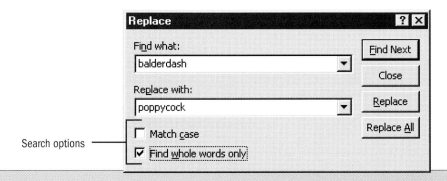

Figure 2.6: To look for data in a file, press CTRL-F, enter the search criteria, and click the Find Next button.

To narrow your search and make it go faster, take advantage of the search options described in Table 2.2. Word users can click the More button to see these options.

Suppose you decide to replace the data you found. To do so, click the Replace button (Word users click the Replace tab) and enter the replacement data in the Replace With text box. Then either click the Replace button to replace the data you recently found or click the Replace All button to replace the data in the Find What box throughout your file with the data in the Replace With box.

Search Option	What It Does
Match Case	Finds upper- or lowercase letters exactly like those in the Find What box.
Find Whole Words (Entire Cells) Only	Finds whole words or the entire contents of cells. For example, a search for **bow** finds that word but not "elbow" or "bowsprit"; a search for **131** finds that number but not "1,131."
Use Wildcards*	Lets you use wildcards (?, *, and others) in searches. For example, **b*r** finds "bur," "beer," and "bachelor." After you click this checkbox, you can click the Special button to choose wildcards.
Sounds Like*	Finds words that sound like the one in the Find What text box. For example, a search for **sit** finds "set" and "sat."
Find All Word Forms*	Searches for plurals, verb endings, and tenses. For example, a search for **sit** finds "sitting," "sits," and "sat."
Format*	Lets you search for formats. Choose an option from the menu and, in the dialog box that appears, choose the format you want to find.
Special*	Lets you search for punctuation marks and special characters.

*Available in Word 2000 only. Click the More button to see these and other search options.

Table 2.2:   Options for Data Searching

CAUTION

The Replace command is very powerful, and can have unexpected consequences. Always save your file before you replace any data. If you regret making the replacements, close your file without saving it to get your original data back.

Decorating Files with Clip Art and WordArt

The easiest way to impress others with your decorating skills is to plop a clip art image or WordArt image, like the ones shown here, into a file. A *WordArt image* is a word (or several words) that has been bent, spindled, or mutilated. Office 2000 comes with hundreds of clip art images that are yours for the taking. Keep in mind that before you can import one of them, the Office 2000 CD must be loaded in your computer's CD-ROM drive, since Office gets the images from the CD.

The upcoming section, "Handling 'Objects' in Files" explains how to change the size and position of a clip art image after you insert it in a file.

Inserting a Clip Art Image into a File

Study Figure 2.7 to learn about selecting clip art images and inserting them into your files.

Click the All Categories button in the Insert ClipArt dialog box to review the various picture categories, no matter where your search takes you. The Back and Forward buttons work like the Back and Forward buttons in a Web browser. Use them to backtrack or go forward as you search for clip art images.

Decorating a File with WordArt

Figure 2.8 explains how to create a WordArt image and insert it into your file.

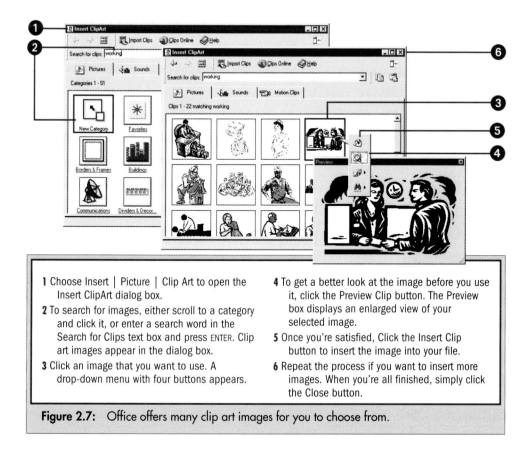

1 Choose Insert | Picture | Clip Art to open the Insert ClipArt dialog box.

2 To search for images, either scroll to a category and click it, or enter a search word in the Search for Clips text box and press ENTER. Clip art images appear in the dialog box.

3 Click an image that you want to use. A drop-down menu with four buttons appears.

4 To get a better look at the image before you use it, click the Preview Clip button. The Preview box displays an enlarged view of your selected image.

5 Once you're satisfied, Click the Insert Clip button to insert the image into your file.

6 Repeat the process if you want to insert more images. When you're all finished, simply click the Close button.

Figure 2.7: Office offers many clip art images for you to choose from.

As I explain shortly, it isn't crucial that you get the font, type size, and other details of your WordArt objects exactly right the first time around. It's easy to go back to the Edit WordArt Text dialog box and revise what you've created. In fact, it's often necessary to wrestle a bit with WordArt images before they come out right. By clicking buttons

See "Handling 'Objects' in Files" just ahead to learn how to change the size and position of a WordArt image.

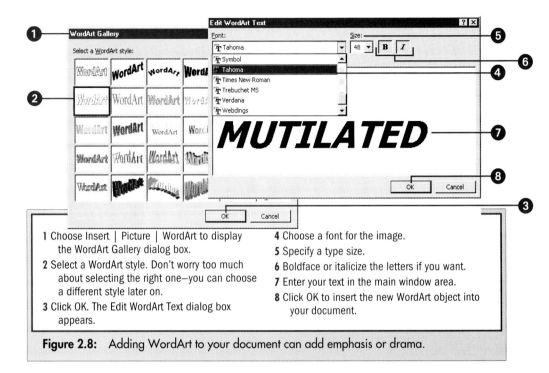

1 Choose Insert | Picture | WordArt to display the WordArt Gallery dialog box.

2 Select a WordArt style. Don't worry too much about selecting the right one—you can choose a different style later on.

3 Click OK. The Edit WordArt Text dialog box appears.

4 Choose a font for the image.

5 Specify a type size.

6 Boldface or italicize the letters if you want.

7 Enter your text in the main window area.

8 Click OK to insert the new WordArt object into your document.

Figure 2.8: Adding WordArt to your document can add emphasis or drama.

on the WordArt toolbar, you can win the wrestling match. Here are some refinements you may want to consider:

- **Change the text, font, and font size** Click the Edit Text button on the WordArt toolbar to open the Edit WordArt Text dialog box (see Figure 2.8) and enter new text or change the font.

- **Change the style** Click the WordArt Gallery button, select a new style in the WordArt Gallery (see Figure 2.8), and click OK.

- **Change the color of your text** Click the Format WordArt button and choose new colors on the Colors and Lines tab of the Format dialog box.

- **Rotate the image**　Click the Free Rotate button. Green selection handles appear on the corners of the image. Click and drag a handle to rotate the image.

Handling "Objects" in Files

After you insert a clip art image, WordArt image, shape, line, text box, or chart in a file, it becomes what Office 2000 calls an "object." You can see seven objects, for example in Figure 2.9. The techniques for manipulating objects like these are the same whether you are dealing with a clip art image, WordArt image, text box, line, or shape. To use objects successfully in a document, you have to know how to position them on the page, change their sizes and shapes, put borders around them, and overlap them. You also need to know how to select an object. Better read on. . .

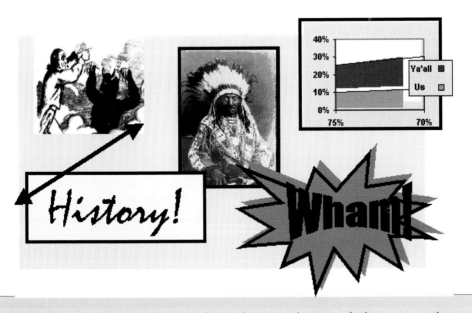

Figure 2.9: The techniques for manipulating objects are the same whether you're working with lines, shapes, autoshapes, clip art images, WordArt images, or graphics.

Selecting Objects

Before you can do anything to an object—change its size or shape, move it, or change its border—you have to select it. To select an object, simply move the pointer over it, wait until you see the four-headed arrow, and click. SHIFT-click to select several objects at once. You can tell when an object has been selected because small squares called *selection handles* appear around it. As this illustration shows, most objects have eight selection handles each; a line, however, has only two:

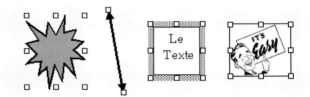

Changing the Location, Size, or Shape of an Object

Select an object and follow these instructions to move it, change its size, or change its shape:

- **Moving an object**   Drag the object to a new location. A dashed outline appears where the object will move when you release the mouse button.

- **Changing an object's size**   Gently move the mouse pointer over a corner selection handle. When you see the two-headed arrow, click and drag. Dragging a corner selection handle changes the object's size but maintains its proportions.

- **Changing an object's shape**   Gently move the mouse pointer over a selection handle on the side, top, or bottom. When you see the two-headed arrow, click and start dragging. The object is stretched or crumpled, depending on which direction you drag the handle.

Adding a Background Color or Border to an Object

Select an object, display the Drawing toolbar, and follow these
instructions to give your object a background color or a border:

- **Background color**   Click the down arrow next to the Fill
  Color button and select a color on the Fill Color menu, as
  shown in Figure 2.10. Choose No Fill to remove the
  background color.
- **Color for the border**   Click the down arrow beside the Line
  Color button and choose a color from the drop-down menu.
- **Line or dashed-line border**   Click the Line Style or Dash
  Style button to open the drop-down menu, and then choose a
  line, as shown in Figure 2.10.

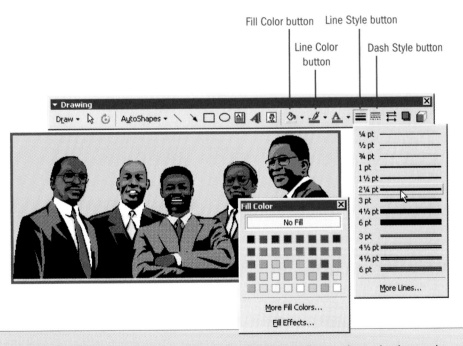

Figure 2.10:   Use the drop-down menus on the Drawing toolbar to choose background
colors and borders for objects like this clip art image.

TIP

The Order commands can be confusing. The easiest way to handle them is to display the Order toolbar and start clicking buttons. To display the toolbar, drag the line at the top of the Order submenu to make the menu "float."

Making Objects Overlap

When objects collide, as they do in the following illustration, one inevitably overlaps the other. And when you throw text into the mix, sometimes objects overlap text and sometimes they don't. How can you control whether objects obscure text and which object appears in front of the other?

To handle this problem, select the object, right-click, and choose Order from the submenu (or else click the Draw button on the Drawing toolbar and choose Order). You see the commands described in Table 2.3. Choose a command and be done with it.

Command	What It Does
Bring to Front	Places the object atop all other objects.
Send to Back	Moves the object behind all other objects.
Bring Forward	In a stack of objects, moves the object higher in the stack.
Send Backward	In a stack of objects, moves the object further down the stack.
Bring in Front of Text*	Places the object in front of text so that the text is obscured.
Send Behind Text*	Sends the object behind text so you can read the text.
*Available only in Word	

Table 2.3: The Order Commands

Printing Your Work

Not so long ago, paper was supposed to become obsolete. But the paperless office is still a pipe dream, and most communication continues to be done on paper. To print a file in its entirety, click the Print button on the Formatting toolbar. If you'd rather pick and choose which part of the file to print, or if you want to print several copies of a file, follow the steps in Figure 2.11

TIP

To examine a file before you print it, click the Print Preview button on the Standard toolbar. You see the Preview screen, which shows what your file will look like on paper.

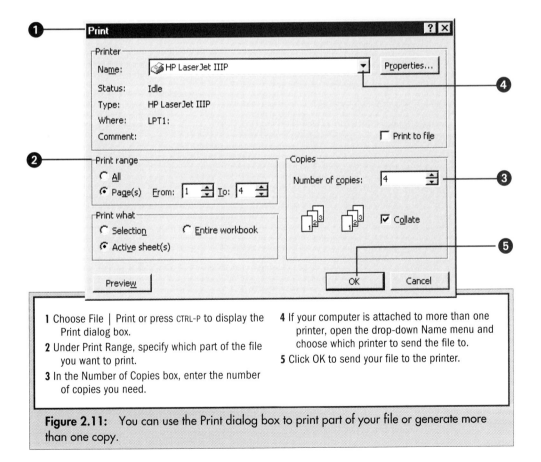

1 Choose File | Print or press CTRL-P to display the Print dialog box.

2 Under Print Range, specify which part of the file you want to print.

3 In the Number of Copies box, enter the number of copies you need.

4 If your computer is attached to more than one printer, open the drop-down Name menu and choose which printer to send the file to.

5 Click OK to send your file to the printer.

Figure 2.11:   You can use the Print dialog box to print part of your file or generate more than one copy.

Up and Running with Word 2000

INCLUDES

- Viewing documents in different ways
- Speed techniques for selecting text
- Indenting text and aligning text with the top and bottom of the page
- Hyphenating, single-spacing, and double-spacing text
- Dividing a document into sections
- Numbering the pages and including headers and footers
- Handling bulleted and numbered lists
- Ways to make pages look better

Change Your View of a Document ➡ pp. 53–54

- Click a View button—Normal View, Web Layout View, Print Layout View, or Outline View—in the lower-left corner of the screen.
- Open the View menu and choose Normal, Web Layout, Print Layout, Outline, or Full Screen.

Select Blocks of Text ➡ pp. 54–56

- With the pointer in the left margin and pointing to the right, click to select a line, click and drag to select several lines, double-click to select a paragraph, or triple-click to select the entire document.
- Click where you want to start selecting text, hold down the SHIFT key, and click at the end of the text you want to select.
- Click where you want to start selecting text, press F8 or double-click EXT on the status bar, and scroll to the end of the text you want to select.

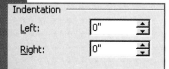

Indent a Section of Text ➡ pp. 57–58

- Drag one of the indent markers—Left Indent, First Line Indent, or Right Indent—on the ruler.
- Choose Format | Paragraph and enter left and right indentation measurements.
- To indent the first line, choose First Line on the Special drop-down menu and enter a measurement in the By text box.

Change the Line Spacing of Text ➥ pp. 59

- Press CTRL-1 to single-space text, CTRL-2 to double-space text, or CTRL-5 to space text by a line and a half.
- Choose Format | Paragraph, choose an option from the Line Spacing drop-down menu in the Paragraph dialog box, and enter an At measurement.

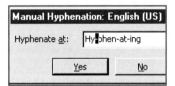

Hyphenate the Words in a Document ➥ pp. 60–62

1. Choose Tools | Language | Hyphenation.
2. To let Word hyphenate the text, click the Automatically Hyphenate Document checkbox and click OK.
3. To decide for yourself where hyphens are placed and words are broken, click the Manual button. In the Manual Hyphenation dialog box, click Yes or No to accept or reject Word's suggestion for placing a hyphen, and keep doing so until the document or text you selected is hyphenated.

Divide a Document into Sections ➥ pp. 64–65

1. Choose Insert | Break.
2. Under Section Break Types in the Break dialog box, choose the kind of section break you want.
3. Click OK.

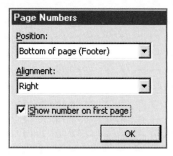

Number the Pages in a Document ➡ pp. 66–67

- Choose Insert | Page Numbers. In the Position and Alignment drop-down menus in the Page Numbers dialog box, tell Word where on the page you want the page numbers to be and click OK.

- Choose View | Header and Footer. Place the cursor in the Header or Footer box where you want the page number to go (click the Switch Between Header and Footer button on the toolbar to see the Footer box), and then click the Insert Page Number button to enter the page number.

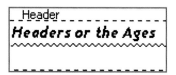

Put Headers and Footers on Document Pages ➡ pp. 67–69

1. Choose View | Header and Footer. You see the Header box. To enter a footer, click the Switch Between Header and Footer button on the Header and Footer toolbar.

2. Type the header or footer. You can click buttons on the Header and Footer toolbar as you do so.

This chapter explains techniques that you will use nearly every time you run Microsoft Word. Study this chapter well and you may just find that you're becoming the resident Word expert.

This chapter teaches you how to select and indent text, view documents in different ways, and hyphenate text. You'll learn how to line-space a document, number the pages, divide a document into sections, and include headers and footers on pages. At the end of the chapter you'll find a few techniques for speeding around in Word, as well as some suggestions for making your documents look better. In true tabloid fashion, this chapter starts by revealing the Microsoft Word family secrets.

By the way, this isn't the only chapter focusing on Microsoft Word. Chapter 4 presents advanced techniques for using the program. And before you read this chapter, be sure you've taken a good look at Chapter 2. It describes tools that are common to all Office 2000 programs, including Word.

> **DEFINITION**
> **Document**: Any report, announcement, or love letter...in this chapter, one that you write using Microsoft Word.

Microsoft Word Family Secrets Revealed!

Before you tackle Microsoft Word, you should know a couple of its family secrets. First, paragraphs are extremely important when you're formatting. Formatting commands apply to the paragraph that the cursor is in or, if you select more than one paragraph, to all the paragraphs you select. To indent a paragraph, for example, all you have to do is click it to place the cursor there, and then give an indent command. To align several paragraphs in a different way, select them and click one of the alignment buttons.

To make this paragraph business even more complicated, a paragraph is simply what you type onscreen before you press the ENTER key. So a heading is considered a paragraph. If you type

SHORTCUT

You can select any part of a paragraph to change the formatting of the whole thing. For example, if you drag the mouse over half of one paragraph and half of the next, and then give a formatting command, both paragraphs are reformatted because you've selected part of each.

Dear Jane at the start of a letter and press ENTER, "Dear Jane" is a paragraph. For formatting purposes, forget what you learned in English class about a paragraph being part of a composition. In Word, a paragraph is just what happens before you press ENTER. You can tell where one paragraph ends and another begins by clicking the Show/Hide ¶ button located on the right side of the Standard toolbar next to the Zoom menu. The paragraph symbol (¶) appears where you or someone else has pressed the ENTER key to end a paragraph:

¶
The·shortest·poem·in·the·English·language·is·thought·to·be·"Upon·the·Eternal·
Recurrence·of·Microbes,"·also·known·by·its·shorter·title,·"Fleas":¶
          Adam.¶
          Had·'em.¶
However,·the·poet·and·boxer·Mohammed·Ali·composed·a·poem·half·as·many·
syllables·long·about·the·necessity·of·citizens·in·a·pluralistic·democratic·society·to·
take·responsibility·for·and·actively·promote·the·well-being·of·others:¶
          Me.¶
          We.¶

Another Word family secret has to do with sections. As "Dividing a Document into Sections" explains later in this chapter, a *section* is a place in a document where formats change dramatically. Before you can change headers and footers in the middle of a document, change the size of margins, or put text in columns, you have to insert a section break. In fact, Word inserts a section break for you if you try to change formats on your own without inserting a section break first.

From time to time, clip art, columns, and other fancy stuff disappears from the screen. Don't panic when that happens. In Word, fancy stuff can be seen only in Print Layout and Web Layout views. When things disappear, switch views to see them again. Speaking of views, better read on...

Viewing Documents in Different Ways

Depending on the task at hand, some views are better than others.
Word offers four different ways to view documents, plus two more if
you count Print Preview and Full Screen as views. To change views of
a document:

- Click a View button—Normal View, Web Layout View,
  Print Layout View, or Outline View—in the lower-left corner
  of the screen.

- Open the View menu and choose Normal, Web Layout, Print
  Layout, Outline, or Full Screen.

Figure 3.1 illustrates four of the six views. Table 3.1 explains why
and when to change your view of a document.

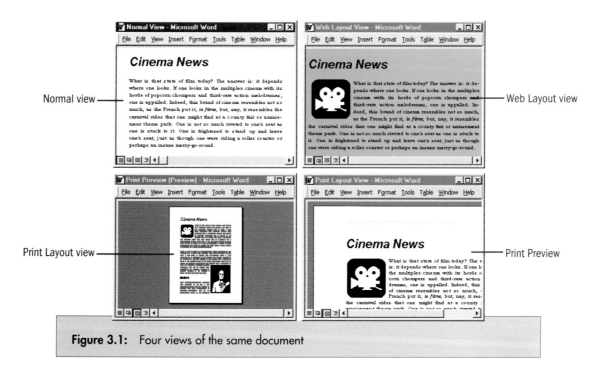

Figure 3.1:   Four views of the same document

View	When to Use It
Normal	Writing first drafts or doing basic editing. In Normal view, you can focus on writing. Sophisticated layouts, including graphics and columns, do not appear.
Web Layout	Laying out Web pages to be displayed online. Color backgrounds appear only in this view. By switching to Web Layout view, you can see what Web pages will look like in a Web browser such as Internet Explorer.
Print Layout	Laying out documents. In this view, you can see where graphics and columns appear, and where each page begins and ends.
Outline	Organizing papers and reports. In Outline view, you can move headings (and the text underneath them) around quite easily.
Print Preview	Seeing what entire pages look like. Use this view to see the big picture and find out whether documents are laid out correctly.
Full Screen	Focusing on the task at hand. In this view, the toolbars, the menu bar, the status bar—everything, in fact—is removed from the screen except the page you are working on. Full Screen view lets you work on a document without being disturbed by the clutter of the Word screen. To give commands, either use keyboard shortcuts, right-click to see shortcut menus, or slide the mouse pointer to the top of the screen to display the menu bar. Press ESC or click Close Full Screen to leave Full Screen view.

Table 3.1: Different Ways to View Word Documents

In Chapter 4, "Outlines for Organizing Your Work" explains Word's Outline view in detail.

Selecting Text in a Word Document

Knowing the different ways to select text is worthwhile because so much word-processing time is spent selecting text. Before you can copy, move, or delete text, you have to select it. You can't change fonts until you select the text. To delete a block of text, select it and click the DELETE key. Word offers numerous ways to select text. You don't need to know all of them, but experiment until you find the four or five that suit you.

Table 3.2 explains how to select text with the mouse. The trick to selecting more than a few words at a time is to click (or double-click) in the margin to the left of the words while the mouse pointer is pointing to the right, not the left. In this illustration, I selected an entire paragraph by double-clicking to its left. Notice that the mouse pointer is pointing to the right:

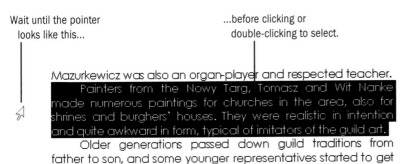

Wait until the pointer
looks like this...

...before clicking or
double-clicking to select.

To Select This...	Do This
A word	Double-click the word.
A few words	Drag over the words.
A line	Click to the left of the line.*
Several lines	Drag up or down to the left of the lines.*
A sentence	Hold down the CTRL key and click in the sentence.
A paragraph	Double-click to the left of the paragraph* (or triple-click inside the paragraph).
A block of text	Click at the start of the text, hold down the SHIFT key, and click at the end of the text.
Several paragraphs	Double-click to the left of a paragraph and then drag up or down.*
A table	Choose Table	Select or hold down the ALT key and double-click in the table.
The whole document	Press CTRL-A or choose Edit	Select All (or triple-click to the left of the text*).

* Make sure the pointer points to the right before clicking, double-clicking, or triple-clicking to the left of the text.

Table 3.2: Techniques for Selecting Text

Suppose you want to select everything from the middle of page 5 to the middle of page 7, including a table or two. In that case, the selection techniques in Table 3.2 can't help, because they're designed for selecting units of text—a line, a paragraph, and so on. However, you can select an unwieldy block of text by following these steps:

1. Click at the start or end of the text you want to select.
2. Either double-click the EXT button on the status bar or press F8. The dark letters EXT on the status bar tell you that you can start selecting text:

3. Scroll or move to the other side of the text you want to select, and click. The text is highlighted to show that it has been selected.

As long as the letters EXT are highlighted on the status bar, you can click elsewhere in your document to change the size of the text block you selected. Perhaps you didn't select enough text; click again to select more words and letters. But after you give a command—to change fonts or copy the block of text, for example—the letters EXT are no longer highlighted on the status bar and you can't click elsewhere to change the size of the text block.

Laying Out the Text

This portion of the chapter looks at the nitty-gritty tasks you have to do to make text fall correctly on the page. These pages explain how to indent text with respect to the left and right margins and also how to align text with respect to the top and bottom of the page. You learn how to line-space a document. Never again will you frown when your teacher, professor, or boss asks you to "double-space it," because double-spacing or single-spacing text is pretty easy. These pages also address the problem of hyphenating text and explain how to break lines and pages.

Indenting Text

Before you know anything else about indenting, you should know that text is indented relative to the margins, not to the edge of the page. If your left margin is 1 inch wide, for example, then indenting your text by 1 inch moves the text 2 inches from the edge of the page (1 inch + 1 inch = 2 inches). Word offers two techniques for indenting text. You can choose Format | Paragraph and enter indentation measurements in the Paragraph dialog box, or you can "eyeball it" by dragging the indent markers on the ruler:

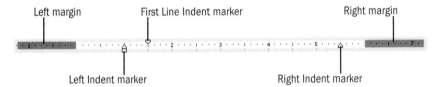

Use the "eyeball it" method when you're in a hurry and you want to indent one or two paragraphs. To use this method, select the paragraph or paragraphs that need indenting, make sure the ruler appears onscreen (choose View | Ruler if you don't see it), and start dragging indent markers on the ruler:

- **Left Indent**   Changes the indentation relative to the left margin.
- **First Line Indent**   Indents the first line in the paragraph or paragraphs relative to the left margin.
- **Right Indent**   Changes the indentation relative to the right margin.

The Paragraph dialog box, shown in Figure 3.2, is the way to go if you want to indent paragraphs by exact amounts, or if you are creating a paragraph style. (Chapter 4 explains styles.) Select one or more paragraphs, and choose Format | Paragraph to open the Paragraph dialog box. Under Indentation are text boxes for indenting text from the left and right margins. To indent first lines, choose First Line from the Special drop-down menu and, in the By text box, enter how much further to indent the first line than the rest of the paragraph. Keep your

SHORTCUT

The fastest way to indent text farther from the left margin is to click the Increase Indent button on the Formatting toolbar. Doing so indents the text by one tab stop, a half-inch if you didn't change the default settings. Clicking the Decrease Indent button moves the text one tab stop toward the left margin.

eye on the Preview box as you enter measurements—it shows precisely what the measurements will do to the text you've selected.

By the way, the Before and After options under Spacing in the Paragraph dialog box (see Figure 3.2) are for telling Word how much space to put before and after each paragraph. These commands are chiefly for use with paragraph styles, when you can carefully weigh which type of paragraph follows which. Indiscriminately entering measurements in the Before and After boxes can have unexpected consequences, since the amount in the After box in one paragraph might be added to the amount in the Before box in the next paragraph to produce a big, ugly gap between the paragraphs.

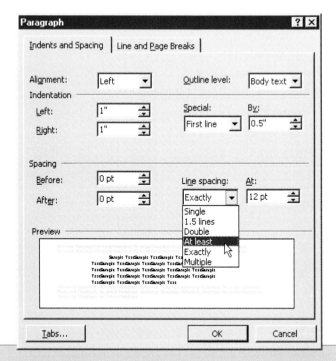

Figure 3.2: The all-purpose Paragraph dialog box is where you indent text and decide how much space to put between lines and paragraphs.

Deciding How Much Space to Put between Lines of Text

Who hasn't been handed a report or term paper only to be told to "double-space it next time"? Fortunately, double-spacing text is pretty easy. So is single-spacing text. And Word offers other line-spacing options as well. To adjust the amount of space between lines of text, select all or part of the paragraphs whose line spacing you want to change, and then choose Format | Paragraph. You see the Paragraph dialog box (see Figure 3.2). Under Line Spacing, choose one of the options and enter a point-size measurement in the At box, if necessary:

- **Single, 1.5 Lines, Double**   Single-spaces, line-and-a-half spaces, or double-spaces lines of text.
- **At Least**   Inserts the amount of space, in points, that you enter in the At box. Line spacing is increased to accommodate tall characters.
- **Exactly**   Inserts the amount of space, in points, that you enter in the At box. Space between lines is *not* increased to accommodate tall characters with this option. Characters taller than the Exactly amount get their heads cut off.
- **Multiple**   Works like double-spacing, but allows for triple-spacing, quadruple-spacing, and other multiple line spacing. Enter a multiple in the At box.

SHORTCUT

To single-space text, select it and press CTRL-1. Press CTRL-2 to double-space text. Pressing CTRL-5 spaces text by a line and a half.

Aligning Text with Respect to the Top and Bottom Margins

Besides aligning text with respect to the left and right margins, you can align text with respect to the top and bottom margins of the page. Align the text on the page with the top and bottom margins when you are working on an announcement or flier and you want the text to

In Chapter 2, "Aligning and Justifying Text" explains how to align text horizontally with respect to the left and right margins of the page.

appear squarely in the middle of the page (the Center alignment option) or to fill the page (the Justified alignment option). Follow these steps to align text vertically on the page:

1. If you want to align all of the pages in a document, it doesn't matter where the cursor is, but if you want to align only the pages in a certain section, click in the section.

2. Choose File | Page Setup and click the Layout tab in the Page Setup dialog box.

3. In the Apply To drop-down menu, choose This Section to change page alignments in the section; This Point Forward to change alignments for the rest of the pages in the document; or Whole Document to change alignments throughout the document.

4. Under Vertical Alignment, choose Top, Center, or Justified, and then click OK. Here is what the three choices do:

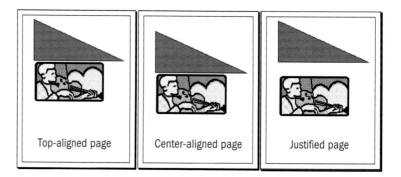

Top-aligned page   Center-aligned page   Justified page

Hyphenating Text

Hyphenating text isn't always necessary. Hyphenated text is harder to read than text that isn't hyphenated. Hyphenate only when you have to squeeze text into narrow columns or you are dealing with justified text and you have to pack more letters on each line to keep gaps from appearing in lines of text. The beauty of hyphenating in Word is that the hyphens appear only where words break at the ends of lines. When a hyphenated word gets shunted to the next line, the hyphens disappear. Word offers two hyphenation methods:

- **Automatic hyphenation**   Word hyphenates the entire document for you. With this technique, you can't tell Word not to hyphenate part of a document. If you change your mind about hyphenating, however, removing the automatic hyphens is simple. (You can hyphenate a document automatically and still keep Word from hyphenating certain paragraphs. To do so, select the paragraphs, choose Format | Paragraph, click the Line and Page Breaks tab in the Paragraph dialog box, and check the Don't Hyphenate checkbox.)

- **Manual hyphenation**   Word suggests hyphenating various words and you say *yes* or *no* to each suggestion. The only way to remove hyphens that were entered manually is to delete them one at a time, which can be time-consuming if you change your mind about hyphenating a document.

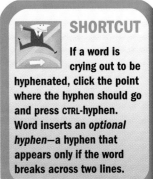

SHORTCUT

If a word is crying out to be hyphenated, click the point where the hyphen should go and press CTRL-hyphen. Word inserts an *optional hyphen*—a hyphen that appears only if the word breaks across two lines.

Automatic Hyphenation

Follow these steps to make Word do the hyphenating for you:

1. Choose Tools | Language | Hyphenation and, in the Hyphenation dialog box, click the Automatically Hyphenate Document checkbox:

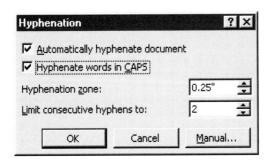

2. Uncheck Hyphenate Words in CAPS if you don't care to hyphenate uppercase words.

3. The Hyphenation Zone text box is for hyphenating left-aligned text. Words that fall in the zone are hyphenated, so a large zone means a less ragged right margin but more ugly hyphens, and a small zone means fewer ugly hyphens but a more ragged right margin.

4. In book publishing, the convention is not to hyphenate more than two consecutive lines, so enter **2** in the Limit Consecutive Hyphens To box if you are bookish. Then click OK.

To unhyphenate a document that you've hyphenated automatically, choose Tools | Language | Hyphenation, uncheck the Automatically Hyphenate Document checkbox, and click OK.

Manual Hyphenation

Follow these steps to pick and choose where hyphens appear:

1. Click where you want to start hyphenating, and choose Tools | Language | Hyphenation.

2. Change the Hyphenation Zone and Limit Consecutive Hyphens To settings, if you so desire. (The previous set of instructions explains how to do this.)

3. Click the Manual button. The Manual Hyphenation dialog box appears, and you see a blinking cursor where Word suggests putting a hyphen:

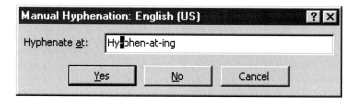

4. Click Yes or No, and keep clicking Yes or No until Word informs you that "Hyphenation is complete."

Breaking Lines and Pages

Pressing ENTER starts a new paragraph, but sometimes it pays to start a new line, or *break a line,* without starting a new paragraph. For example, consider the heading in Figure 3.3 and the lines of text below the heading. The first heading is top-heavy, so I broke it after the word "Sucker" to make the heading easier to read. In the lines of text, I broke the second line after the word "Kiwanis" to make the right margin more even. To break a line, click where you want the break to occur and press SHIFT-ENTER.

When you come to the bottom of a page, Word starts a new page for you automatically, but if you want to start a new page before you reach the bottom, press CTRL-ENTER. You can also start a new page by choosing Insert | Break and selecting the Page Break option in the Break dialog box. Break the page after you enter the text on a title page, for example. Whatever you do, don't press ENTER over and over to reach the bottom of a page.

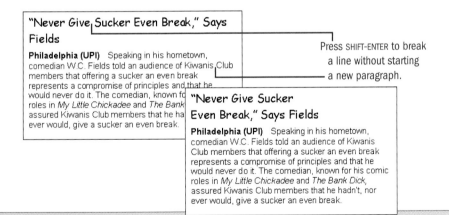

Figure 3.3: Breaking a line can make text easier to read. (Fields was right. Never give a sucker an even break.)

arlier in this chapter, "Viewing Documents in Different Ways" explains how views work in Word.

Recognizing a page break in Normal view is easy because the words "Page Break" and two dotted lines appear onscreen. In Print Layout view, however, page breaks look exactly like the page breaks that Word introduces when you reach the end of a page:

You see the bottom of one page and the top of the next. To erase a page break, switch to Normal view, click the words "Page Break," and press the DELETE key.

Dividing a Document into Sections

In order to put text in columns, change the margins, change page-numbering schemes, or change headers and footers in the middle of a document, you have to create a new section. Word 2000 is very touchy about sections. If you try to change margin settings or introduce columns without creating one, Word takes over and creates a new section for you. You can tell if a document has been divided into sections and which section the cursor is in by glancing at the status bar along the bottom of the screen. Next to the page number are the letters *Sec* followed by the number of the section that the cursor is in:

Figure 3-4 shows you how to introduce a section break in a document. Word offers four kinds of section breaks:

- **Next Page**   Starts a new section at the top of the next page.
- **Continuous**   Starts a new section immediately, with no page break. Choose Continuous, for example, to run text in columns starting in the middle of a page.

- **Even Page**   Starts a new section at the top of the next even-numbered page.

- **Odd Page**   Starts a new section at the top of the next odd-numbered page. In conventional publishing, a new chapter always begins on an odd page. Choose this kind of section break when headers and footers change from chapter to chapter and you want to start a new chapter in your document on an odd-numbered page.

The next part of this chapter explains how to insert page numbers, and how to include them in your headers or footers.

The only way to delete a section break or to be sure where a new section starts is to switch to Normal view, where you can see where each break is and even what kind of section break you are dealing with. To delete a section break, click it and then press the DELETE key.

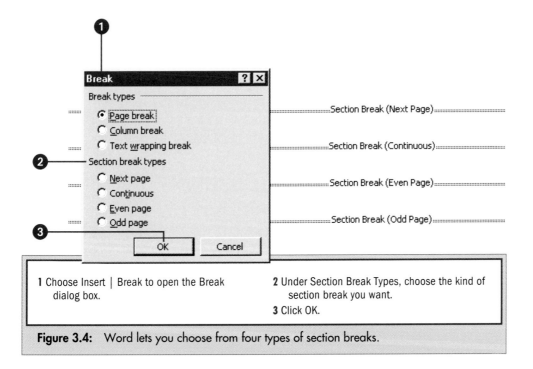

1 Choose Insert | Break to open the Break dialog box.

2 Under Section Break Types, choose the kind of section break you want.

3 Click OK.

Figure 3.4:   Word lets you choose from four types of section breaks.

Numbering the Pages in a Document

Word offers two techniques for numbering your pages automatically. Choose Insert | Page Numbers (see Figure 3.5) to place a number on each page, but choose View | Header and Footer to include page numbers as part of a longer header or footer. Whichever technique you choose, sequential page numbers will appear in the top or bottom margin of your document. What's more, you can change the page-numbering scheme with either method, and specify Roman numerals instead of Arabic numerals, or letters instead of numbers.

EXPERT ADVICE

Choose Insert | Page Numbers if all you want is a simple number on each page. Don't use this command, however, if you intend to include headers or footers in your document. Instead, set up your header or footer to generate the page numbers. (The page numbering feature does not work harmoniously with the header and footer features; a page number entered with Insert | Page Numbers will not fit or align properly beside text that you include in a header or footer.)

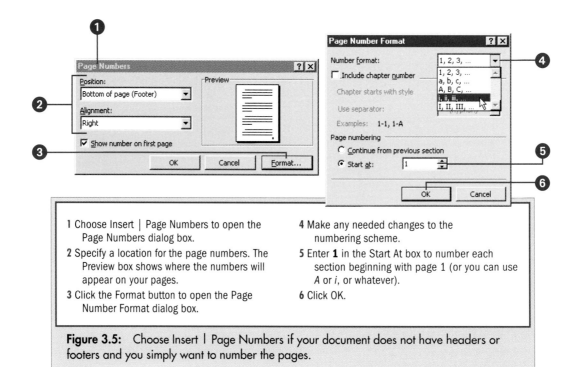

1 Choose Insert | Page Numbers to open the Page Numbers dialog box.

2 Specify a location for the page numbers. The Preview box shows where the numbers will appear on your pages.

3 Click the Format button to open the Page Number Format dialog box.

4 Make any needed changes to the numbering scheme.

5 Enter **1** in the Start At box to number each section beginning with page 1 (or you can use A or *i*, or whatever).

6 Click OK.

Figure 3.5: Choose Insert | Page Numbers if your document does not have headers or footers and you simply want to number the pages.

To remove page numbers you've entered with the Insert | Page Numbers command, choose View | Header and Footer. The Header box appears, as does the Header and Footer toolbar. Click the Switch Between Header and Footer button on the toolbar, if necessary, to see the page number in the Footer box. When you can see the page number, gently slide the mouse pointer over it, and then click when you see the four-headed arrow. If you do this correctly, eight black squares appear around the page number. When you see them, press the DELETE key.

Putting Headers and Footers on Pages

A *header* is a bit of text in the top margin of the page that tells readers what's what. Headers usually list the title of the document, its author, and the page number. *Footers* serve the same general purpose as headers, except that they do it in the bottom margin instead of the top margin. In this book, the headers on even pages display the current chapter title, while the headers on odd pages show you the current main topic heading.

To grace the pages of your own document with a header or footer, follow these steps:

1. Choose View | Header and Footer. You see the Header box at the top of the page:

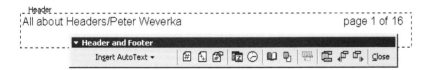

2. Click the Switch Between Header and Footer button to see the Footer box at the bottom of the page if you want to create a footer instead of a header.

3. Type your header or footer. You can call on nearly all of the formatting commands as you do so. Boldface the text, for example, or change fonts, or click an alignment button.

4. Click the Close button when you are finished entering your header or footer.

Try clicking these buttons on the Header and Footer toolbar to spruce up your header or footer:

- **Insert AutoText**   Opens a drop-down menu so that you can insert document information—the filename or author's name, for example.

- **Insert Page Number**   Includes the page number in the header or footer.

- **Insert Number of Pages**   Indicates the total number of pages in the document.

- **Format Page Number**   Opens the Page Number Format dialog box so that you can change numbering schemes (see Figure 3.5).

- **Insert Date**   Displays the date on which the document is printed (which is not necessarily the current date, nor the date when you created the header or footer). To choose your own format for the date (or time), don't bother with the Insert Date or Insert Time button. Instead, choose Insert | Date and Time, select a date or time format in the Date and Time dialog box, and click OK.

- **Insert Time**   Indicates the time at which the document was printed.

- **Page Setup**   Opens the Layout tab of the Page Setup dialog box so you can make different headers and footers for odd and even pages or change the header or footer on the first page of a document or section:

Even Page Header
All about Odd and Even Headers/Peter Weverka   page 2 of 16

- **Show/Hide Document Text**   Hides or shows the text in the document so you can see what it looks like in relation to the header or footer text.

EXPERT ADVICE

According to convention, headers and footers don't appear on the first page of documents. To keep them from appearing, click the Page Setup button on the Header and Footer toolbar (or choose File | Page Setup). On the Layout tab in the Page Setup dialog box, check the **Different First Page** checkbox. Check the **Different Odd and Even** checkbox on the Layout tab if you intend to print on both sides of the paper and you want the headers and footers on even and odd pages to be different, as they are on the pages of this book, for example. Then enter the headers or footers in the Even Page Header and Odd Page Header boxes (or their footer equivalents).

- **Same as Previous**   This button is for creating different headers or footers for different sections in a document. ("Dividing a Document into Sections" earlier in this chapter explains how to work with sections.) In a document that has been divided into sections, the Header or Footer box lists which section you are working in. When the Same as Previous button has been "pressed," the Header or Footer box reads "Same as Previous," and the header or footer in the previous section of the document is the same as the one in the section you are working in:

To make the header or footer different from the one in the previous section, click the Save as Previous button so that it isn't pressed down, and enter a new header or footer.

- **Switch Between Header and Footer**   Shows the Header box at the top of the page or the Footer box at the bottom so that you can enter a header or footer.

- **Show Previous**   Shows the header or footer in the previous section of a document that has been divided into sections. Click this button to see what the previous section's header or footer is.

- **Show Next**   Shows the header or footer that will appear in the next section.

SHORTCUT

However faintly, headers and footers appear at the top and bottom of pages in Print Layout view. To edit a header or footer in that view, simply double-click it. You see the Header or Footer box without having to choose View | Header and Footer.

Creating Numbered and Bulleted Lists

The Numbering button and the Bullets button on the Formatting toolbar make numbering a list or attaching bullets to a list very easy. In printing terminology, a *bullet* is a black filled-in circle or other character. Attach bullets to a list when you want to present alternatives to the reader or present a list in which the items are not ranked in any order:

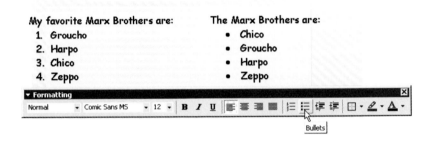

To select a list, click to the left of the first item and drag the mouse down the left margin. "Selecting Text in a Word Document" earlier in this chapter explains the numerous ways to select text.

The easiest way to create a numbered or bulleted list is to type the list, select it, and click the Numbering or Bullets button. You can also click the Numbering or Bullets button before you start typing the list. Each time you press ENTER to end one line and start the next, Word attaches a number or bullet to the line.

As you can see here, Word offers different numbering schemes and bullet types for lists:

1) Snap	I. Snap	A. Snap	a) Snap	a. Snap
2) Crackle	II. Crackle	B. Crackle	b) Crackle	b. Crackle
3) Pop	III. Pop	C. Pop	c) Pop	c. Pop
o Snap	▪ Snap	▫ Snap	❖ Snap	➢ Snap
o Crackle	▪ Crackle	▫ Crackle	❖ Crackle	➢ Crackle
o Pop	▪ Pop	▫ Pop	❖ Pop	➢ Pop

To choose a numbering scheme or bullet type apart from the standard numbers and bullets you get by clicking the Numbering or Bullets button, either right-click the list and choose Bullets and Numbering on the shortcut menu or choose Format | Bullets and Numbering.

You see the Bullets and Numbering dialog box shown in Figure 3.6. Click a numbering scheme or bullet in the dialog box and click OK.

Occasionally you have to interrupt a numbered list. Suppose you enter points 1 and 2 in the list, type a few paragraphs of commentary, and then want to resume the list at point 3. To do that, click the Numbering button in the paragraph where you want to resume the list. After Word incorrectly starts the list with the number 1, right-click and choose Bullets and Numbering from the shortcut menu. You see the Numbered tab of the Bullets and Numbering dialog box (see Figure 3.6). Click the Continue Previous List option button, and then click OK. Occasionally Word tries to start a list at step 3, 4, or whatever. When that happens, click the Restart Numbering option button in the Bullets and Numbering dialog box.

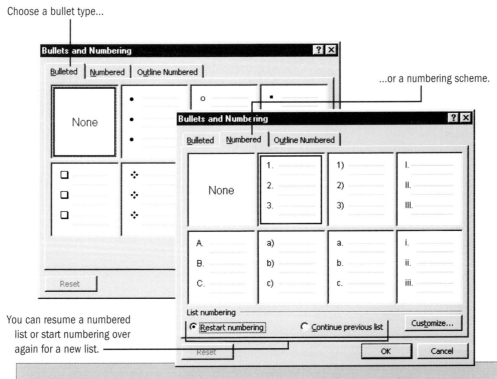

Choose a bullet type...

...or a numbering scheme.

You can resume a numbered list or start numbering over again for a new list.

Figure 3.6: In the Bullets and Numbering dialog box, you can choose different numbering schemes and bullet types.

EXPERT ADVICE

Word creates a numbered list automatically when you enter 1., type an item, and press the enter key. Some people find that annoying and want to be able to type numbered lists on their own without Word's interference. If you are one of those people, choose Insert | AutoText | AutoText, click the AutoFormat As You Type tab in the AutoCorrect dialog box, and uncheck the Automatic Numbered Lists checkbox.

Speed Techniques for Getting Around in Long Documents

As documents get longer, going here and there gets harder and harder. Here are a handful of techniques for getting there fast. Read on to find out how to place bookmarks in a document and use the Document Map.

Bookmarking the Important Places in a Document

When you want to return to an important place in a document, bookmark it. Then all you have to do is double-click the bookmark's name in the Bookmark dialog box, as shown in Figure 3.7, and you'll return to your place instantly. To create or use a bookmark, choose Insert | Bookmark (or press CTRL-SHIFT-F5). Then, in the Bookmark dialog box, do one of the following:

- **Create a bookmark**   Make sure the insertion point is where you want the bookmark to be before you choose Insert | Bookmark. In the Bookmark dialog box, enter a name in the Bookmark Name text box and click the Add button or press ENTER. Bookmark names cannot include blank spaces. The first character must be a letter, not a number.

- **Go to a bookmark**   Double-click a bookmark name in the Bookmark dialog box. To find names, use the scroll bar if necessary. You can also choose a Sort By option to arrange the names in alphabetical or location order.

Click any heading in the Document Map window to move to that point in your document.

Document Map button

Double-click the name of a bookmark and you instantly move to the marked location.

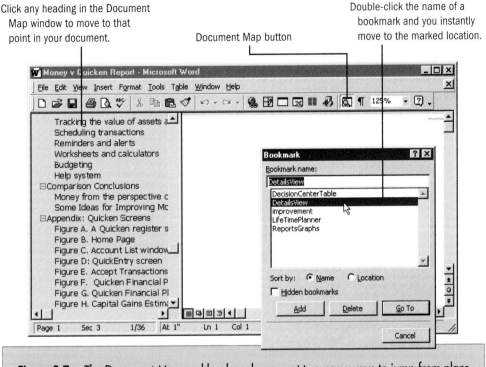

Figure 3.7: The Document Map and bookmarks present two easy ways to jump from place to place in a document.

Going Here and There with the Document Map

As long as you've assigned heading styles to the headings in a document, you can jump from place to place by means of the Document Map. To see the Document Map, click the Document Map button or choose View | Document Map. A list of headings appears on the left side of the screen (see Figure 3.7). Click a heading and Word takes you there immediately. If you can't read a heading on the Document Map, rest the pointer on top of it. The heading name appears in a pop-up box. To choose which headings are shown, right-click the Document Map and choose which headings you want to see from the drop-down menu.

In Chapter 4, "Styles for Consistent and Easy Formatting" explains what styles are and how to apply them to headings.

Six Ways to Make Pages Look Better

Herewith are a few simple techniques you can use to make pages look better. You don't have to be a Microsoft Word guru to use these techniques, and they go a long way toward sprucing up pages.

TIP

What if your drop cap doesn't look quite right? Easy! Just click anywhere in the paragraph, choose Format | Drop Cap again, and play with the settings until you like what you see.

1. DROP IN A DROP CAP A *drop cap,* or *drop-capital letter,* is a large letter that falls two, three, or four lines into the text. Drop caps look good on the first page of a chapter, and they're easy to place in your document. Figure 3.8 shows you how to drop in a drop cap.

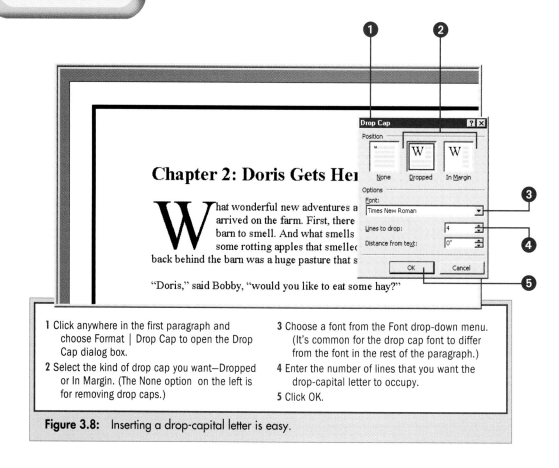

1 Click anywhere in the first paragraph and choose Format | Drop Cap to open the Drop Cap dialog box.

2 Select the kind of drop cap you want—Dropped or In Margin. (The None option on the left is for removing drop caps.)

3 Choose a font from the Font drop-down menu. (It's common for the drop cap font to differ from the font in the rest of the paragraph.)

4 Enter the number of lines that you want the drop-capital letter to occupy.

5 Click OK.

Figure 3.8: Inserting a drop-capital letter is easy.

2. PUT A BORDER AROUND THE PAGE   A page border helps make a flier or announcement stand out. To insert a page border like the one you see in Figure 3.8, choose Format | Borders and Shading and click the Page Border tab in the Borders and Shading dialog box. Under Setting, click the Box, Shadow, or 3-D option. Then choose a line style from the Style menu and a width for the border from the Width drop-down menu and click OK.

3. PUT A LINE BELOW HEADERS AND ABOVE FOOTERS

One of the easiest ways to spruce up a document is to draw a line below headers and above footers. The line separates the header or footer from the main text in the document. In Word, you can choose from many different line styles:

Earlier in this chapter, "Putting Headers and Footers on Pages" explains how to put headers at the top of pages and footers at the bottom.

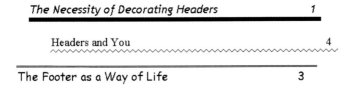

Follow these steps to place a line—that is, a border line—below a header or above a footer:

1. Choose View | Header and Footer to see your header. If you want to draw a line above the footer, click the Switch Between Header and Footer button on the Header and Footer toolbar.

2. Choose Format | Borders and Shading, and click the Borders tab in the Borders and Shading dialog box.

3. Under Setting, click the Box option.

4. On the Style menu, find and click the kind of line you want, and then choose a width for the line from the Width drop-down menu.

5. Borders appear around all four sides of the Preview box. Click to remove the lines from three of the four sides:

- **For a header** Click the left, right, and top lines. Only the bottom line remains. This line will appear underneath the header.

- **For a footer** Click the left, right, and bottom lines. Only the top line remains. It will appear above the footer.

6. Make sure Paragraph appears in the Apply To drop-down menu, and click OK.

4. PRINT A WATERMARK ON EACH PAGE According to the Microsoft Corporation, a *watermark* is a faint image that appears behind the text in the same place on each page (a watermark is really a faint imprint made directly onto the paper). Odd as it may seem, you create a watermark by choosing View | Header and Footer, clicking in the Header box, and then importing a clip art image and placing it in the middle of the page. Because the clip art image is technically part of the header, it appears on every page, as a header does. And it appears behind the text, in the background.

Watermarks are elegant indeed. They are a good way to impress your impressionable friends and co-workers:

In Chapter 2, "Decorating Files with Clip Art and WordArt" explains how to import a clip art image. "Handling 'Objects' in Files" in the same chapter explains how to position clip art on the page.

TIP

On the Picture toolbar, click the Image Control button and then choose Grayscale from the drop-down menu to turn a color watermark gray so it doesn't obscure text on the page.

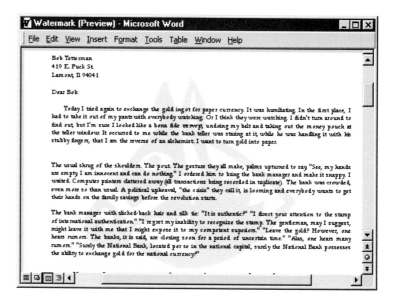

5. MAKE USE OF TEXT EFFECTS   Maybe the fastest way to spruce up a heading is to select it, open the Font dialog box, and choose one of the unusual text effects—Shadow, Outline, Emboss, or Engrave. For this illustration, I've selected Shadow and Outline. Choose Format | Font and experiment with the text effects—you never know what will happen:

The Shadow Knows...

6. USE HANGING HEADINGS   A *hanging heading* is one that "hangs" in the margin. If you want to see a hanging heading, look no further than this book. Notice on the pages of this book how the major headings jut into the margin. Hanging headings are good for technical manuals and reports where you have to look up information. They are easy to find and read.

   To create hanging headings, make sure that the paragraph text is indented further from the left margin than the heading text. That's all there is to it. At the beginning of the next chapter, "Styles for Consistent and Easy Formatting" explains how to create a style for paragraph text and make sure that paragraphs are indented further than headings.

CHAPTER 4

Advanced Word 2000

INCLUDES

- Applying and creating styles
- Laying out and formatting tables
- Tricks for handling tables
- Running text in newspaper-style columns
- Using the Thesaurus
- Organizing your work in Outline view
- Generating a table of contents
- Including footnotes and endnotes in documents

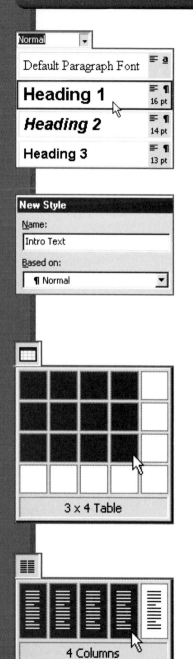

Apply a Style to Text ➥ pp. 82–85

1. Click the paragraph whose style you want to change, or select several paragraphs.
2. Click the down arrow to open the drop-down Style menu, and then choose a style.

Create a New Style to Format Text Quickly ➥ pp. 85–89

- Format a prototype paragraph to model the style after, and then click in the Style menu box. Type a short but descriptive name for the style and press ENTER.
- Choose Format | Style, click the New button in the Style dialog box, and choose a style type and style options in the New Style dialog box.

Create a Table ➥ pp. 89–99

- Click the Insert Table button on the Standard toolbar, and click on the grid to tell Word how many rows and columns to put in the table.
- Choose Table | Draw Table and sketch the table yourself with the Draw Table pointer.
- Choose Table | Insert | Table and enter the number of columns and rows you want in the Insert Table dialog box.

Arrange Text in Newspaper-Style Columns ➥ pp. 99–101

- Type the text, select it, click the Columns button, and choose the number of columns you want from the drop-down menu.
- Select the text, choose Format | Columns, and choose or enter the number of columns you want in the Columns dialog box.

Use the Thesaurus to Find a Synonym ➥ pp. 101–102

1. Click the word for which you need a synonym and press SHIFT-F7.
2. Start searching for a synonym and click Replace when a good synonym appears in the Replace with Synonym box.

   • Click a word in the Meanings box to turn the search in another direction.
   • Click a word in the Replace with Synonym list and click the Look Up button to find synonyms for it.

Move Text in Outline View ➥ pp. 103–104

1. Click the Outline View button or choose View | Outline to switch to Outline view.
2. Click a Show Heading button (1 through 7) to see headings only.
3. Click a heading and click the Move Up or Move Down button to move it, as well as its text and subheadings, forward or backward in the document.

Create a Table of Contents ➥ pp. 104–106

1. Choose Insert | Index and Tables and click the Table of Contents tab in the Index and Tables dialog box.
2. Choose a TOC design from the drop-down Formats menu.
3. In the Show Levels box, enter a number to tell Word which headings to include in the table of contents, and then click OK.

Put Footnote Text in a Document ➥ pp. 106–107

1. Click where you want the footnote citation to appear, and choose Insert | Footnote.
2. In the Footnote and Endnote dialog box, click Custom Mark and enter a symbol if you would rather mark the footnote with a symbol than a number.
3. Click OK and type your footnote.

This chapter picks up where Chapter 3 left off and takes you headlong into the advanced realm of Word 2000. In this chapter, you take the bull by the horns. You take command, stay the course, and put the pedal to the metal. Here you discover how styles can make formatting easier, and how you can use them to create professional-looking documents. You also learn how to create and lay out tables, run text in newspaper-style columns, use Word's Thesaurus, rearrange documents in Outline view, generate a table of contents, and add footnotes and endnotes.

Styles for Consistent and Easy Formatting

A *style* is a collection of commands and formats that have been bundled under one name. By using styles, you free yourself from having to visit and revisit numerous dialog boxes whenever you want to change the formatting of a paragraph. Styles save a lot of time. When you want to reformat a paragraph, you simply choose a style name from the drop-down Style menu. The paragraph is reformatted instantly. What's more, you can rest assured that all parts of the document that were assigned the same style are laid out the same and look the same. By using styles, you make sure that various parts of your document are consistent with one another and that your documents have a professional look.

Read on if styles interest you—and they should if you intend to do any serious work whatever in Microsoft Word. Styles can save a ridiculous amount of time that you would otherwise spend formatting and wrestling with text. And many Word features rely on styles. To generate a table of contents, organize a document with an outline, see the Document Map, or refer to a heading in a cross-reference, you must have assigned heading styles to the headings in your document.

You can even turn a Word document into a Web page if you thoughtfully assign styles in the document.

These pages explain how to apply a style, create a style of your own, and modify a style. First, however, a little background concerning styles...

How Styles Work

To get a sense of how styles work, open the drop-down Style menu on the left side of the Formatting toolbar, as shown in Figure 4.1. The styles you see are the ones that are available in the current document. Different templates offer different styles. In Figure 4.1, I am working in a document I created with the Normal template, the one you get when you create a new document by clicking the New button or pressing CTRL-N, so the list of styles is fairly short.

You can tell which style has been assigned to a paragraph by clicking the text and glancing at the Style menu box, which lists the name of the style. Names on the Style menu hint at what styles look

At the beginning of Chapter 2, "Opening a New File" explains what templates are.

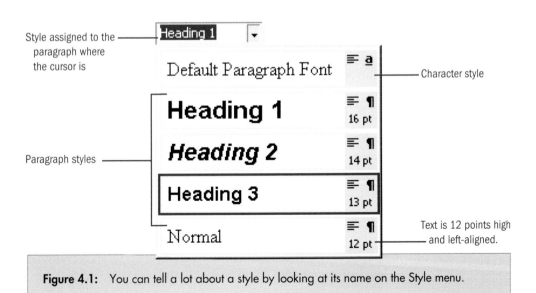

Style assigned to the paragraph where the cursor is

Character style

Paragraph styles

Text is 12 points high and left-aligned.

Figure 4.1: You can tell a lot about a style by looking at its name on the Style menu.

like, and if you look closely at the box to the right of style names you can tell a lot about a style:

- Whether the style is a paragraph or a character style. Paragraph styles show the ¶ symbol; character styles are marked by an underlined letter *a*.
- Whether the text is left-aligned, right-aligned, centered, or justified. The alignment symbols on the Style menu look like the alignment buttons on the Formatting toolbar.
- The font size of the text, which is listed in points.

At the beginning of Chapter 3, "Microsoft Word Family Secrets Revealed!" explains how formatting commands, including styles, affect the paragraph the cursor is in or the paragraphs that you've selected.

Word offers two kinds of styles, *paragraph styles* and *character styles*. Most styles are paragraph styles. Character styles apply to characters you select, whereas paragraph styles apply to entire paragraphs:

- **Paragraph style**   When you select a paragraph style from the Style menu, the style's format and font settings apply to all the text in the paragraph that the cursor is in (or to several paragraphs, if you selected all or part of them before assigning the style). A paragraph style can include these settings: font, paragraph, tab, border, language, and bullets and numbering. In other words, any setting you can make by choosing Format | Font, Format | Paragraph, Format | Tabs, Format | Borders and Shading, Tools | Language | Set Language, or Format | Bullets and Numbering and filling out a dialog box can be included in a paragraph style.
- **Character style**   Character styles apply to text, not to paragraphs. You must select text before you can apply a character style. Create a character style for text that is hard to lay out (such as small capitals) or for foreign-language text. A character style can include these settings: font (Format | Font command), border (Format | Borders and Shading), and language (Tools | Language | Set Language). When you apply a character style to text, the character-style settings override the paragraph-style settings. If the paragraph style calls for a

12-point Times Roman font but the character style calls for a
10-point Arial font, the 10-point Arial font wins.

Applying a Style

Follow these steps to apply a style in a document:

1. Place the insertion point in the paragraph whose style you want
   to change, or select several paragraphs. To apply a character
   style, select the text.

2. Open the drop-down Style menu on the Formatting toolbar
   (see Figure 4.1), and choose a style.

The Style menu only lists styles that have already been used in the
document. If you want to select a style that hasn't been used yet, choose
Format | Style, choose a style from the Styles list in the Style dialog
box, and click the Apply button. By the way, open the drop-down List
menu and choose Styles in Use, All Styles, or User-Defined Styles to
shorten or lengthen the list and find the style you need.

I n Chapter 3, "Selecting Text
in a Word Document" explains
all the ways to select text,
including paragraphs.

Creating a New Style

To create a style of your own, you can select an example paragraph
and use it as a model for creating a style, or you can build it from the
ground up by describing the style in the New Style dialog box. The
example method is fastest, but with the ground-up method you can
tell Word to update the style automatically as you change paragraph
formats and do a couple of other things besides. Both methods are
described here. You have to use the ground-up method to create a
character style.

Creating a Style by Example

To create a style by example, start by formatting a paragraph. Make
your paragraph look exactly like the paragraphs to which you will
apply the style. Use all the commands you deem necessary to make the
paragraph look just so: font commands, formatting commands, and
border and shading commands, for example. Figure 4.2 demonstrates
how to create a style from an example paragraph.

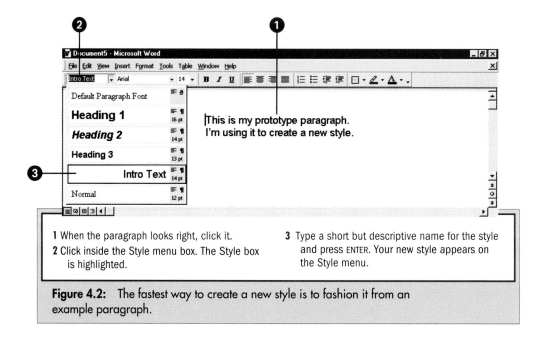

1 When the paragraph looks right, click it.
2 Click inside the Style menu box. The Style box is highlighted.

3 Type a short but descriptive name for the style and press ENTER. Your new style appears on the Style menu.

Figure 4.2:   The fastest way to create a new style is to fashion it from an example paragraph.

EXPERT ADVICE

Choosing a style from the Based On menu saves time because you inherit formats and thereby get a head start on the new style. But basing a style on another style can have unexpected consequences: if you change the base style, any styles based on that style will inherit those changes, for good or ill. To be on the safe side, choose the Normal style or another bare-bones style, or choose No Style to make sure your style keeps to itself.

Creating a Style from the Ground Up

Figure 4.3 shows you how to create a style from the ground up. Once you get the hang of it, creating a style this way is pretty simple, although the following options in the New Style dialog box may take a bit of getting used to:

- **Based On**   Specifies a style to use as the basis for the new style you are creating.

- **Style for Following Paragraph**   Choose a style from this drop-down menu if the style you are creating is always to be followed by an existing style. For example, if Heading 1 is always followed by Intro Text, choose the Intro Text style. This way, users who enter a first-level heading and press ENTER don't have to choose the Intro Text style for the paragraph following the heading.

- **Add to Template**   Adds the style you are creating to the template with which you created the document. If you check this box, a user who creates a document with the template in the future can make use of your new style. Unless this box is checked, new styles are available only in the document for which they were created.

- **Automatically Update**   Tells Word to redefine the style each time a paragraph to which the style has been assigned is reformatted. In other words, if you change the indentation of a paragraph assigned to your new style, all other paragraphs assigned the new style are indented as well. I recommend clicking this checkbox—it's the easiest way to make sure that paragraphs are up to date when you reformat a style.

Modifying a Style

What if a paragraph doesn't look quite right when you assign a style to it? You can fix that by modifying the style. Modifying styles is similar to creating them in that you can do it by example or by visiting the Modify Style dialog box, which looks and works much like the New Style dialog box.

- **Visiting the Modify Style dialog box**   Choose Format | Style to open the Style dialog box, select the style you want to modify from the Styles list, and click the Modify button. You see the Modify Style dialog box, whose options are identical to those on the New Style dialog box (see Figure 4.3), with one exception: You can't choose between a paragraph or character style on the drop-down Style Type menu. Your choice of style types, I'm afraid, is set in stone and can't be altered.

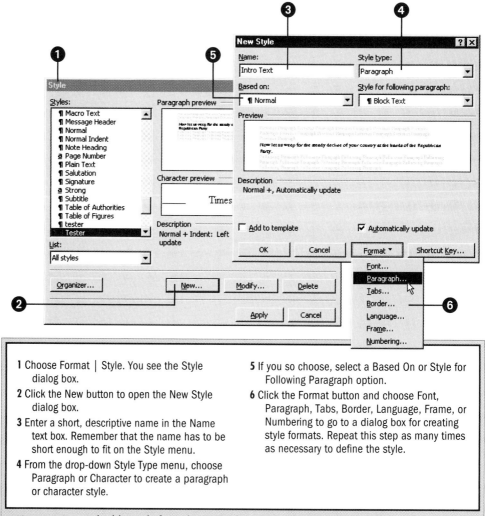

1 Choose Format | Style. You see the Style dialog box.

2 Click the New button to open the New Style dialog box.

3 Enter a short, descriptive name in the Name text box. Remember that the name has to be short enough to fit on the Style menu.

4 From the drop-down Style Type menu, choose Paragraph or Character to create a paragraph or character style.

5 If you so choose, select a Based On or Style for Following Paragraph option.

6 Click the Format button and choose Font, Paragraph, Tabs, Border, Language, Frame, or Numbering to go to a dialog box for creating style formats. Repeat this step as many times as necessary to define the style.

Figure 4.3: To build a style from the ground up, go to the New Style dialog box.

EXPERT ADVICE

As long as you check the Automatically Update check box in the New Style dialog box (see Figure 4.3) when you create a style, paragraphs assigned to the style are modified whenever you change the format of a single paragraph to which the style was assigned. If you want to be able to modify a style automatically, choose Format | Style to open the Style dialog box and select the style on the Styles list. Then click the Modify button and check the Automatically Update checkbox in the Modify Style dialog box.

- **Modifying a style by example**   Reformat a paragraph whose style needs changing and, with the cursor still in the paragraph, click in the Style menu box and press the ENTER key. You see the Modify Style message box, which asks whether you want to update the style. Click OK. While you're at it, you can also check the Automatically Update the Style from Now On checkbox so that formatting changes made to paragraphs in the future are made to the style as well.

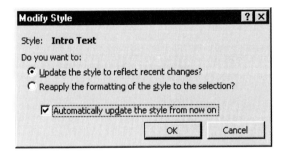

Constructing the Perfect Table

Tables are so problematic that Microsoft Word devotes an entire menu to creating and formatting them. On the Table menu are numerous commands for handling tables. Read on to find out how to create tables, enter the text, lay out a table, and format a table. At the end of this section, for you and you alone, are ten tricks for constructing tables.

Before you can work on tables, you need to learn a few vocabulary words:

- **Cells**   The boxes that hold data items. A cell is formed where a row and column intersect.
- **Heading row**   The top row of the table, where labels are displayed that explain what is in the columns below. Also called the *header row.*
- **Borders**   The lines in the table. You decide what the lines look like and how thick they are.

- **Gridlines**   The gray lines that show where the columns and rows are. Gridlines are not printed—they appear on the screen merely to help you enter data. To see or remove the gridlines, choose Table | Show Gridlines or Table | Hide Gridlines.

Heading row

State	State Highway	Interstate Highway	Total
Arkansas	437	183	620.00
Louisiana	523	294	817.00
Mississippi	392	301	693.00

Cells   Gridlines

Laying Out the Columns and Rows

Word offers no fewer than three different ways to lay out the columns and rows for a table. You can click the Insert Table button, choose Table | Insert | Table, or, believe it or not, sketch a table. Don't worry about formatting the table at this point. Lay out the columns and rows and enter the data before you consider the table's appearance.

Later in this chapter, "Changing the Table Layout" explains how to remove or add new columns and rows. Don't worry about getting the right number of columns and rows when you create a table.

The fastest way to lay out a table is to click the Insert Table button on the Standard toolbar. Click the button and you see an empty table grid, but by moving the pointer onto the grid, you can tell Word how many rows and columns to include in the table. Click when the bottom of the menu lists the number of rows and columns you want. Click and drag the mouse sideways and downward on the grid to create a table larger than 4 rows by 5 columns:

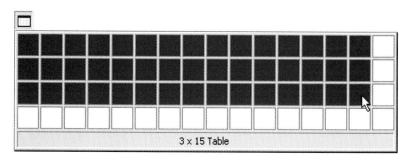

3 x 15 Table

Choose Table | Draw Table to sketch the table yourself. The pointer changes to a pencil, and the Tables and Borders toolbar appears. Drag the pencil pointer to draw the table. If you make a mistake, click the Eraser button on the toolbar and rub out your mistake with the new pointer, which looks like an eraser.

TIP
Draw the outer boundaries of the table first; then fill in the middle.

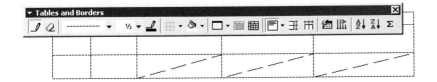

When you want a say in how wide the table and its columns should be, use the Insert Table dialog box, as shown in Figure 4.4. The box contains a number of options, under AutoFit Behavior, that make it easy to get your table looking its best:

- **Fixed Column Width** Enter a measurement to make all columns the same width. Choosing Auto in the text box creates a table with columns of equal size that goes from margin to margin (choosing Auto is tantamount to choosing the AutoFit to Window option).

- **AutoFit to Window** This option, which is used for laying out Web pages, makes the table fill the window when the table is shown in Web Layout view or seen through a Web browser.

- **AutoFit to Contents** Choosing this option makes each column wide enough to accommodate its widest entry. You get very narrow columns to begin with. As you enter data, Word adjusts the size of columns and rows to make rows and columns roughly the same size.

You can delete a table, if you regret having ever created it, by choosing Table | Delete | Table.

CAUTION
Many people find it hard to enter data in a table that was created with the AutoFit to Contents option because row and column boundaries shift continuously as you enter data when this option is turned on. However, you can always enter the data and apply the AutoFit To Contents command later. To do so, click your table and choose Table | AutoFit | AutoFit to Contents.

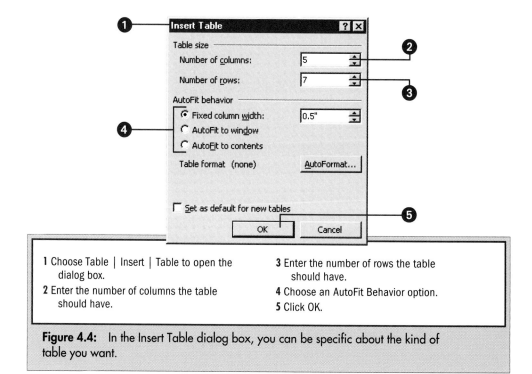

Figure 4.4: In the Insert Table dialog box, you can be specific about the kind of table you want.

The callouts in the figure read:

1 Choose Table | Insert | Table to open the dialog box.
2 Enter the number of columns the table should have.
3 Enter the number of rows the table should have.
4 Choose an AutoFit Behavior option.
5 Click OK.

Entering the Data

To enter the data for a table, start typing. As you do so, you can click in different cells or use the navigation techniques in Table 4.1 to go here and there in the columns and rows.

SHORTCUT

If you need to add a row at the bottom of the table, place the cursor in the last column of the last row and press the TAB key.

Changing the Table Layout

Tables have minds of their own, and they tend to grow or shrink in spite of the plans their creators make for them. Suppose you have to insert a row or column in the middle of a table, or you want to delete a row or column. Depending on whether you want to insert or delete

Press	To Go Here
TAB	Next column in the row
SHIFT-TAB	Previous column in the row
DOWN ARROW	Row below
UP ARROW	Row above
ALT-HOME	Start of row
ALT-END	End of row
ALT-PAGE UP	Top of column
ALT-PAGE DOWN	Bottom of column

Table 4.1: Getting Around in Word Tables

a column or row, choose these options from the Table menu and its submenus:

- **Insert a column**   Choose Table | Insert and, on the submenu, choose Columns to the Left or Columns to the Right to insert a column to the left or right of the one you clicked in step 1.
- **Insert a row**   Choose Table | Insert and, on the submenu, choose Rows Above or Rows Below to add a row above or below the one you clicked in step 1.
- **Delete a column or row**   Choose Table | Delete and either the Columns or Rows option on the submenu.

SHORTCUT
After you insert one column or row, press F4 to insert another. Keep pressing F4 to insert more columns or rows.

Formatting a Table

Half the commands on the Table menu have to do with formatting tables, but here's a little secret: You don't really have to learn the table-formatting commands. Instead, you can let Microsoft Word do the job—and a very good job, too—of formatting your table. Figure 4.5 demonstrates how to choose a prefabricated format for your table.

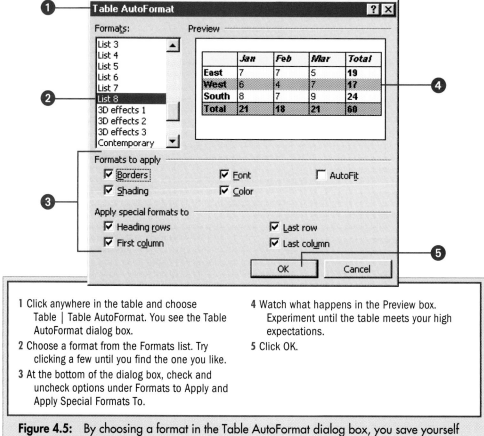

1 Click anywhere in the table and choose Table | Table AutoFormat. You see the Table AutoFormat dialog box.

2 Choose a format from the Formats list. Try clicking a few until you find the one you like.

3 At the bottom of the dialog box, check and uncheck options under Formats to Apply and Apply Special Formats To.

4 Watch what happens in the Preview box. Experiment until the table meets your high expectations.

5 Click OK.

Figure 4.5: By choosing a format in the Table AutoFormat dialog box, you save yourself the trouble of formatting the table on your own.

In a document with more than one table, the tables should be laid out the same way for consistency's sake. Take note of the format you choose in the Table AutoFormat dialog box so you can apply it again to the next table. Remember, you can always click in a table and choose Table | Table AutoFormat to choose a different format.

Ten Tricks for Handling Tables

Here are 10 tricks for working with tables. Some of these tricks require the use of the Tables and Borders toolbar, which you can display by choosing View | Toolbars | Tables and Borders.

1. TURNING ROW LABELS SIDEWAYS TO SAVE SPACE   When
a table gets too wide to fit on the page, you have a problem. One way
to solve the problem is to turn the heading row labels sideways so that
the columns aren't as wide, as was done in the table shown here. To
turn cell contents sideways, drag over the cells to select them and then
click the Change Text Direction button on the Tables and Borders
toolbar. Click it as many times as it takes for the text to face the
right direction.

Another way to fit a wide table on a page is to turn the page sideways and print the page in landscape mode. See "Choosing a Paper Size and Orientation" in Chapter 2.

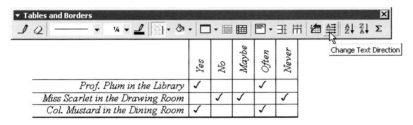

2. ALIGNING TEXT IN COLUMNS AND ROWS   Aligning text
in columns is easy enough. To do so, select the column (by choosing
Table | Select Column) and click an alignment button—Align Left,
Center, Align Right, or Justify—on the Formatting toolbar. Aligning
the text across rows is more problematic:

1. Select the rows whose text you want to align. To do so, drag
   the mouse downward across the rows, right-click, and choose
   Table | Select | Row.

2. Right-click, choose Cell Alignment, and click a cell alignment
   option button on the shortcut menu.

   or

   Click the arrow beside the Cell Alignment button on the Tables
   and Borders toolbar, and click a cell alignment button there.

3. MAKING COLUMNS OR ROWS A UNIFORM SIZE   To make
all the columns or all the rows in a table the same size, click the table,
choose Table | AutoFit, and then choose either Distribute Rows Evenly
or Distribute Columns Evenly from the submenu. All rows are made
as tall as the formerly tallest row in the table or as wide as the
heretofore widest column.

4. ARRANGING A TABLE ON THE PAGE   Normally, a table fits against the left margin of the page, but you can center a table in the middle of the page or make it fit against the right margin. To do so, click in the table and choose Table | Table Properties to open the Table Properties dialog box. Under Alignment on the Table tab, choose Center to center the table or Right to place it against the right margin. You can also indent it from the left margin by entering a measurement in the Indent from Left text box.

5. MAKING TABLE HEADINGS APPEAR ON SUBSEQUENT PAGES   If a table breaks across pages, make sure the heading row—the top row of the table that tells what is in the rows below—appears on the second page. Without the heading row, readers can't easily tell what the information in the table means. To make the headings appear on all pages that the table falls on, click in the heading row and choose Table | Heading Rows Repeat.

6. MERGING CELLS TO CREATE LARGER CELLS   In the table shown here, I merged the cells in the middle row to create one large cell. Then I typed the title of the table in the middle row. Kind of elegant, I think. To merge cells, select the cells you want to merge by dragging over them, and then either click the Merge Cells button on the Tables and Borders toolbar, or right-click and choose Merge Cells.

1993	1994	1995	1996	1997	1998
Mark McGuire's Home Runs					
46	53	51	52	58	70

7. SPLITTING CELLS TO CREATE SMALLER CELLS   The opposite of merging is *splitting*. You can split cells in a table as well as merge them. Splitting cells is chiefly of use in creating paper forms like the one shown here. Gridlines appear in the illustration, but if you were seeing this form after it was printed and you couldn't see the gridlines, you would never know that this form is really a table:

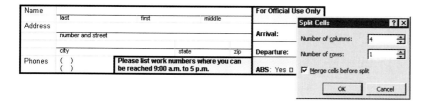

To split cells in a table:

1. Select the cells to be split by dragging the mouse over them.
2. Click the Split Cells button on the Tables and Borders toolbar, or right-click and choose Split Cells. You see the Split Cells dialog box.
3. Enter the number of columns and rows you want to see in the cells you selected and click OK.

The cells you selected in step 1 are divided equally among the number of columns you entered in step 3.

SHORTCUT A fast way to split cells is to click the Draw Table button on the Tables and Borders toolbar and simply draw lines where you want to split cells. This way, you can create cells of unequal size.

8. DOING THE MATH IN TABLES
Please don't do the math in a table yourself —get Word to do it. To compute the data in a table, place the cursor in the cell that will hold the sum or product of the cells above, below, to the right, or to the left, and follow these steps:

1. Choose Table | Formula. You see the Formula dialog box:

TIP If you merely want to total the cells above the location of the cursor, click the AutoSum button on the Tables and Borders toolbar.

2. Choose a function from the drop-down Paste Function menu, and when the function name appears in the Formula box, enter **left**, **right**, **above**, or **below** in the parentheses to tell Word where the figures that you want to compute are. Make sure an equal sign (=) appears before the function name.

3. From the Number Format box, choose a format for your number; then click OK.

You can copy formulas from one cell to another to save yourself the trouble of opening the Formula dialog box by using Word's Copy and Paste commands. To update all the computations in a table, select the table (choose Table | Select | Table) and press F9.

9. ALPHABETIZING TABLE DATA   On the Table menu is a command that you can use to quickly alphabetize the data in a table column. Choose Table | Sort and you see the Sort dialog box. To begin with, the dialog box wants to alphabetize the first column in the table, but you can choose another column by selecting it from the drop-down Sort By menu. Click OK and your table is alphabetized.

10. TURNING AN ADDRESS LIST INTO A TABLE   Suppose you need to turn an address list into a table—perhaps so you can generate mailing labels from the address list. Yes, you can do this, but not in the twinkling of an eye. The Table menu offers a command called Convert | Text to Table, but to use it you have to get the list ready first. To do so, go through the list and do the following for each addressee:

- Remove the spaces, commas, or whatever it is that divides each part of the address, and press the TAB key where the division mark is now. For example, if the address is divided into five parts (first and last name, street address, city, state, and zip code), make sure a tab space and nothing else appears after each part. When the conversion is done, the columns will begin and end where you entered the tab spaces.
- Make sure each address is divided by tab spaces into the same number of parts—for example, first and last name, street address, city, state, and zip code.

- Make sure each addressee appears on his or her own line in the list. In other words, each addressee should appear in a paragraph. After the conversion, each paragraph will turn into a row in the table.

To convert the list into a table, select it and choose Table | Convert | Text to Table. You see the Convert Text to Table dialog box. Make sure the Tabs option button is selected under Separate Text At in the bottom of the dialog box. Also make sure that the number in the Number of Columns text box is the same as the number of parts in your address list. If the two numbers aren't the same, something is amiss in your list, and you have to examine the list to see where you forgot to enter a tab space. If all is well and the numbers match, click OK to convert the list into a table.

Putting Newspaper-Style Columns in a Document

Probably the easiest way to prove your word-processing prowess is to run text in newspaper-style columns. Columns look great, and you can pack a lot of words into them. To lay out text in columns, you can either click the Columns button on the Standard toolbar or choose the Format | Columns command. For no-frills columns, type the text, select it, click the Columns button, and choose the number of columns you want from the drop-down menu. To create more than four columns, click and drag outward with the mouse.

When you introduce columns in a document, Word creates a new section automatically. "Dividing a Document into Sections" in Chapter 3 explains sections. Columns appear only in Print Layout view and Print Preview view. See "Viewing Documents in Different Ways" in Chapter 3.

News on the Marsh

This week saw an upsurge in the number of tadpoles on the marsh. The little creatures, bursting with spring vitality, were spotted Sunday last by Ms. Anita Browles during her morning constitutional.

This year's crop looks exceptionally healthy, according to Rick Nichols of the Forest Service, who observed that there seem to be more tads on the marsh this year than in past years.

"Of course, counting tadpoles is a fool's game," he said. "But I really think there are more on the marsh than ever before."

To demonstrate his assertion, Ranger Nichols reached into the marsh and pulled out a handful of the wriggling little creatures. "Look at that, will ya?" he said. "It makes an old ranger's heart glad. Why, I haven't seen this many tads since the historic spring of '63."

EXPERT ADVICE

Text in columns, especially narrow columns, looks better when it is hyphenated and justified. To justify text, select it and click the Justify button on the Formatting toolbar. In Chapter 3, "Hyphenating Text" explains hyphenation techniques.

By choosing the Format | Columns command, you can take advantage of the various amenities in the Columns dialog box shown in Figure 4.6. Either select the text to be laid out in columns or place the cursor where you want to introduce the columns, then choose Format | Columns, and negotiate these options:

- **Presets**   Choose a preset number of columns. The One option is for removing columns.
- **Number of Columns**   Enter a number if you want more than three columns.

Click to draw lines between columns.

Choose preformatted columns . . .

. . . or format the columns yourself.

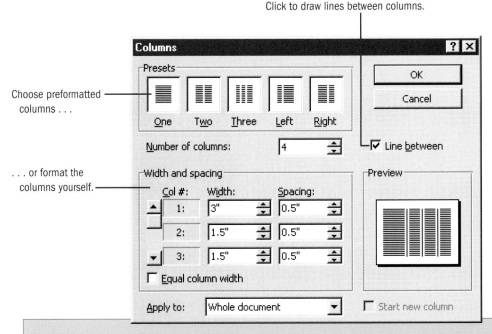

Figure 4.6:   Choose Format | Columns to draw lines between columns or create columns of different widths.

- **Line Between**   Check this box to draw lines between the columns.
- **Col #**   If you create more than three columns, use the scroll bar to enter the width and spacing measurements for columns 4 and up.
- **Width**   If you uncheck the Equal Column Width box, you can create columns of different sizes. Enter a width measurement in each Width box.
- **Spacing**   Enter measurements to put blank spaces to the right of columns.
- **Equal Column Width**   Checking this box creates columns of equal width.
- **Apply To**   Choose which part of the document gets columns— selected text, the section the cursor is in, this point forward in your document, or the whole document.
- **Start New Column**   Click to break a column before it reaches the bottom of the page.

TIP

Rather than visiting the Columns dialog box and clicking the Start New Column checkbox, you can break a column before it reaches the bottom of the page by placing the cursor where you want the break to be and pressing CTRL-SHIFT-ENTER. **Or you can choose Insert | Break and click the Column Break option button.**

Finding the Right Word with the Thesaurus

Choosing the right word is so important in writing that Microsoft has included a thesaurus with its word processor. Use Word's Thesaurus to find *synonyms*—words that have the same or a similar meaning. To find a synonym for a word, click the word in question and either press SHIFT-F7 or choose Tools | Language | Thesaurus. You see the Thesaurus dialog box shown in Figure 4.7. Use these boxes and buttons to find the synonym you so desperately seek:

- **Looked Up**   Lists the words you investigated in your search for a synonym. Choose a word from the drop-down menu to backtrack.
- **Meanings**   Lists the various ways in which the word can be used. Click a word to steer the search in a different direction.

Click to see a list of synonyms for the current replacement word.

Click to see a list of the words you've looked up.

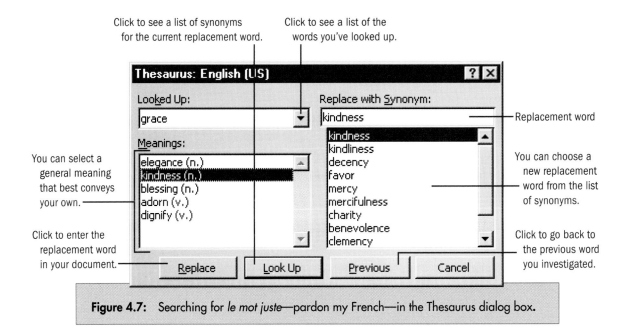

Replacement word

You can select a general meaning that best conveys your own.

You can choose a new replacement word from the list of synonyms.

Click to enter the replacement word in your document.

Click to go back to the previous word you investigated.

Figure 4.7: Searching for *le mot juste*—pardon my French—in the Thesaurus dialog box.

SHORTCUT

You can type your own replacement word in the Replace with Synonym box.

- **Replace with Synonym** Lists what the program thinks is the best synonym for the word in the Looked Up box. Click a word in the box below to make it the replacement word—the word that goes in your document when you click the Replace button.

- **Replace** Enters the word in the Replace with Synonym box in the document. Click this button when your search is done.

- **Look Up** Tells the program to find synonyms for the word in the Replace with Synonym box. Click to see a new batch of synonyms.

- **Previous** Lists synonyms for the last word you investigated. Click this button to backtrack.

Tools for Reports and Scholarly Papers

The rest of this chapter is dedicated to the brave men and women who have to write reports and scholarly papers and do it in a hurry. As you break new ground, as you expand the storehouse of scientific knowledge or sweep away the cobwebs of history or dig deep into the vagaries of the world economy, you certainly don't want to waste any time word processing. These pages describe techniques for writing reports and white papers. Here you will find out how outlines can help you stay organized, how to generate a table of contents, and how to include footnotes in documents.

Outlines for Organizing Your Work

As long as you've assigned heading styles to the headings in your report, you can switch to Outline view and see how the different parts of your report fit together. If they don't fit together, you can rearrange headings and simultaneously move text backward or forward in the document. You can also promote and demote headings. To switch to Outline view, click the Outline View button or choose View | Outline. Your screen looks something like Figure 4.8. Do you recognize the headings in the figure? Why, that's Chapter 4 all over again!

Editing headings in Outline view is very easy. All you have to do is click and start typing or deleting text. Click the 1, 2, 3, or one of the other number buttons on the Outlining toolbar to see only first-, second-, third-, or fourth-level headings. Or click the All button to see all headings and the first line of each paragraph in the document. While you are staring at your headings, take advantage of these techniques:

- **Moving headings (and the text beneath them)** To move a heading and the text and subheadings beneath it forward or backward in a document, click the heading and then click the Collapse button. Then click the Move Up or Move Down button and watch the heading move backward or forward in the document.

- **Promoting and demoting headings** To promote a heading to a higher level or demote a heading by a level, click the Promote or Demote button, or else choose a new heading style from the Style menu.

Styles are explained in "Styles for Consistent and Easy Formatting" at the start of this chapter. See "Viewing Documents in Different Ways" in Chapter 3 to learn about views.

Click to promote or demote headings and text.

Move headings and text forward or backward in the document.

See or hide headings and text under the selected heading.

See headings of different levels.

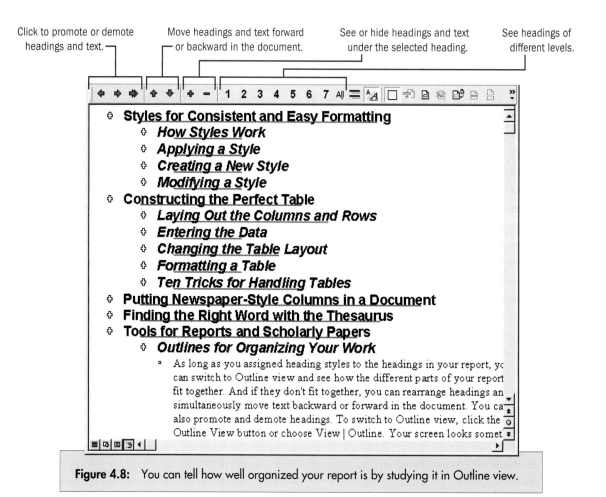

Figure 4.8:   You can tell how well organized your report is by studying it in Outline view.

Generating a Table of Contents

Every reference work needs a table of contents (TOC) so readers can find what they need to find in the work. As long as you conscientiously applied heading styles to the headings in your document, generating a TOC is very, very easy. Here's how to do it:

See "Styles for Consistent and Easy Formatting" at the beginning of this chapter to learn how to apply styles, including heading styles, to your text.

1. At the start of the document, type **Table of Contents** and press ENTER.

2. Choose Insert | Index and Tables and click the Table of Contents tab in the Index and Tables dialog box. You see the Table of Contents tab:

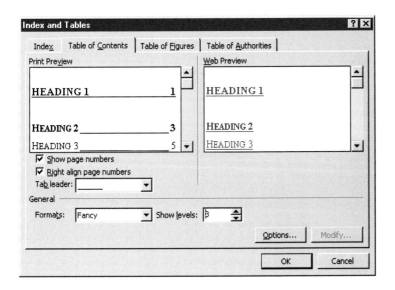

3. From the drop-down Formats menu, choose a design. Watch the Print Preview box to see what your design looks like.

4. In the Show Levels box, tell Word how deep the TOC should be. Entering 2, for example, includes only headings assigned the Heading 1 and Heading 2 styles.

5. Choose a tab leader, and indicate whether to show page numbers and whether to right-align them. (A *tab leader* is a punctuation mark that appears between the heading and the page number in a TOC.) As you make these decisions, keep your eye on the Print Preview box.

6. Click OK.

CAUTION

Don't include too many headings in your table of contents. Readers go to the table of contents to look up information quickly. Having to read through many headings defeats the purpose.

Later, if you need to update your table of contents because you added or deleted headings, right-click it and choose Update Field. You see the Update Table of Contents dialog box. Choose Update Entire Table and click OK.

In Chapter 3, "Dividing a Document into Sections" explains how to create a new section, and "Putting Headers and Footers on Pages" explains how to impose different page-numbering schemes on the different sections in a document.

Put your table of contents in its own section, and start numbering the pages in the section after the TOC. If you don't follow my advice, your TOC will appear on page 2 or 3, and the first page in the document will not be marked page 1, but page 4 or 5, for example.

Putting Footnotes and Endnotes in Documents

Footnotes are references, explanations, or comments that appear along the bottom of a page. *Endnotes* are the same as footnotes, except that they appear at the end of the chapter. When you write footnotes and endnotes, you still have to list authors, their works, the dates their works were published, and the rest of the scholarly hoopla, but at least you don't have to worry about formatting, deleting, or moving the notes. Word handles that for you.

Follow these steps to insert a footnote or endnote:

1. Click in the document where you want to place the *note citation,* the number or symbol that marks the footnote or endnote.

2. Choose Insert | Footnote. You see the Footnote and Endnote dialog box.

3. Click Footnote to enter a footnote or Endnote to enter an endnote.

4. Under Numbering, make the citation a number or a symbol:

   • **AutoNumber**   Click this option to number the notes automatically.

   • **Custom Mark**   Click this option to mark the note with a symbol. Then either enter the symbol yourself or click the Symbol button and enter it by way of the Symbol dialog box.

5. Click OK. In Print Layout view, you go to the bottom of the page or to the end of the document or section, where, beside the symbol or number, you can type the footnote or endnote. In Normal view, you see a box for typing the footnote or endnote:

6. Type the footnote or endnote.

7. Click Close if you are in Normal view to leave the Notes box. In Page Layout view, scroll up the page.

To read a footnote or endnote, all you have to do is gently move the pointer over its citation in the text. A pop-up box appears so you can read the note. Do the following to edit, move, or delete a note:

> Foster, David Wallace, "Sometimes Text Is Just a Cigar," Harper's, March 1999, 66-71.

- **Editing a note** Double-click the note's citation. You see the Notes box at the bottom of the page if you are in Normal view, or at the end of the chapter if you are in Print Layout view. Edit the note.

- **Moving a note** Select the note's citation in the text and either cut and paste or drag it to a new location. When you move a note, all other notes are renumbered, if necessary.

- **Deleting a note** Select the note's citation and press the DELETE key. The remaining notes are renumbered, if necessary.

CHAPTER 5

Up and Running with Excel 2000

INCLUDES

- Analyzing data with worksheets
- Speedy ways to enter data
- Selecting, deleting, copying, and moving data
- Formatting numbers
- Aligning and centering numbers and text in columns and rows
- Inserting, deleting, and changing the size of columns and rows
- Drawing borders in and applying colors to worksheets
- Rearranging, inserting, and deleting worksheets in a workbook

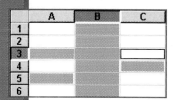

Enter Data Quickly in Cells ➡ pp. 114-118

- Click in a cell and start typing. Press ENTER when you're ready to move to the next cell in the column.
- To enter serial data, enter the first piece of data (or the first and second in the case of numbers and dates) and start dragging the AutoFill handle, the small black square in the lower-right corner of the cell.

Select Cells So You Can Format Data ➡ pp. 118-119

- Drag across adjacent cells to select them.
- Drag diagonally across a block of cells to select it, or else click one corner and SHIFT-click the opposite corner.
- Hold down the CTRL key and click or drag across different cells to select them.
- Click a row number or drag across several row numbers to select rows.
- Click a column letter or drag across several column letters to select columns.

Use the Format Buttons to Change Number Formats ➡ pp. 120-121

- Click the Currency Style button to put dollar signs on numbers.
- Click the Percent Style button to display numbers as percentages.
- Click the Comma Style button to place commas in numbers.
- Click the Increase Decimal or Decrease Decimal button to increase or decrease the number of decimal places in numbers.

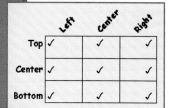

Align Text and Numbers in Columns and Rows ➡ pp. 121-123

- Select numbers in columns and click the Align Left, Center, or Align Right button to align numbers horizontally.
- Select numbers in rows, choose Format I Cells, and click the Alignment tab to align numbers vertically.
- Select a heading as well as cells adjacent to it and click the Merge and Center button to center text across several cells.

Insert or Remove Rows and Columns ➡ pp. 123-124

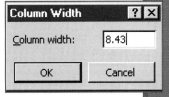

- **Inserting**   Right-click a row number or column letter and choose Insert from the shortcut menu. To insert several rows or columns at once, drag across row numbers or column letters before right-clicking.
- **Removing**   Drag across the row numbers or column letters, right-click, and choose Delete from the shortcut menu.

Change the Size of Columns and Rows ➡ pp. 124-125

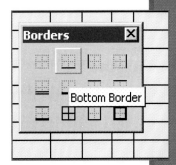

- Move the pointer into the row headings or column headings, and drag the border of the column or row whose size you want to change.
- Select columns or rows and choose either Format | Column | Width or Format | Row | Height. In the Column Width or Row Height dialog box, enter new measurements.

Draw Borders Around Worksheet Data ➡ p. 126

1. Select the cells that you want to draw borders around.
2. Click the down arrow beside the Borders button on the Formatting toolbar and click a border button.

Rename or Delete Worksheets in a Workbook ➡ p. 127

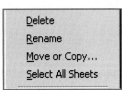

1. Right-click a worksheet tab at the bottom of the Excel window.
2. Choose Rename or Delete from the shortcut menu.
3. Either enter a new name for the worksheet or click OK to delete it.

This is the first of two chapters that explain Excel 2000, the official bean counter of Office 2000. Use Excel to track, tabulate, and analyze data. Use it to plan next year's budget, find out last year's profits, or analyze Elvis sightings in North America. After you enter your numbers in Excel and tell the program how to tabulate them, the rest is easy, because Excel does the math for you. All you have to do is sit back and see how the numbers stack up.

In Chapter 2, "Opening a New File" explains how to open a new Excel workbook file.

This chapter explains how to enter the data in Excel. Here you'll learn what worksheets and workbooks are, how to enter the numbers, and how to lay out worksheets so that others can read and understand them. The next chapter takes on the onerous task of building formulas to compute the numbers you've so carefully entered.

Introducing Worksheets and Workbooks

	B
1	
2	
3	**1996**
4	178
5	561
6	89
7	828

Before you learn anything else about Excel, you need to know about worksheets. A *worksheet* is a table where you enter data and data labels. Figure 5.1 shows a worksheet with data about Elvis sightings. Notice how the worksheet is divided by gridlines into columns (A, B, C, and so on) and rows (1, 2, 3, and so on). The rectangles where columns and rows intersect are called *cells,* and each cell can hold one data item.

In Figure 5.1, for example, cell B4 holds 178, the number of Elvis sightings in Canada in 1996. Meanwhile, as the Formula bar at the top of the screen shows, cell B7 holds the formula B4+B5+B6, the sum of the numbers in cells B4, B5, and B6. Cell B7 shows the number 828, the result of the formula (178+561+89)—the total number of Elvis sightings in Canada, the United States, and Mexico in 1996.

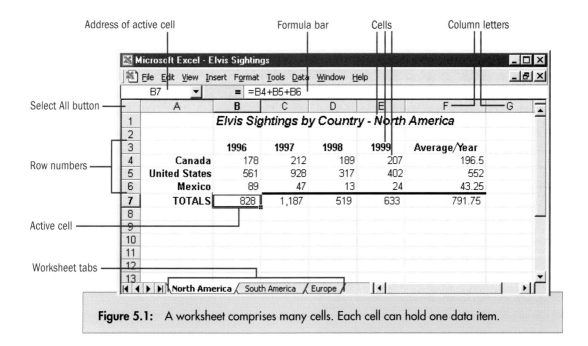

Figure 5.1:   A worksheet comprises many cells. Each cell can hold one data item.

The beauty of Excel is that the program does all of the calculations and recalculations for you. If I were to change the number in cell B4, Excel would instantly recalculate the total number of Elvis sightings in 1996 and enter the new total in cell B7. You don't have to worry about the math—all you have to do is make sure that the data and the formulas are entered correctly.

Each worksheet has 256 columns and 65,536 rows—not that anyone outside the federal government needs that many. The rows are numbered, and columns are labeled A to Z, then AA to AZ, then BA to BZ, and so on. The important thing to remember is that each cell has an address whose name comes from a column letter and a row number. The first cell in row 1 is A1, the second is A2, and so on. You need to enter cell addresses in formulas to tell Excel which numbers to compute. To learn a cell's address, either study the gridlines to see which column and row it lies in or click the cell and glance at the

Formula bar. The left side of the Formula bar lists the address of the *active cell,* which is the cell most recently clicked. Here I've clicked cell G10:

| G10 | ▾ | ✕ ✓ = | B10+C10+D10+E10+F10 |

At the end of this chapter, "Handling the Worksheets in a Workbook" explains how to delete, add, rename, and change the order of worksheets in a workbook.

When you open a new Excel file, you open a *workbook,* a file with three worksheets in it. The worksheets are called Sheet1, Sheet2, and Sheet3, and you can go from one to the other by clicking tabs along the bottom of the Excel screen. Why three worksheets? Because you might need more than one worksheet for a single project. Think of a workbook as a stack of worksheets. Besides calculating the numbers in cells across the rows or down the columns of a worksheet, you can make calculations throughout a workbook by using numbers from different worksheets in a calculation.

Entering and Editing the Data

In Chapter 6, "All About Formulas" explains how formulas work, and "Entering a Formula" demonstrates how to enter a formula in a cell.

The first step in creating a glorious worksheet is to enter the data and data labels. These pages explain the basic techniques for doing that as well as some speed techniques to make entering data easier. You will also find instructions here for getting around in a worksheet and for selecting, copying, moving, and deleting data.

Entering Data in a Worksheet

Don't worry too much about putting data in the right places on the worksheet. Later I'll show you how to move data, insert rows and columns, remove rows and columns, and enlarge rows and columns. Follow these steps to enter the data or a label in a worksheet:

1. Click the cell where you want to enter the data or label. A square appears around the cell to show that it is the active cell. If you're not sure which cell you are about to enter data in, glance at the left side of the Formula bar. It lists the cell address.

2. Start typing, or, if you find typing in the Formula bar easier, click and start typing there. As soon as you type the first character, you see the Cancel button (an ×), the Enter button (a checkmark), and the Edit Formula button (an equal sign) on the Formula bar.

3. Do any of the following after you type the data:
   - Press an arrow key on the keyboard. Doing so enters the data and moves the cursor to the adjacent cell.
   - Press the ENTER key. The cursor moves down a cell.
   - Click the Enter button (the checkmark) on the Formula bar.

When a number is too large to fit in a cell, Excel displays pound signs (###) instead of a number or displays the number in scientific notation. You can always solve the problem of not being able to see numbers in their entirety by making the columns wider, as explained in "Changing the Width of Columns and the Height of Rows" later in this chapter.

To accommodate text entries that are too wide to fit in a column, Excel lets the text spill into the next cell, unless there happens to be something there as well. To solve this problem, either widen the column or shorten the text entry. Whether or not Excel can display what is in a cell, the program retains the entire number or text entry in memory and uses it for all calculations. Nothing gets lost when it can't be displayed onscreen.

Speed Techniques for Entering Data

Entering data in a worksheet is a tedious business, so Excel offers a few speed techniques to take the sting out of the job. These pages explain how AutoFill can help you enter things like serial numbers and months faster. You also learn how to "freeze" panes so that data labels always appear onscreen no matter where you go in a worksheet.

AutoFill for Entering Serial Data

Certain kinds of data fall in the "serial" category—month names and consecutive numbers and dates, for example. Instead of laboriously

TIP

Look on the Formula bar to see precisely what number or text entry is in a cell.

To enter data more easily, you can make the screen look larger or smaller. See "Learn to Zoom In and Zoom Out" in Chapter 1.

entering serial data one piece at a time, you can get Excel's help to enter it all at once. Believe it or not, Excel recognizes certain kinds of serial data and will enter it for you as part of the AutoFill feature. Follow these steps to "autofill" cells with serial data:

SHORTCUT

To enter the same number or text in several different cells, either drag over the cells to select them or select each cell by holding down the CTRL key as you click it. Next, type a number or some text and press CTRL-ENTER.

1. Click the cell that is to be first in the series. For example, if you intend to list the months in consecutive cells, click where the first month is to go.

2. Enter the first item in the series, or, if you want to enter numbers or dates, enter the first and second items in adjacent cells. Excel needs the first and second items in the case of numbers and dates so it can tell how much to increase or decrease the given amount or time period in each cell. For example, entering 2000 and 2001 tells Excel to increase the number by 1 each time, so that the next serial entry is 2002.

3. Select the cells or cells. To select a single cell, click it; drag over the cells to select two.

   At the lower-right corner of your selection is a tiny black square called the AutoFill handle. When you move the mouse pointer over it, it changes into a black cross.

4. Click the AutoFill handle and start dragging in the direction in which you want the data series to appear on your worksheet. The black cross follows you as you drag, and the serial data appears in a pop-up box:

AutoFill handle

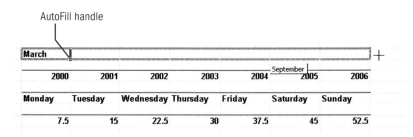

Freezing Panes So You Always See Data Labels

Suppose your adventures in Excel take you to a faraway cell address, like Z26. Out there, it's hard to tell where to enter data because you can't see the data labels that describe what the data in the worksheet is. However, you can solve this problem by "freezing" the labels to make the data in one column and one row appear wherever you go in a worksheet.

In Figure 5.2, cell G19 is the active cell, yet you can still see the data labels in row 1 (Property, Management Fee, and so on) and column A (the property addresses) because row 1 and column A are frozen onscreen. Without any trouble, you can tell that cell G19 is where you enter the cost of removing the trash at 6177 North Creel Street.

To freeze panes so you can always see the data labels, follow these steps:

1. Click the cell located directly below the row you want to freeze and in the column to the right of the column you want to freeze.

   In Figure 5.2, for example, I clicked cell B2, row 2 being below row 1, the row with the column labels (Property, Management Fee, and so on), and column B being to the right of column A, the column with the row labels (the property addresses).

A nother way to always see the column headings is to split the Excel window. See "Splitting a File Window to Work in Two Sections at Once" in Chapter 1.

Lines onscreen indicate which row(s) and column(s) you've frozen.

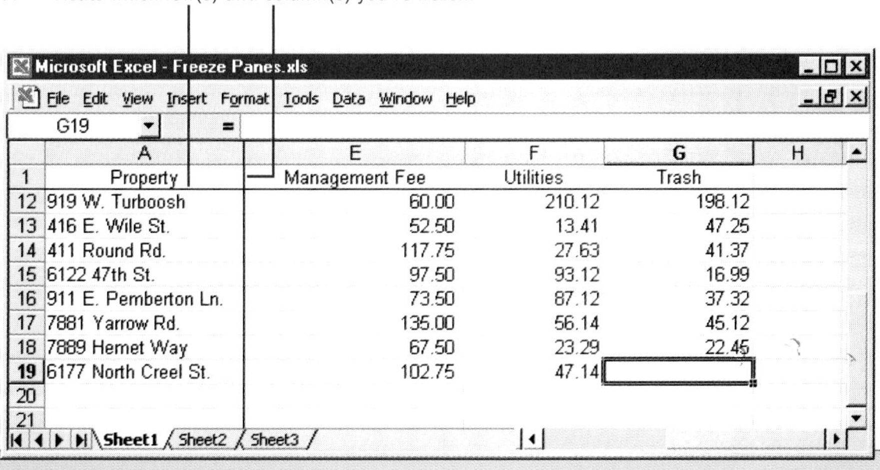

Figure 5.2: Freeze the labels in large worksheets so you can be sure you are entering data in the right cells.

2. Choose Window | Freeze Panes. Notice that lines are drawn onscreen to show the row and column where your panes are frozen.

Now you can move where you will in the worksheet, and the sections that you've frozen stay visible onscreen. When you no longer require frozen window panes, simply choose Window | Unfreeze Panes.

Moving Around in a Worksheet

As a worksheet gets larger, going from place to place gets harder. Table 5.1 lists keyboard shortcuts you can use to move around in a large worksheet. While you're at it, try these techniques for getting around as well:

- **Scroll bars**   Use the vertical and horizontal scroll bars to get from place to place.
- **Go to a specific cell**   Choose Edit | Go To (or press CTRL-G) to open the Go To dialog box. Enter a cell address in the Reference box and click OK to go directly to the cell.
- **Find text**   Choose Edit | Find (or press CTRL-F) to open the Find dialog box. Enter the text you seek in the Find What box and click the Find Next button.

Selecting Cells in a Worksheet

Before you can format data, copy it, move it, or delete it, you have to select it. Here are instructions for selecting cells and the data inside them:

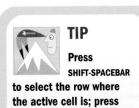

TIP

Press SHIFT-SPACEBAR to select the row where the active cell is; press CTRL-SPACEBAR to select the column the active cell is in.

- **Adjacent cells in the same row or column**   Drag across the cells.
- **A block of cells**   Drag diagonally across the worksheet from one corner of the block of cells to the opposite corner. You can also click one corner and SHIFT-click the opposite corner.

Press	To Move the Cursor
CTRL-HOME	To cell A1, the first cell in the worksheet
CTRL-END	To the last cell with data in it
HOME	To column A of the current row
CTRL-RIGHT ARROW, CTRL-LEFT ARROW, CTRL-UP ARROW, or CTRL-DOWN ARROW	In one direction toward the nearest cell with data in it or to the first or last cell in the column or row
PAGE UP or PAGE DOWN	Up or down one screenful of rows
ALT-PAGE UP or ALT-PAGE DOWN	Left or right one screenful of columns

Table 5.1: Keyboard Shortcuts for Moving Around in Worksheets

- **Cells in various places**   Hold down the CTRL key and click different cells, drag across different cells, and click row numbers and column letters.
- **A row or rows**   Click the row number to select an entire row. Click and drag down the row numbers to select several rows.
- **A column or columns**   Click the column letter to select an entire column. Click and drag across letters to select several columns.
- **The entire worksheet**   Click the Select All button, which is the blank square to the left of the column letters and above the row numbers.

Deleting, Copying, and Moving Data

To empty cells of their contents, select the cells and either press the DELETE key or right-click and choose Clear Contents.

In Chapter 2, "Copying and Moving Data" explains how to copy and move data in an Office 2000 program.

Use the standard Cut, Copy, and Paste commands to copy or move data in an Excel worksheet. When you paste the data, click where you want the first cell of the block of cells you are copying or moving to go. Be careful not to overwrite cells with data in them when you copy or move data. And don't forget the Undo button when you copy and move data. You can click it to reverse your last command, which you sometimes have to do when you paste data in the wrong location.

As for the drag-and-drop method of copying and moving text, you can use it as well. Move the pointer to the edge of the cell block, click when you see the arrow, and start dragging.

Laying Out a Worksheet

A worksheet doesn't have to look drab and solemn. If you intend to print your worksheet or show it to others, you may as well dress it in its Sunday best. And you can do a number of things to make worksheets easier to read and understand. You can change character fonts. You can draw borders around or shade important cells. You can also format the numbers so that readers know, for example, whether they are staring at dollar figures or percentages. Read on to find out how to make a gaudy patchwork-quilt worksheet like this one:

Formatting the Numbers

On the Formatting toolbar are five buttons—Currency Style, Percent Style, Comma Style, Increase Decimal, and Decrease Decimal—that you can click to determine how numbers are formatted in worksheets.

Select cells with numbers in them and then click one of these buttons to change the numbers' formatting:

Button	Name	What It Does
$	Currency Style	Places a dollar sign before the number and gives it two decimal places.
%	Percent Style	Places a percent sign after the number and converts it to a percentage.
,	Comma Style	Places commas in the number.
+.0 .00	Increase Decimal	Increases the number of decimal places by one.
.00 +.0	Decrease Decimal	Decreases the number of decimal places by one.

Aligning Numbers and Text in Columns and Rows

To begin with, numbers are right-aligned in cells and text is left-aligned, but you can change that by selecting cells and clicking an alignment button on the Formatting toolbar. Suppose you want to change the way that text and numbers are aligned across the rows. Read on. These pages explain how to change the alignment of data in rows, change the orientation of cells, and center text across several cells.

In Chapter 2, "Aligning and Justifying Text" explains how to align text with the alignment buttons on the Formatting toolbar.

Changing the Alignment of Data in Rows

Changing the alignment of data across rows is done by way of the Format | Cells command. You can place the data at the top, center, or bottom of the cells:

Top	3	Constantinople	4	Timbuktu	5
Center	3	Constantinople	4	Timbuktu	5
Bottom	3	Constantinople	4	Timbuktu	5

Figure 5.3 shows you how to change the alignment of text and numbers across a row or several adjacent cells.

Changing the Orientation of Text

Notice the Orientation box and the Degrees slider box on the Alignment tab (see Figure 5.3). By clicking and dragging the orange diamond in the Orientation box or entering a number in the Degrees

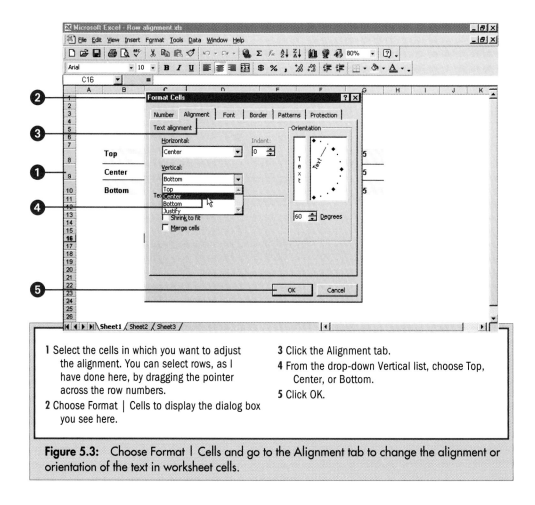

1 Select the cells in which you want to adjust the alignment. You can select rows, as I have done here, by dragging the pointer across the row numbers.

2 Choose Format | Cells to display the dialog box you see here.

3 Click the Alignment tab.

4 From the drop-down Vertical list, choose Top, Center, or Bottom.

5 Click OK.

Figure 5.3:   Choose Format | Cells and go to the Alignment tab to change the alignment or orientation of the text in worksheet cells.

box, you can change the orientation of text in cells. I chose a 75-degree orientation for the column labels in this worksheet:

Centering Text Across Several Cells

In the following example, notice that "Sales Totals by Regional Office" is centered across five cells:

	Sales Totals by Regional Office				
Montana	Idaho	Wyoming	South Dakota	North Dakota

Merge and Center

Normally, text is left-aligned, but if you want to center it across several cells, drag across the cells to select them and then click the Merge and Center button, as I've done here.

Inserting and Removing Rows and Columns

At some point, you'll have to insert new columns and rows and delete those that are no longer needed. Inserting and deleting rows and columns is easy to do, but make sure before you delete a row or

---

EXPERT ADVICE

Changing the orientation of text in cells is an elegant solution to the problem of keeping a worksheet from getting too wide. Numbers are usually a few characters wide, but heading labels can be much wider than that. By changing the orientation of a heading label, you make columns narrower and keep worksheets from growing too fat to fit on the page.

column that you don't delete data you really need. To insert and delete rows and columns, follow these instructions:

- **Inserting rows**   Right-click the row number below where you want the new row to be, and choose Insert from the shortcut menu. For example, to insert a new row above row 9, right-click the row 9 heading number and choose Insert. Alternatively, you can simply click in the worksheet below where you want the row to appear and choose Insert | Rows. To insert more than one row at a time, select more than one row number or more than one cell before giving the Insert command.

- **Inserting columns**   Right-click the column letter to the right of where you want the new column to be, and choose Insert from the shortcut menu. You can also click in the worksheet and choose Insert | Columns.
Select more than one column or select adjacent cells to insert more than one column at one time with the Insert command. You can also simply insert one column and keep pressing F4 until you've inserted all of them.

- **Deleting rows or columns**   Drag across the heading numbers or letters of the rows or columns you want to delete to select them. Then right-click and choose Delete from the shortcut menu.

Changing the Width of Columns and the Height of Rows

Rows are 12.75 points high, but Excel makes them taller when you enter letters or numbers that are taller than 12.75 points. Columns are 8.43 characters wide. To make columns wider, you have to widen them yourself. (You can change the 8.43-character standard width for columns in a worksheet by choosing Format | Column | Standard Width.)

Follow these instructions to make columns wider or rows taller:

- **Changing the height of rows**   To change the height of a single row, move the mouse pointer onto the row heading numbers and point to the bottom border of the row whose height you want to change. When the pointer changes to a double-headed arrow, click and drag the border up or down. A pop-up box tells you how tall the row will be when you release the mouse button.

  To change the height of several rows, select them and choose Format | Row | Height. In the Row Height dialog box, enter a row height larger or smaller than the default 12.75 points and click OK.

- **Changing the width of columns**   To make a single column wider or narrower, move the mouse pointer onto the column heading letters and point to the border to the right of the column whose size you want to change. When you see the double-headed arrow, click and drag the border left or right. A pop-up box tells you how wide the column will be when you release the mouse button.

  To make several rows the same width, select them and choose Format | Column | Width. Then enter the number of characters you want to fit in the column and click OK.

Earlier in this chapter, "Selecting Cells in a Worksheet" explains how to select rows and columns.

EXPERT ADVICE

Rather than changing the width of columns one at a time, you can tell Excel to make columns as wide as their widest entries. This way, you can be sure that data in each cell appears onscreen. To adjust the width of columns to their widest entries, select the columns and choose Format | Column | AutoFit Selection.

Borders and Colors for Worksheets

Gridlines are not printed when you print a worksheet—their job is simply to help you line up numbers and letters in cells. Because gridlines are not printed, drawing borders on worksheets is absolutely necessary if you intend to print your worksheet. Use borders to steer the reader's eye to the most important parts of a worksheet—the totals, column labels, and heading labels. You can also decorate worksheets with colors. This part of the chapter explains how to put borders and colors on worksheets.

Drawing Borders on Worksheets

To draw borders on a worksheet, start by selecting the cells around which you want to place borders. Then click the down arrow beside the Borders button on the Formatting toolbar and choose a border. Usually, you have to wrestle with the Borders buttons until you come up with borders you like. By the way, don't be afraid to click the Undo button and start all over, or to select a new set of cells and press F4 to apply the same kind of border a second time.

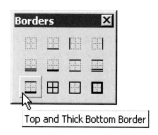

Top and Thick Bottom Border

The Border tab in the Format Cells dialog box offers different lines and colors for your borders. Choose Format | Cells and click the Border tab if you want to try your hand at applying borders by way of the dialog box.

Decorating Worksheets with Colors

To fill your cells with background color, select the cells, click the down arrow beside the Fill Color button, and choose a color from the drop-down menu. Choose No Fill from the drop-down menu to remove any color from the selected cells. You can also choose Format | Cells and click the Patterns tab in the Format Cells dialog box. Click the Pattern down arrow and choose a pattern for the cells, if that idea tickles your fancy.

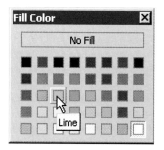

Handling the Worksheets in a Workbook

As you know if you read the start of this chapter, each workbook comes with three worksheets. Herewith are instructions for moving among, adding, deleting, renaming, and changing the order of worksheets:

- **Moving among worksheets** To go from one worksheet to another, click a tab along the bottom of the screen. You can also click the buttons to the left of the worksheet tabs.

- **Deleting a worksheet** Right-click the worksheet tab, choose Delete from the shortcut menu, and click OK.

- **Renaming a worksheet** Right-click the worksheet tab, choose Rename from the shortcut menu, type a new name, and press ENTER.

- **Inserting a worksheet** To start a new worksheet, choose Insert | Worksheet. Then type a name for your worksheet on the new worksheet tab and press ENTER.

- **Rearranging worksheets** To change the order of worksheets, click and drag the worksheet tabs to their new locations. As you drag a worksheet tab, a tiny black arrow and page icon appear. Release the mouse button when the tiny black arrow points to where you want the worksheet to be:

CHAPTER 6

Advanced Excel 2000

INCLUDES

- How formulas work
- Entering a formula in a worksheet cell
- Speedy ways to enter cell references in formulas
- Copying formulas from cell to cell
- Using Excel's functions in formulas
- Creating a chart from worksheet data
- Changing the layout and appearance of a chart
- Choosing a new chart type and sub-type for a chart

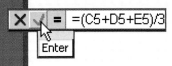

Enter a Formula to
Calculate Worksheet Data ➡ pp. 132–136

1. Click the cell where you want to enter the formula, click in the Formula bar, and enter an equal sign (=).

2. Enter the formula, making sure all cell addresses are entered correctly, and either press ENTER or click the Enter button.

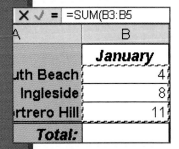

Enter Cell References in Formulas
by Clicking or Selecting Cells ➡ pp. 136–137

• As you enter a formula, click the cell on the worksheet that you want to refer to. Shimmering marquee lights appear around the cell, and its address is entered on the Formula bar.

• Drag across cells to enter a range in a formula. Marquee lights appear around the cells you selected, and the range is entered on the Formula bar.

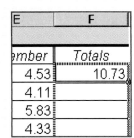

Copy Formulas from
Row to Row or Column to Column ➡ pp. 137–138

1. Click the cell whose formula needs copying.

2. Drag the AutoFill handle to copy the formula down rows or across columns.

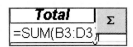

Quickly Total the Numbers in a
Column or Row with the SUM Function ➡ p. 139

1. Click at the end of a column or row where you want the sum of the adjacent cells to appear.

2. Click the AutoSum button on the Standard toolbar.

Compute Data with
One of Excel's Functions ➦ pp. 139–140

1. Type = in the Formula bar and click the Paste Function button.
2. Choose a function category and function name in the Paste Function dialog box and click OK.
3. In the Function palette, enter the arguments for the function and click OK.

Create a Chart from Your Data ➦ pp. 141–142

1. Select the data you want to plot in a chart.
2. Click the Chart Wizard button.
3. Choose a chart type and sub-type in the first Chart Wizard dialog box.
4. Choose options in the other three Chart Wizard dialog boxes and click Finish.

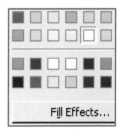

Change the Appearance of a Chart ➦ pp. 143–144

1. Double-click the part of the chart—the chart area, category axis, or legend, for example—that needs changing.
2. Choose options and settings in the Format dialog box and click OK.

Choose a New Chart Type ➦ p. 144

- Click the down arrow beside the Chart Type button on the Chart toolbar, and choose a new chart.
- Click the Chart Wizard button on the Formatting toolbar. Click the Back button, if necessary, to go to the Chart Type dialog box, and then choose a new chart and chart sub-type.

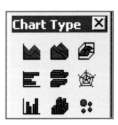

This chapter continues the Excel saga by describing techniques for crunching numbers. In the last chapter, you learned how to enter and format data in a worksheet. This chapter shows you how to analyze the data. Here you learn how to enter formulas in a worksheet—and find out what to do when a formula doesn't compute. You also discover speed techniques for entering formulas and learn how to make use of functions, the predefined formulas that come with Excel. The last part of this chapter shows you how to create a glorious chart from the data you've so laboriously assembled, entered, and computed.

All About Formulas

A *formula,* as you probably remember from your school days, is a statement that calculates numbers. For example, 2+2=4 is a formula. What makes Excel formulas different is that they can include cell references as well as numbers. When a formula refers to a cell, the number in the cell is used to calculate the formula.

To see the value of using cell references in formulas, consider the following worksheet, which calculates scoring in a football game across four quarters. Cell F2 contains a conventional formula for tabulating the score: 7+10+14+0. If the 49ers score 7 points in the fourth quarter, I have to enter 7 in cell E2 and replace the 0 in the cell F2 formula with a 7 to update the score:

	A	B	C	D	E	F
1		*1Qtr*	*2Qtr*	*3Qtr*	*4Qtr*	
2	**49ers**	7	10	14	0	=7+10+14+0
3	**Broncos**	0	7	0	0	=B3+C3+D3+E3

By contrast, the formula in cell F3 calculates the Broncos' score by referring to the numbers in cells B3, C3, D3, and E3, not by listing points scored. The formula totals the numbers in cells B3, C3, D3, and E3, whatever they happen to be. If the Broncos score 7 points in the fourth quarter, all I have to do is enter 7 in cell E3 to instantly recalculate the Broncos' score, because the formula in cell F3 includes a reference to cell E3.

Besides referring to cells with numbers in them, you can refer to formula results in cells. For example, consider the worksheet shown here. The first worksheet shows the formulas, and the second shows formula results. In columns B, C, and D, expenses are subtracted from income to show profits. Rows 2 and 3 total income and expenses, respectively. The formula in cell E4 (E2-E3) subtracts total expenses in cell E3 (B3+C3+D3) from total income in cell E2 (B2+C2+D2) to arrive at a total profit figure:

	A	B	C	D	E
1		Jan	Feb	Mar	Totals
2	Income	15080	14960	12300	=B2+C2+D2
3	Expenses	12780	12600	12500	=B3+C3+D3
4	Profits	=B2-B3	=C2-C3	=D2-D3	=E2-E3
5					

	A	B	C	D	E
1		Jan	Feb	Mar	Totals
2	Income	15,080	14,960	12,300	42,340
3	Expenses	12,780	12,600	12,500	37,880
4	Profits	2,300	2,360	(200)	4,460
5					

Addition and subtraction aren't the only operators you can use in formulas. Table 6.1 explains the arithmetic operators you can use and the key you press to enter each operator.

Operation	Keypress	Sample Formula	Answer that Excel Will Calculate and Display
Addition	+	=A1+A2+A3	The sum of the numbers in those cells
Division	/	=B3/4	The number in cell B3 divided by 4
Exponentiation	^	=10^2	10^2, or 100
Multiplication	*	=C2*3	The number in cell C2 multiplied by 3
Percentage	%	=10%	10 percent, or 0.1
Subtraction	–	=F5-4	The number in cell F5 minus 4

Table 6.1: Arithmetic Operators for Use in Formulas

In the worksheets shown in Figure 6.1, five arithmetic operators are used to calculate the individual costs of, total cost of, and six monthly payments on the components of a home entertainment center. The upper worksheet shows the results of the calculations, and the lower worksheet shows the formulas that produce those results. Take a close look—you can see how formulas can reference other formulas and how, with all the operators at work, you can create a very sophisticated and useful worksheet.

When a formula includes more than one operator, the order in which you enter the operators becomes important. Consider this formula: =3+4*5. Will it result in 35 (that is, 7×5) or 23 (you know, 3+20)? The answer is 23, because Excel performs multiplication (4×5=20) before addition (3+4=7) in formulas. In other words, multiplication takes precedence over addition. The order in which calculations are made in a formula that includes different operators is called the *order of precedence*. Table 6.2 lists the order of precedence. Be sure to keep it in mind when you construct any formula with more than one operator.

	A	B	C	D	E	F
1	Item	Quantity	Cost Per Item	Cost of Items	10% Discount	Price
2	Stereo	1	$ 459.99	$ 459.99	$ 46.00	$ 413.99
3	Big Screen TV	1	$ 1,029.99	$ 1,029.99	$ 103.00	$ 926.99
4	Speakers	2	$ 174.99	$ 349.98	$ 35.00	$ 314.98
5	VCR	1	$ 239.99	$ 239.99	$ 24.00	$ 215.99
7					Price For All Items	$ 1,871.96
8					Sales Tax	$ 121.68
9					Total Price	$ 1,993.63
10		**Your six low monthly payments are only**				**$ 332.27**

	A	B	C	D	E	F
1	Item	Quantity	Cost Per Item	Cost of Items	10% Discount	Price
2	Stereo	1	459.99	=B2*C2	=D2*10%	=D2-E2
3	Big Screen TV	1	1029.99	=B3*C3	=D3*10%	=D3-E3
4	Speakers	2	174.99	=B4*C4	=D4*10%	=D4-E4
5	VCR	1	239.99	=B5*C5	=D5*10%	=D5-E5
7					Price For All Items	=F2+F3+F4+F5
8					Sales Tax	=F7*6.5%
9					Total Price	=F7+F8
10		**Your six low monthly payments are only**				**=F9/6**

Figure 6.1: A complex worksheet showing formula results (above) and the formulas used to produce them (below)

Operators	Name
1. %	Percent
2. ^	Exponentiation
3. * and /	Multiplication and division (leftmost operations are calculated first).
4. + and -	Addition and subtraction (leftmost operations are calculated first).

Table 6.2: The Order of Precedence for Calculating with Operators

---

EXPERT ADVICE

You can override the order of precedence by enclosing parts of formulas in parentheses. Operations in parentheses are calculated before all other parts of the formula. For example, the formula =3+4*5 usually equals 23, but it equals 35 when it is written this way: =(3+4)*5.

Entering a Formula

This part of the chapter explains the basics of entering a formula. After you have read this section, be sure to read the next, "Speed Techniques for Entering Formulas." Excel offers plenty of techniques for taking the tedium out of entering complex formulas. You need to know all of these techniques if you intend to do any serious work in Excel.

To enter a formula, follow these basic steps:

1. Click the cell where you want to enter the formula.
2. Click in the Formula bar.
3. Enter an equal sign (=).
4. Enter the formula. Make sure you enter all cell addresses correctly. By the way, you can enter lowercase letters in cell references. Excel changes them to uppercase when you finish entering the formula.
5. Either press ENTER or click the Enter button (the green checkmark). The result of the formula appears in the cell.

CAUTION
You must be sure to enter the equal sign before you enter a formula. Without it, Excel thinks you are entering text, not a formula.

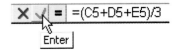

Sometimes you enter a formula but it doesn't compute and you get an error message, a cryptic three or four letters preceded by a pound sign (#). Here are some common error messages—and what you can do about them:

- **#N/A** The formula refers to an empty cell, so no data is available for computing the formula. Enter a number or formula in the empty cell or revise the formula.
- **#NULL** The formula refers to a range that Excel can't understand. Make sure the range is entered correctly in the formula.
- **#VALUE** The formula includes a function that is used incorrectly. Make sure the function uses the right argument.
- **####** The result of the formula can't fit in the cell. Make the column wider.

Speed Techniques for Entering Formulas

Yes, entering formulas and making sure that all cell references are correct is a chore, so Excel offers four or five techniques to make entering formulas easier. Read on to find out how to enter cell references by pointing and clicking or by using ranges. You will also find instructions here for copying formulas and for using functions, the built-in formulas that come with Excel.

Clicking and Selecting to Enter Cell References

The hardest part of entering a formula is entering the cell references correctly. You may have to squint to see which row and column the cell is in that you want to refer to. You have to be careful when typing in the column letter and row number. However, instead of typing the cell reference, you can simply click the cell itself. As soon as you click the cell, Excel enters its address on the Formula bar. What's more, shimmering marquee lights appear around the cell to show you which one you are referring to in the formula:

SUM	▾	✕ ✓ =	=B3+B4+B5		
	A	B	C	D	E
1	Home sales so far this year:				
2		January	February	March	Total
3	South Beach	14	26	23	
4	Ingleside	8	7	15	
5	Portrero Hill	11	19	12	
6	Total:	=B3+B4+B5			

In this worksheet, I've clicked cell B5 instead of entering its address. Notice that the reference B5 appears on the Formula bar, and that the marquee lights appear around cell B5.

Besides clicking a single cell, you can select a *range* of cells to refer to them in a formula. In the following worksheet, I've selected cells B3, C3, and D3 by dragging over them. Excel entered the range B3:D3 on the Formula bar and put the marquee lights around cells B3 through D3:

Cell ranges are for use with functions, as "Working with Functions" explains later in this chapter.

SUM	▾	✕ ✓ =	=SUM(B3:D3		
	A	B	C	D	E
1	Home sales so far this year:				
2		January	February	March	Total
3	South Beach	14	26	23	=SUM(B3:D3
4	Ingleside	8	7	15	
5	Portrero Hill	11	19	12	
6	Total:	33			

Copying Formulas

Often in worksheets, the same formula but with different cell references is used across a row or down a column. Take the worksheet shown in

DEFINITION

AutoFill handle: The tiny black square in the lower-right corner of the cell. When you move the mouse pointer over it, the AutoFill handle changes into a black cross.

Figure 6.2, for example. Column F of the worksheet totals the rainfall figures in rows 3 through 7. To enter formulas for totaling the numbers in rows 3 through 7, you could laboriously enter formulas in cells F3, F4, F5, F6, and F7. But a faster way is to enter the formula once in cell F3 and then copy the formula in F3 down the column to F4, F5, F6, and F7. Follow the steps shown in Figure 6.2 to copy a formula.

When you copy a formula to a new cell, Excel adjusts the cell references in the formula so that the formula works in the cells to which it has been copied. Amazing! Not only that, but opportunities to copy formulas abound on most spreadsheets. And copying formulas is the fastest and safest way to enter formulas in a worksheet.

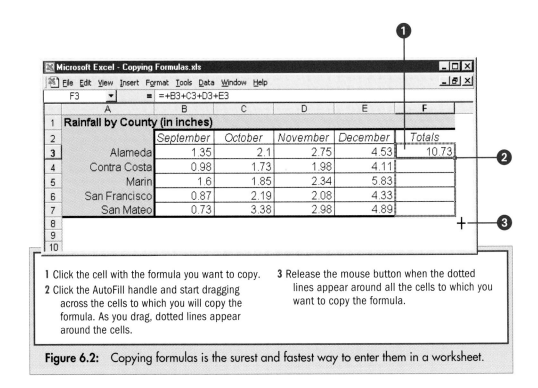

1 Click the cell with the formula you want to copy.
2 Click the AutoFill handle and start dragging across the cells to which you will copy the formula. As you drag, dotted lines appear around the cells.
3 Release the mouse button when the dotted lines appear around all the cells to which you want to copy the formula.

Figure 6.2: Copying formulas is the surest and fastest way to enter them in a worksheet.

Working with Functions

A *function* is a canned formula that comes with Excel. Excel offers hundreds of functions, some of which are very obscure, fit only for use by rocket scientists. Other functions are very practical. For example, you can use the SUM function to quickly total the numbers in a cell. Instead of entering =F4+F5+F6+F7 on the Formula bar, you can enter =SUM(F4:F7), which tells Excel to total the numbers in the range F4 through F7.

A function takes one or more *arguments*—the cell references or numbers, enclosed in parentheses, that the function acts upon. For example, AVG(D1:D4) returns the average of the numbers in cells D1 through D4; PRODUCT(6.5,F4) returns the product of multiplying the number 6.5 by the number in cell F4. When a function requires more than one argument, enter a comma between the arguments.

You can enter a function the conventional way by typing it and its arguments on the Formula bar, or you can seek the help of the Function Wizard, as detailed in Figure 6.3. The Function Wizard tells you which arguments the function requires and calculates the result of the function and its arguments before entering them in a worksheet. This way you can see if you are indeed entering the function correctly.

SHORTCUT

To quickly total the numbers in a range of cells, click the cell where you want the total to appear and then click the AutoSum button on the Standard toolbar. Marquee lights appear around the cells that Excel wants to add up. Press ENTER if the lights appear around the correct cells. Excel uses the SUM function to total the numbers.

TIP

To enter a cell address or a range of cells as an argument, you can drag the Formula palette to the side of the screen and either click a cell or drag across several cells.

EXPERT ADVICE

To reuse the function that you've entered most recently, you can click the Most Recently Used category in the Paste Function dialog box. You can also select functions from the Most Recently Used list by clicking the down arrow on the left side of the Formula bar and choosing a function name.

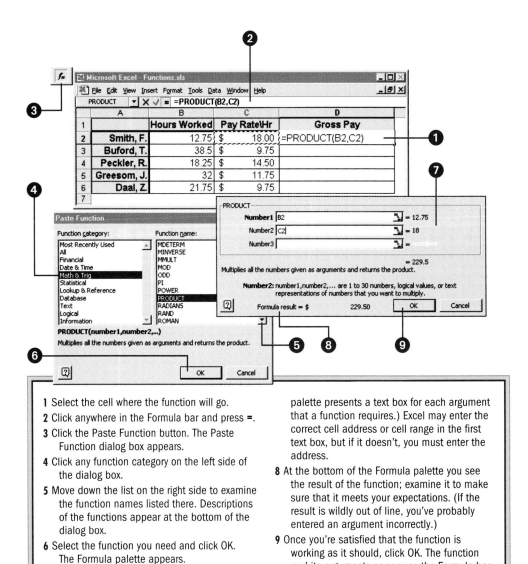

1 Select the cell where the function will go.

2 Click anywhere in the Formula bar and press **=**.

3 Click the Paste Function button. The Paste Function dialog box appears.

4 Click any function category on the left side of the dialog box.

5 Move down the list on the right side to examine the function names listed there. Descriptions of the functions appear at the bottom of the dialog box.

6 Select the function you need and click OK. The Formula palette appears.

7 Enter as many arguments as the function requires, clicking OK each time. (The Formula palette presents a text box for each argument that a function requires.) Excel may enter the correct cell address or cell range in the first text box, but if it doesn't, you must enter the address.

8 At the bottom of the Formula palette you see the result of the function; examine it to make sure that it meets your expectations. (If the result is wildly out of line, you've probably entered an argument incorrectly.)

9 Once you're satisfied that the function is working as it should, click OK. The function and its arguments appear on the Formula bar, and the result appears in the cell you selected in step 1.

Figure 6.3: If entering detailed functions on the Formula bar makes you weary, let the Function Wizard be your guide.

Building Charts from Your Data

Here's some good news: The Excel Chart Wizard has made it very easy to create charts. Excel offers 15 kinds of charts, which is good, but even better is the fact that you can transform a chart you created into a different kind of chart merely by clicking a couple of buttons. And editing a chart is easy, too. Following are instructions for creating and editing charts.

Creating a Chart with the Chart Wizard

Figure 6.4 shows an "Elvis Sightings" worksheet and a column chart that I created from data in the worksheet. To create charts like these, you fill out Chart Wizard dialog boxes. As you fill in the dialog boxes, you watch your chart take shape. You can always revisit the Chart Wizard dialog boxes to edit your chart, as the next part of this chapter explains. Meanwhile, follow these steps to create a chart:

1. Select the data that you want to chart.

2. Click the Chart Wizard button. You see the Chart Type dialog box, the first of four Chart Wizard dialog boxes.

3. From the Chart Type list, choose the kind of chart you want, choose a sub-type from the Chart Sub-type options, and click the Next button.

   Be sure to try out different chart types and sub-types before you make your choice. And be *absolutely* sure to hold down the Click and Hold to View Sample button. When you hold down this button, you see your chart in miniature, and you can tell right away if you've made the right choice of charts.

4. In the Chart Source Data dialog box, choose which data series should appear in rows and which in columns by clicking the Rows or Columns option button; then click Next.

   Once again, keep your eye on the sample chart—it shows precisely what your choices mean as you construct your chart.

CAUTION

Don't select a totals column or row for charts. The purpose of a chart is to compare and contrast data. Including a totals column or row creates an unrealistic comparison, because the totals data is inevitably much, much larger than the other data and you end up with an extra-large pie slice or bar, for example, in your chart.

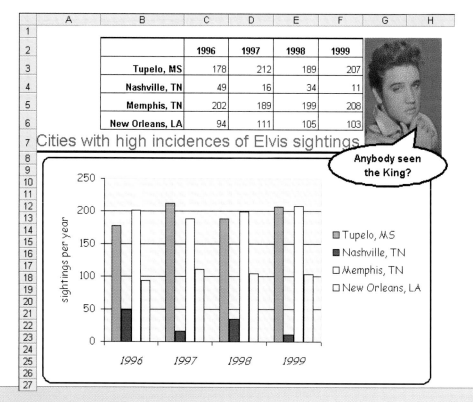

Figure 6.4: To create a chart, select the data you want to chart and click the Chart Wizard button.

5. In the Chart Options dialog box, enter a title and, optionally, labels for the X-axis data and Y-axis data; then visit the various tabs to choose where gridlines and the legend appear, for example; click Next when you're done.
   Again, watch the sample chart to see where your title and labels will appear.

6. In the Chart Location dialog box, choose the As New Sheet option to place the chart on a new worksheet or the As Object In option to place the chart on the same worksheet as the data you selected in step 1; then click the Finish button.

Editing a Chart

After you create a chart, the Chart toolbar appears onscreen (click your chart if you don't see it, or else choose View | Toolbars | Chart). Use the Chart toolbar to change the appearance of a chart—the color scheme, the letters' font and font size, and the width and shape of the borders. To change a chart's layout, go back to the Chart Wizard dialog boxes. Very likely, your chart needs a tweak here and a tweak there. Here are the specifics of editing a chart.

A chart is considered an object. See "Handling 'Objects' in Files" in Chapter 2 to learn how to move or change the size and shape of a chart.

Changing the Appearance of a Chart

A chart is composed of different areas—the category axis, chart area, and chart title, among others. The drop-down Chart Objects menu on the Chart toolbar lists all of these areas, and you can also read their names in pop-up boxes by slowly moving the pointer around the chart. Figure 6.5 shows how, with the help of the Format button, you can change an area's background colors, font settings, or borders. Choose Edit | Undo and start all over if your changes to the chart didn't work out. Usually, you have to wrestle with Format dialog boxes for five minutes or so before the chart starts smelling like a rose.

Changing the Layout

To change the layout of a chart, click to select it and then click the Chart Wizard button. You return to the Chart Wizard and its four dialog boxes, where you can choose a new chart sub-type, specify which data series should be put in columns and rows, rewrite titles and legends, and do everything else you can do in the Chart Wizard dialog boxes. Click the Back or Next button to go from dialog box to dialog box. Click Finish when you are done overhauling your chart.

EXPERT ADVICE

The legend, plot area, and chart title on a chart are objects in their own right. As such, you can drag them to different positions in the chart area. To move an object, click to select it. When you see the black selection handles, start dragging. A dotted line shows where the object will land when you release the mouse button.

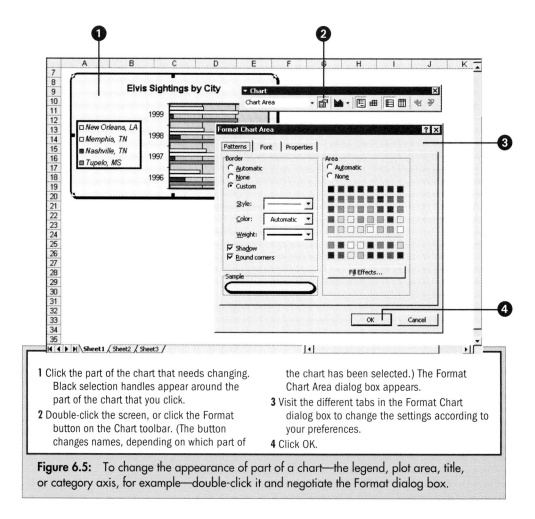

1 Click the part of the chart that needs changing. Black selection handles appear around the part of the chart that you click.

2 Double-click the screen, or click the Format button on the Chart toolbar. (The button changes names, depending on which part of

the chart has been selected.) The Format Chart Area dialog box appears.

3 Visit the different tabs in the Format Chart dialog box to change the settings according to your preferences.

4 Click OK.

Figure 6.5: To change the appearance of part of a chart—the legend, plot area, title, or category axis, for example—double-click it and negotiate the Format dialog box.

Changing the Chart Type

The fastest way to change chart types is to click the down arrow beside the Chart Type button on the Chart toolbar and choose a new chart from the drop-down menu. To choose a new sub-type, however, you have to click the Chart Wizard button on the Formatting toolbar. Doing so opens the Chart Wizard, where you can choose a chart sub-type in the Chart Type dialog box. Click the Back button to get there, if necessary.

CHAPTER 7

Outlook 2000: Managing Your E-Mail and Your Time

INCLUDES

- Composing and sending e-mail messages
- Sending a file along with an e-mail message
- Receiving and reading e-mail
- Organizing messages in subfolders
- Keeping a Contacts list address book
- Importing addresses into the Contacts list
- Scheduling meetings and appointments
- Managing tasks with the Tasks list

Go Quickly from
Outlook Screen to Outlook Screen ➡ pp. 148–149

- Click an icon in the Outlook bar.
- Click the down arrow beside a screen's name and choose a new screen from the drop-down list.

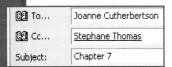

Address and Send an E-Mail Message ➡ pp. 150–151

1. In the Inbox, click the New Mail Message button, enter a subject in the Message window, and type the message.
2. Click the To button to open the Select Names dialog box, click the recipient's name, click the To button, and click OK.
3. Click Send in the Message window.

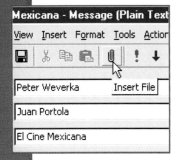

Send a File Along with a Message ➡ p. 152

1. In the Message window, click the Insert File button.
2. Find and select the file in the Insert File dialog box, and click Insert.

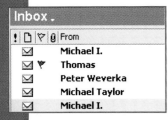

Send, Receive, and Read Your E-Mail ➡ pp. 155–156

1. In the Inbox, click the Send and Receive button.
2. Enter a password and click OK in the Connect dialog box.
3. In the Inbox, click a message to read it, or double-click a message to read it in a window.

Move an E-Mail Message to a Subfolder ➡ pp. 157–158

1. Choose View | Folder List to open the Folder List bar, and then click the plus sign next to the Inbox folder to see its subfolders.
2. Select the message from the Inbox and drag it to the subfolder.

Find a Contact in the Contacts List ➡ p. 160

- Use the scroll bar.
- Click a letter on the right side of the screen.
- Click the Find button. In the Look For text box, enter a word or two, and click the Find Now button.

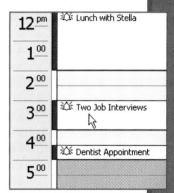

Schedule an Appointment in the Calendar ➡ pp. 162–163

1. Switch to Day view and click the hour in which the appointment is to start.
2. Enter a brief description of the appointment and press ENTER.
3. If necessary, drag the bottom of the appointment downward to make it longer than half an hour.

Enter a Task on the Tasks List ➡ pp. 164–165

1. Click at the top of the screen, where it says "Click here to add a new Task."
2. Type a few words to describe the task.
3. Enter the due date in the Due Date box.

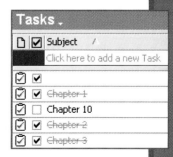

Outlook 2000 is really two programs in one. On one hand, Outlook is an e-mail program. You can use it to send e-mail messages to and receive e-mail messages from friends, co-workers, and colleagues. On the other hand, the program offers a Calendar, Contacts list, and Tasks list so that you can make order out of chaos and manage your time and appointments better. This chapter explores both sides of Outlook. On these pages you find out how to send and receive e-mail, keep track of important addresses, schedule meetings and appointments, juggle tasks, and write reminder notes to yourself. Outlook does not field phone calls or make coffee, but otherwise the program operates much like a personal secretary.

A Trip Around the Outlook Screen

The first thing you notice about Outlook is that it looks very different from the other Office 2000 programs. Why all those strange icons on the left side of the screen? What's up with those shortcut buttons? Figure 7.1 breaks it down for you.

   Here are some details about what the various icons and buttons do:

- **Outlook Shortcuts**   Displays the Outlook icons in the Outlook bar.
- **Outlook Today**   Brings up a screen that lists calendar appointments, tasks, and the number of incoming and outgoing messages.
- **Inbox**   Takes you to the Inbox screen, where you can write and receive e-mail messages.
- **Calendar**   Displays the Calendar, where you can schedule your appointments and meetings electronically.

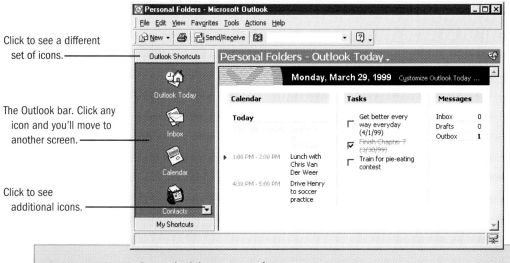

Click to see a different set of icons.

The Outlook bar. Click any icon and you'll move to another screen.

Click to see additional icons.

Figure 7.1: Use the Outlook bar to move from screen to screen.

- **Contacts**   Opens the Contacts screen so you can look up phone numbers and other contact information.
- **Tasks**   Displays the Tasks screen to help you plan your projects.
- **Notes**   Brings up the Notes screen, which is useful for jotting down notes and reminders.
- **Deleted Items**   Shows the Deleted Items screen, where deleted e-mail messages, contacts, and tasks are kept.
- **My Shortcuts**   Displays icons that you can click to visit the Drafts, Inbox, Sent Items, and Deleted Items folders. (See "Storing and Managing Your E-Mail" later on in this chapter.)

To get from screen to screen, click an icon. To see some of the icons, you have to click a button—Outlook Shortcuts or My Shortcuts—first. Another way to get from screen to screen is to click the down arrow beside a screen's name and choose a new screen from the drop-down list. In the example you see here, I've clicked the down arrow in the Inbox screen.

Inbox: Composing, Sending, and Receiving E-Mail Messages

The pages that follow explain how to do a bunch of different things from the Inbox. You find out how to write and address e-mail messages, send files over the Internet, send the same message to many different people, reply to and forward e-mail messages, send and read e-mail, and manage the messages you've received so you can reply to them in a timely fashion.

Writing and Addressing an E-Mail Message

Later in this chapter, "Replying to and Forwarding E-Mail Messages" explains how to reply directly to a message you've received or forward it to a third party.

Writing and addressing an e-mail message is pretty darn easy, especially if you've entered the recipient's e-mail address on the Contacts list. (Updating your Contacts list is explained later in this chapter.) Figure 7.2 shows you how to write an e-mail message.

Suppose you change your mind about a message you've sent. To keep it from being delivered, click the My Shortcuts button on the Outlook bar. Then click the Outbox icon to see outgoing messages,

select the message you regret writing, and click the Delete button (or press CTRL-D).

Copies of the e-mail messages you've sent are kept in the Sent Items folder. To review this folder, click the My Shortcuts button on the Outlook bar, and then click the Sent Items icon. Finally, in the list of messages, double-click any sent message that you want to read.

SHORTCUT

Instead of opening the Select Names dialog box, you can simply type each recipient's name in the To box of the Message window—as long as you've recorded the name and correct e-mail address on the Contacts list.

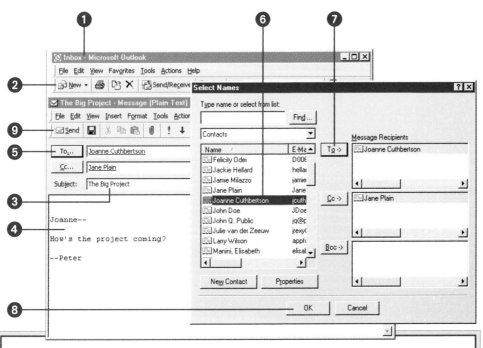

1 Click the Inbox icon (Remember? It's on the Outlook bar) to move to the Inbox screen.

2 Click the New Mail Message button (or press CTRL-N). The Message window appears.

3 Briefly describe the message you'll be sending. (When others receive it, the first thing they'll see is what you've typed on the Subject line.)

4 Type your message.

5 Click the To button. You see the Select Names dialog box, listing the names of people in your Contacts list who have e-mail addresses.

6 Click the name of the person you want to send the message to. (You can CTRL-click multiple names if your message is meant for more than one person.)

7 Click the To button. The name or names that you've selected will appear in the Message Recipients box. (You can also send a copy or a blind copy of a message; simply repeat this step, but click the Cc or Bcc button instead of To.)

8 Click OK. The Select Names dialog box closes, and the name(s) you've chosen appear in the Message window.

9 Click the Send button. If your computer is connected to a network, the message is sent immediately. Otherwise, it lands in the Outbox, where it remains until you click the Send and Receive button.

Figure 7.2: Compose your message in the Message window (left). Decide who will receive the message in the Select Names dialog box (right).

Later in this chapter, "Storing Files That Have Been Sent to You" explains what to do when you receive a file by e-mail.

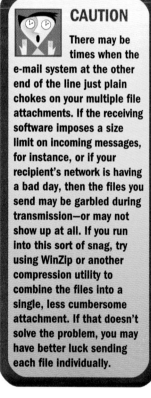

CAUTION

There may be times when the e-mail system at the other end of the line just plain chokes on your multiple file attachments. If the receiving software imposes a size limit on incoming messages, for instance, or if your recipient's network is having a bad day, then the files you send may be garbled during transmission—or may not show up at all. If you run into this sort of snag, try using WinZip or another compression utility to combine the files into a single, less cumbersome attachment. If that doesn't solve the problem, you may have better luck sending each file individually.

Sending a File Along with a Message

Yes, it can be done. You can send a file—or several files—along with an e-mail message. Just follow these steps:

1. With the Message window open, either click the Insert File button or choose Insert | File. You see the Insert File dialog box.

2. Locate and select the file that you want to send. CTRL-click filenames to select more than one file.

3. Click the OK button. As you can see here, the name of each file you've chosen appears in a box along the bottom of the Message window:

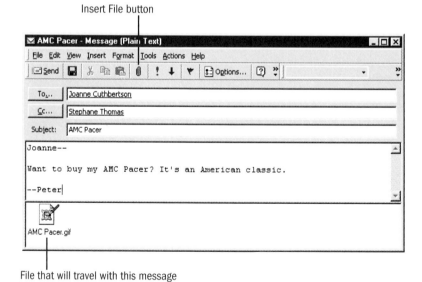

Insert File button

File that will travel with this message

4. Click Send, as usual. Your message will be sent on its way, and the file(s) you've attached will travel with it.

Sending the Same Message to Several People at Once

Suppose you are the captain of a softball team and every week you have to send an e-mail message to each team member to tell him or her where the next game is played. Composing and sending twelve or fifteen different messages to team members is a drag. To keep from having to do that, you can create a *distribution list*, a list of several different e-mail contacts. That way, you only have to write the message once and then choose the name of the distribution list in the Select Names dialog box, as shown in Figure 7.3, to send the message to everyone on the list.

Follow these steps to bundle e-mail contacts into a distribution list:

1. Click the Contacts icon to access the Contacts screen.

2. Click the down arrow beside the New Contact button, located on the left end of the toolbar at the top of the screen.

3. From the menu that appears, choose Distribution List. You see the Distribution List dialog box, as shown in Figure 7.3.

4. Enter a descriptive name in the Name text box.

5. Click the Select Members button.

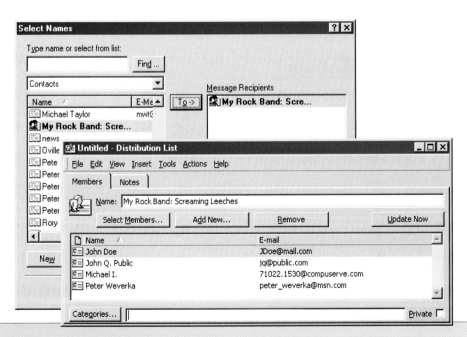

Figure 7.3:   Create a distribution list (right), and then you can easily send the same message to a number of different recipients (left).

6. In the dialog box that appears, CTRL-click the name of each person you want to include on your distribution list.

7. Click the Add button, and click OK.

8. Click the Save and Close button in the Distribution List dialog box.

Now all you have to do to send the same e-mail message to several people at once is address the message in the usual way but choose the name of the distribution list in the Select Names dialog box, as shown in Figure 7.3.

To add names to or remove names from a distribution list, go to the Contacts list and double-click the name of the distribution list that needs altering. In the Distribution List dialog box, select names and click the Remove button to remove names from the list. To add names, click the Select Members button, CTRL-click the names of people you want to add to the list, click the Add button, and click OK.

Replying to and Forwarding E-Mail Messages

Replying to and forwarding messages is as easy as pie. For one thing, you don't need to know the recipient's e-mail address to reply to a message. In the Inbox, select the message you want to reply to or forward and do the following:

- **Reply to author**   Click the Reply button. The Message window opens with the sender's name already entered in the To box and the original message in the text box below. Write a reply and click the Send button.

- **Reply to all parties who received the message**   Click the Reply to All button. The Message window opens with the names of all parties who received the message in the To: and Cc: boxes and the original message in the text box. Type your reply and click the Send button.

- **Forward a message** Click the Forward button. The Message window opens with the text of the original message. Click the To button to open the Select Names dialog box (see Figure 7.2) and choose the names of the parties to whom the message will be forwarded. Click OK, add a word or two to the original message if you like, and click the Send button.

By the way, you can find out someone's e-mail address by double-clicking a message they've sent you in the Inbox. In the Message window that appears, glance at the address beside the sender's name to learn his or her e-mail address. To add the person to Contacts list, right-click the sender's name and choose Add to Contacts.

In Chapter 11, "Finding Addresses and Phone Numbers on the Internet" explains how to find others' e-mail addresses by going online.

Sending, Receiving, and Reading Your E-Mail

To simultaneously send e-mail messages and collect the messages that have been sent to you, click the Send and Receive button (or press F5). If you are not on a network, you shortly see a Connection dialog box. Enter your password, if necessary, and click the Connect button.

Messages arrive in the Inbox window, as shown in Figure 7.4. Unread messages are shown in boldface type and have open envelope icons next to their names; read messages are shown in Roman type and appear beside closed envelopes. To read a message, click its name in the top of the window and read it in the bottom. You can click the From, Subject, or Received column headings to re-sort, or rearrange, the messages in the window.

TIP

Double-click a message to open it in its own window, where you'll be able to read it better.

Later in this chapter, "Storing and Managing Your E-Mail" explains how to store messages in folders so you can keep better track of them.

EXPERT ADVICE

Are you getting too much junk mail? To keep from receiving unwanted e-mail from the same source again and again, click the message you got from the junk mailer and choose **Actions | Junk E-mail | Add to Junk Senders List.**

Messages that have been read   Double-click any message to read it.

Unread messages

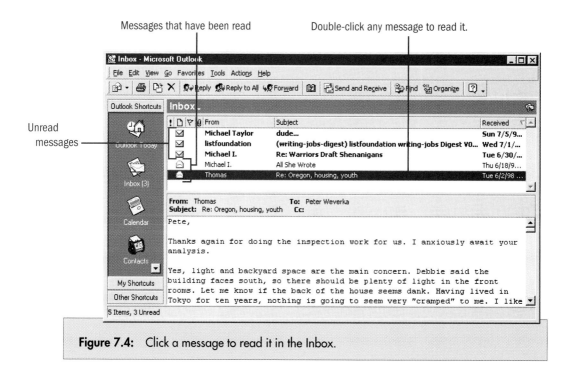

Figure 7.4: Click a message to read it in the Inbox.

Storing Files That Have Been Sent to You

You know when someone has sent you a file along with an e-mail message because a paperclip appears next to the sender's name in the top half of the Inbox window. To view the file, right-click the message to which it was attached, choose View Attachments from the shortcut menu, and click the file's name. You can also double-click the message to see it in a window and then double-click the file icon in the bottom of the window.

No matter how or when you view the file, you should store it safely in a folder so you'll know where to find it later on. To do so, follow these steps:

1. Select the e-mail message in the Inbox and choose File | Save Attachments, and then the file's name. You see the Save Attachment dialog box.

2. Find and click the folder in which you want to save the file.

3. Click the Save button.

Storing and Managing Your E-Mail

These days, many people receive more e-mail than they do regular mail, which says a lot about how many people now rely on e-mail more than snail mail. The next few pages explain how to create special folders for storing e-mail, read messages that you've stored in folders, and delete e-mail messages.

One way to remind yourself to respond to a message is to select it and choose Actions | Flag for Follow Up. In the dialog box that appears, click the Due By down arrow and then click a date on the mini-calendar. In the Inbox, a flag appears next to the message so you know it needs attention. If you double-click the message, you can read the follow-up date in the Message window:

> ❶ Follow up by Tuesday, September 21, 1999 5:00 PM.

Creating Subfolders for Storing E-Mail

Many people receive ten, twenty, or thirty e-mail messages a day. If you are one of those unfortunate souls, you owe it to yourself to create subfolders for storing e-mail messages. Create one subfolder for each project you are working on. That way, you know where to find e-mail messages when you want to reply to or delete them. Figure 7.5 shows you how to create a subfolder.

Storing E-Mail Messages in Subfolders

Choose View | Folder List to open the Folder List bar, and then follow these instructions to handle messages in subfolders:

- **Moving to a subfolder**   To move an e-mail message to a subfolder, click the plus sign next to the Inbox folder to see its subfolders. Then select any message from the Inbox and drag it to the subfolder.

- **Seeing and reading messages in a subfolder**   Click a subfolder in the Folder list to see the messages that you've stored in it. You might have to click the plus sign next to the Inbox to see the subfolders. Click a message in the subfolder to read it.

- **Deleting and renaming subfolders**   Right-click a subfolder and choose Delete or Rename from the shortcut menu.

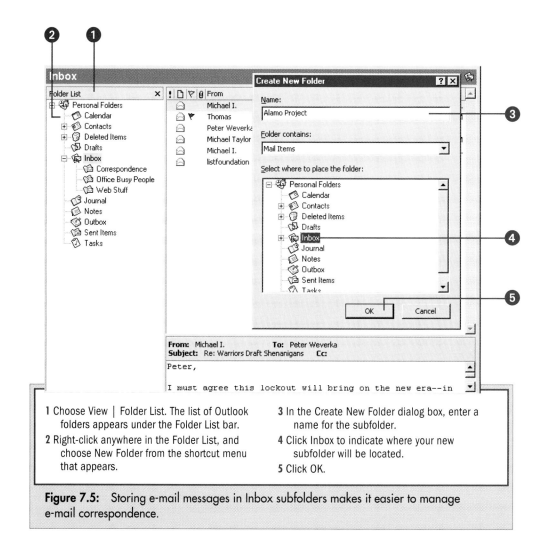

1 Choose View | Folder List. The list of Outlook folders appears under the Folder List bar.

2 Right-click anywhere in the Folder List, and choose New Folder from the shortcut menu that appears.

3 In the Create New Folder dialog box, enter a name for the subfolder.

4 Click Inbox to indicate where your new subfolder will be located.

5 Click OK.

Figure 7.5:   Storing e-mail messages in Inbox subfolders makes it easier to manage e-mail correspondence.

Deleting E-Mail Messages

All you have to do to delete an e-mail message is select it and click the Delete button or press DELETE. To delete many messages in a row, click the first one, SHIFT-click the last, and then click the Delete button. To delete messages that are not listed together, CTRL-click each of them and click the Delete button.

Keep in mind that when you delete a message, it is not obliterated immediately. Instead, it is moved to the Deleted Items folder. Deleted contacts and tasks land there as well. To delete old and forgotten items once and for all, click the Outlook Shortcuts button in the Outlook bar, click the Deleted Items icon, select the items you want to delete in the window, and click the Delete button or press DELETE.

SHORTCUT

Choose Tools | Empty "Deleted Items" Folder to remove all of the messages from the Deleted Items folder at once.

Contacts: Keeping Information about Others

The Contacts list is a sort of high-powered address book. As you know if you've read the first part of this chapter, Outlook gets e-mail addresses from the Contacts list. You can also stockpile addresses and phone numbers of all varieties (including fax numbers and pager numbers) on the Contacts list, along with miscellaneous information such as birthdays. Read on to find out how to enter a contact on the Contacts list and look up a contact.

Adding a Contact to the Contacts List

To place someone on the Contacts list, click the Contacts icon in the Outlook bar to get to the Contacts screen, and then either click the New Contact button or choose File | New | Contact. You see the Contact window. Start entering what you know about the contact. On the General and Details tabs are lots of places for describing how to reach the person or business in question. Click the Save and Close button when you are done.

Be sure to write a few words at the bottom of the General tab to describe how and where you met the contact. When the time comes to weed the list, reading the descriptions helps decide who is important and should remain on the list.

I n Chapter 10, "Generating Form Letters and Labels" explains how you can print mailing labels for people on the Contacts list.

EXPERT ADVICE

Microsoft Outlook offers several attractive ways to print the Contacts list. Before you print, choose File | Page Setup and then Card Style, Small Booklet Style, or one of the other options. In the Page Setup dialog box, choose a font and make other choices for formatting the list. Then click the Print Preview button to see what your list will look like and, finally, click the Print button in the Print Preview window to print the list.

Searching for a Contact on the List

The Contacts list, shown in Figure 7.6, can grow very large, so Outlook offers a number of ways to search it:

- **Scrollbar** You can move through the list by either clicking the arrows or dragging the scrollbox across the bar.

- **Letter buttons** Click a letter button on the right side of the screen to move to a specific letter in the list.

- **Find button** If you can't quite remember a contact's name but you can remember, say, the company that he or she works for, simply click the Find button on the toolbar. When the Look For text box appears, type a word or two and click the Find Now button.

- **Views** Select View | Current View. A menu appears that lets you display your contacts as individual address cards, detailed address cards, or a phone list. You can also arrange contacts by category, company, or location.

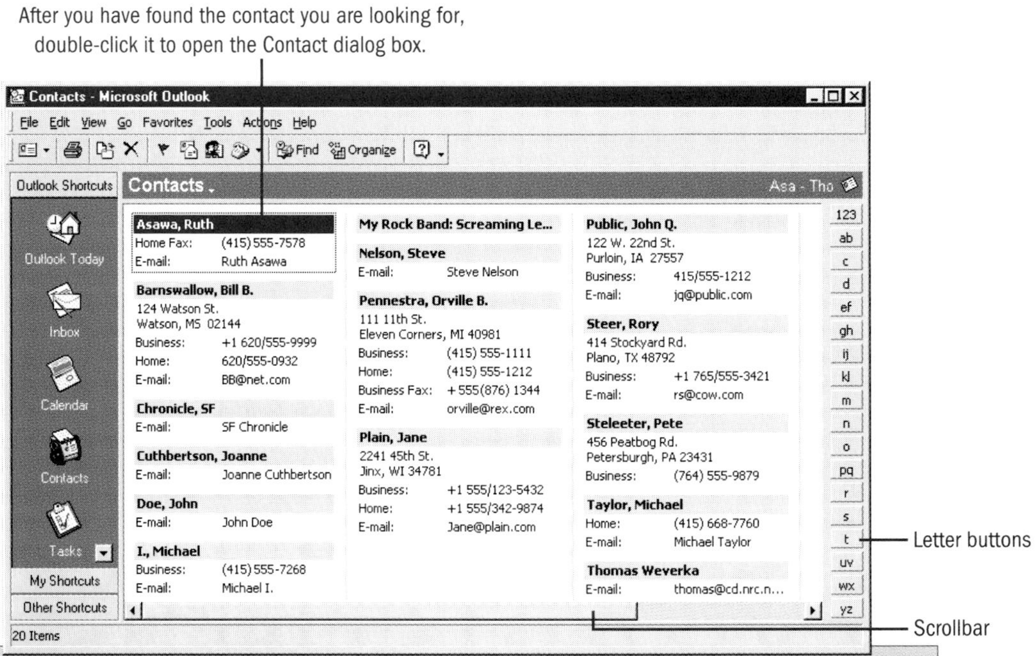

After you have found the contact you are looking for, double-click it to open the Contact dialog box.

Figure 7.6: It's easy to find the name you're looking for on the Contacts list.

Calendar: Scheduling Meetings and Appointments

Use the Calendar to juggle appointments and meetings and make sure you get there on time. You can gaze at the Calendar screen, shown in Figure 7.7, and see precisely where you are supposed to be on a given day, work week (Monday through Friday), week, or month. And as if you weren't busy enough, the TaskPad in the Calendar window also lists the tasks you are supposed to do. Read on to find out how to get around in the Calendar screen and schedule appointments.

Calendar

Getting Around in the Calendar

Finding your way around the Calendar is pretty simple. Unless you're in Month view, you can click a date in the calendar or calendars in the upper-right corner of the screen to go to a different date. If necessary, click an arrow beside a month name to go backward or forward by a month. Days on which meetings or appointments are scheduled appear in boldface on the calendar.

TIP

No matter how far you stray, you can see today's date in the Calendar window by clicking the Go to Today button.

Use these buttons to change your view of time.

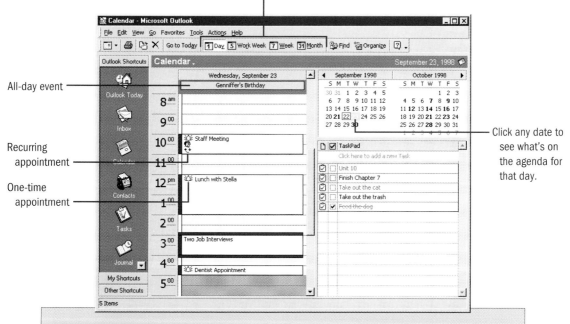

All-day event

Recurring appointment

One-time appointment

Click any date to see what's on the agenda for that day.

Figure 7.7: By clicking dates and viewing appointments and meetings by day, work week, week, or month, you can see precisely where you are supposed to be.

Use the scroll bar in the middle of the screen to travel from hour to hour in Day view or from day to day in Week or Work Week view. If you need more room to see your schedule or you want to make the TaskPad wider or see two calendars instead of one, drag the border between the schedule area and the calendar to the left or right. To do so, gently move the mouse pointer over the border, and click and drag when you see the double-headed arrow.

Scheduling Appointments and Meetings

For scheduling purposes, Outlook makes a distinction between appointments, events, and meetings. If your computer is connected to a network and the network uses the Microsoft Exchange Server, you can schedule meetings and invite others on the network to come to the meetings. But if your computer is not on a network, don't bother with meetings. Schedule appointments and all-day events instead. You can schedule the following activities:

- **Appointment** An activity that occupies a specific time period—for example, a meeting that takes place between 2 and 3 o'clock.

- **Recurring appointment** An appointment that takes place daily, weekly, or monthly on the same day and same time each day, week, or month; for example, a weekly staff meeting. When you schedule a recurring appointment, it is entered on the calendar ad infinitum.

- **All-day event** An activity that lasts all day; for example, an all-day trade show or a birthday.

- **Meeting** Same as an appointment, except you can invite others to attend. See your network administrator for details.

To schedule recurring appointments, all-day events, or appointments by way of a dialog box, click the date on which the activity is to occur, open the Actions menu, and choose New Appointment, New All Day Event, or New Recurring Appointment. You'll see a dialog box for naming the appointment or event, stating its starting and ending time, and choosing whether and when you

SHORTCUT

To schedule a half-hour appointment, switch to Day view and click the hour in which the appointment is to start. Then type a brief description of the appointment and press ENTER. To make the appointment longer than half an hour, gently move the mouse pointer to the bottom of the appointment box, and then click and drag downward to make the box longer.

want to be alerted to its occurrence (see Figure 7.8). If you've specified
a recurring appointment, you also see a dialog box for stating when
and how often the appointment occurs. Click the Save and Close
button when you are done describing the activity.

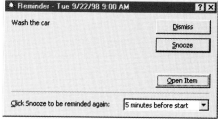

If you check the Reminder box and ask to be alerted before
the activity, you see the Reminder message box however many
minutes in advance of the activity you asked to be alerted.
Click the Dismiss button to heed the warning right away, or
else choose an option from the Click Snooze drop-down menu,
and then click the Snooze button to be reminded again later.

Canceling, Rescheduling, and Altering Activities

Canceling, rescheduling, and altering appointments and all-day events
is pretty easy:

- **Canceling**   Click an activity on the schedule, and then click
  the Delete button. When you cancel a recurring appointment,
  a dialog box asks if you want to delete all occurrences of the
  appointment or just the appointment on the day you selected.
  Choose an option and click OK.

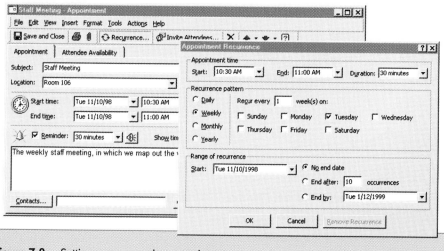

Figure 7.8: Setting up a recurring appointment

- **Rescheduling**   Simply drag the activity to a new location on the schedule. If necessary, switch to Work Week, Week, or Month view in order to do so. To reschedule several months in advance, display the calendar month to which the activity will be moved in the upper-right corner of the screen and drag the activity to a day on the calendar.
- **Altering**   Double-click the activity to reopen the Appointment or Event dialog box and change the particulars of the activity.

Tasks: Seeing What Needs to Get Done

As Figure 7.9 shows, the Tasks list is a simple tool that shows you what needs to be done, when it is due, and whether it is overdue. On this list, due dates clearly show how smartly the whip is being cracked and how close you are to deadlines. A gray line appears across tasks that are done. Tasks that are overdue appear in red.

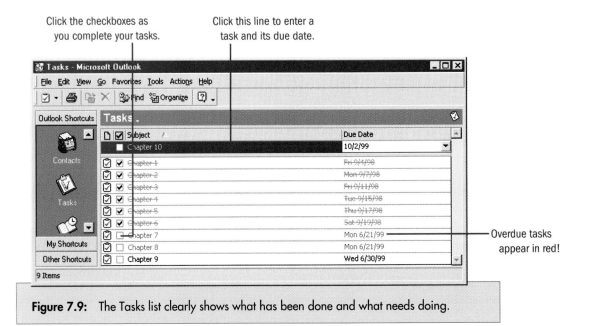

Figure 7.9: The Tasks list clearly shows what has been done and what needs doing.

To enter a task on the list, click the line at the top, just below the Subject head, that says "Click here to add a new Task." Type a few words to describe the task, and enter the due date in the Due Date box. Click the checkbox when a task is complete. To delete a task from the list, simply select it and click the Delete button.

CHAPTER 8

PowerPoint 2000: Creating Professional Presentations

INCLUDES

- Choosing a design for the slides
- Adding slides to presentations
- Entering the text and writing notes for a presentation
- Rearranging, deleting, and copying slides
- Changing the appearance of slides
- Printing handout copies of a presentation
- Giving an in-person and a kiosk-style presentation
- Making presentations livelier

Create a New Slide Show Presentation ➡ pp. 170–172

1. Choose File | New (or press CTRL-N) to open the New Presentation dialog box.
2. On the General tab, select Blank Presentation to create a presentation from scratch or AutoContent Wizard to get the help of the AutoContent Wizard; or, on the Design Templates tab, choose a design.

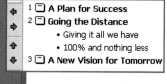

Add a Slide to a Presentation ➡ pp. 173–174

1. In Normal or Outline view, select the slide that the new slide will come after and choose Insert | New Slide.
2. In the New Slide dialog box, select an AutoLayout and click OK.

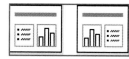

Enter Text on the Slides ➡ p. 176

1. Click the Outline View button to switch to Outline view.
2. Start typing. You can open the Outlining toolbar and use it to promote or demote text and move lines of text, among other things.

Rearrange the Slides in a Presentation ➡ p. 177

1. Switch to Slide Sorter view.
2. Click the slide you want to move, and drag it to a new location.

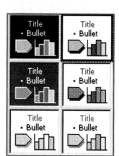

Change the Background Color or Scheme of Your Slides ➡ pp. 178–180

1. Choose Format | Background or Format | Slide Color Scheme.
2. In the Background dialog box, choose a new color from the drop-down menu; in the Color Scheme dialog box, select a new scheme.
3. Click the Apply to All button to apply your changes to all the slides in the presentation, or click the Apply button to apply your changes to the slide or slides you've selected.

Print Handout Copies of the Presentation ➥ p. 181

1. Choose File | Print (or press CTRL-P) to open the Print dialog box.
2. In the drop-down Print What menu, choose Handouts.
3. In the drop-down Slides per Page box, enter the number of slides you want on each page, and then click OK.

Give the Presentation ➥ pp. 181–184

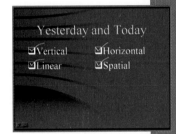

1. Choose View | Slide Show or click the Slide Show button to start.
2. Press the N or PAGE DOWN key, or right-click and choose Next, to move forward slide by slide.
3. Press the P or PAGE DOWN key, or right-click and choose Previous, to go backward.
4. Press ESC, or right-click and choose End Show, to end the presentation.

Use the Pen to Mark Slides
During a Presentation ➥ pp. 184–185

1. With a slide onscreen, right-click, choose Pointer Options from the shortcut menu, and choose Pen. The pointer turns into a pen.
2. Draw with the pen.

This chapter explains how to create a slide presentation, but don't be put off by the word *slide*. No, you don't need a slide projector to show these slides. *Slide* is simply the PowerPoint term for the images you create with the program. In fact, if you've spent any time in an office, you know that slides are things of the past, since you can now plug a laptop or other computer into special monitors that display PowerPoint slides.

In this chapter, you'll find out how to create professional presentations that dazzle or persuade an audience. These pages explain how to create the presentation, enter the text for the slides, insert and rearrange slides, and write notes for reading during the presentation. You'll also learn how to fiddle with the appearance of slides, give a presentation, and prepare a timed kiosk-style presentation. Last but not least, this chapter includes seven techniques for making your presentations livelier.

Three Ways to Create a Presentation

As Figure 8.1 shows, PowerPoint offers no fewer than three ways to create a new presentation. You can use what the program calls the AutoContent Wizard, start from a design template, or start with a blank presentation:

- **AutoContent Wizard**   With this technique, PowerPoint asks questions about the kind of presentation you want. When you are done answering, the program chooses a presentation design for you, complete with generic headings and text. All you have to do is enter your own headings and text and be done with it. Use this paint-by-numbers technique if you are in a hurry. Here you see the generic "Communicating Bad News" presentation. Check out the somewhat amusing generic text:

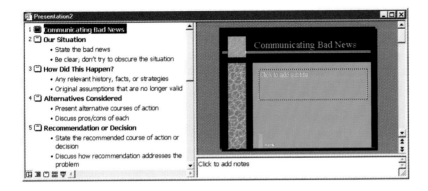

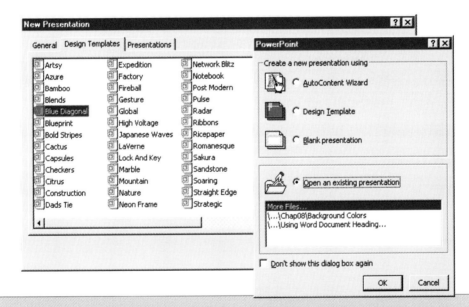

Figure 8.1: To start work on a presentation, either choose an option in the PowerPoint dialog box (right) or choose File | New and make a choice on the General, Design Templates, or Presentations tab of the New Presentation dialog box (left).

- **Design template**   With this technique, you choose a presentation design from a dialog box. You have to insert the slides and write the text yourself, but at least you get to examine slide designs before you choose one, which isn't the case with the AutoContent Wizard.

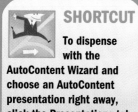

SHORTCUT

To dispense with the AutoContent Wizard and choose an AutoContent presentation right away, click the Presentations tab in the New Presentation dialog box (see Figure 8.1), choose a presentation name, and click OK.

- **Blank presentation**   You're on your own. With this technique, you have to fashion a design yourself and insert the slides one by one. I don't recommend this technique unless you know PowerPoint well and you have an artistic flair. Why make your own design when you can rely on a professional design from the AutoContent Wizard or a template? Even if you have to tweak a design you've inherited from someone else, tweaking it with the AutoContent Wizard or a template is the better way to go.

Creating a New Presentation

To create a PowerPoint presentation if you just started the program, choose an option in the PowerPoint dialog box (see Figure 8.1) and click OK. Otherwise, choose File | New (or press CTRL-N) to open the New Presentation dialog box (see Figure 8.1) and then do one of the following:

- **Design template**   Click the Design Templates tab and then click a template name. The Preview box shows what the template design looks like. When you find a design you like, click OK. You see the New Slide dialog box. (Skip ahead to "Putting a New Slide in a Presentation.")
- **Blank presentation**   On the General tab of the New Presentation dialog box, click Blank Presentation and click OK. You see the New Slide dialog box.
- **AutoContent Wizard**   On the General tab, click AutoContent Wizard and click OK. You see the first AutoContent Wizard dialog box. Click Next and keep answering questions and clicking Next until the time comes to click the Finish button.

EXPERT ADVICE

No matter which design you inherited or chose when you created your presentation, you can change your mind and choose a new design. To do so, choose Format | Apply Design Template. In the Apply Design Template dialog box, choose a new template and click Apply.

Putting a New Slide in a Presentation

By choosing an AutoLayout, you get a preformatted slide and you save yourself the trouble of laying out text and graphics yourself. What's more, six AutoLayouts—Text & Chart, Chart & Text, Organization Chart, Chart, Text & Clip Art, and Clip Art & Text—offer special buttons you can click that make creating charts and inserting clip art images easier.

EXPERT ADVICE

If you mistakenly choose the wrong AutoLayout for a slide, you can choose another. Select the slide and choose Format | Slide Layout, choose a new AutoLayout, and click the Reapply button.

To put a new slide in a presentation, follow the steps in Figure 8.2.

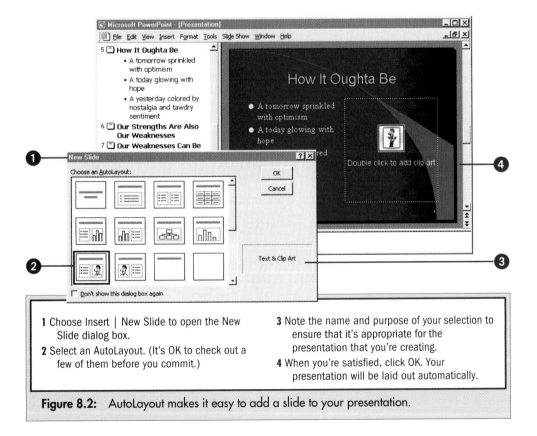

1 Choose Insert | New Slide to open the New Slide dialog box.

2 Select an AutoLayout. (It's OK to check out a few of them before you commit.)

3 Note the name and purpose of your selection to ensure that it's appropriate for the presentation that you're creating.

4 When you're satisfied, click OK. Your presentation will be laid out automatically.

Figure 8.2: AutoLayout makes it easy to add a slide to your presentation.

SHORTCUT

A fast way to insert a slide is to select one that's already there, choose Insert | Duplicate Slide, and then change the text on the duplicate slide and move it elsewhere.

The procedure for inserting an additional slide is very similar:

1. In Normal or Outline view ("Changing the View" later in this chapter explains views), select the slide that you want the new slide to come after.

2. Choose Insert | New Slide or press CTRL-M. The New Slide dialog box appears (see Figure 8.2).

3. Select an AutoLayout and click OK.

Viewing and Working on Slides

This part of the chapter explains the grunt work of creating a presentation. You didn't think it was going to be easy, did you? The presentation templates and AutoContent presentations make designing slides very, very easy, but you have to write the presentation yourself. You have to decide how many slides are needed. You have to put yourself in the place of the audience and carefully consider the best way to communicate what you want to communicate. To help you, these pages explain how to change views of a presentation, enter the text, write notes to work from as you give the presentation, and rearrange the slides.

Changing the View

When you work on a presentation, some views are better than others. Table 8.1 describes the six ways to view a presentation and tells why you would choose one view over another. Figure 8.3 shows four of the six views. To change views, either click a View button in the lower-left corner of the screen or open the View menu and choose Normal, Slide Sorter, Notes Page, or Slide Show.

EXPERT ADVICE

A boring PowerPoint presentation is the best cure for insomnia. To keep the attention of the audience, hit the high points and don't go into too much detail on the slides. Slide text should serve the same purpose as the headings in a report and the headlines in a newspaper—it should announce the topic of discussion, not describe the topic in detail. Titles and text on PowerPoint slides should be short, sweet, and to the point.

View	What It Shows You
Normal	The text in the presentation, a slide, and any notes. Normal is the all-purpose view.
Outline*	Just the text in the presentation. Good for entering and editing text.
Slide*	A single slide—but unlike Slide Show view, Slide view offers buttons for going quickly to any slide in the presentation. Good for rehearsing a presentation.
Slide Sorter	Thumbnails of all the slides in the presentation. Slide Sorter view is good for moving and deleting slides.
Slide Show	A single slide, which fills the screen. Presentations are given in Slide Show View. (Press ESC to leave this view.)
Notes Page	The notes that you've written to help you with the presentation. Good for entering notes. This view is available only on the View menu.

*Available only by clicking a View button in the lower-left corner of the screen.

Table 8.1: Ways of Viewing a Presentation

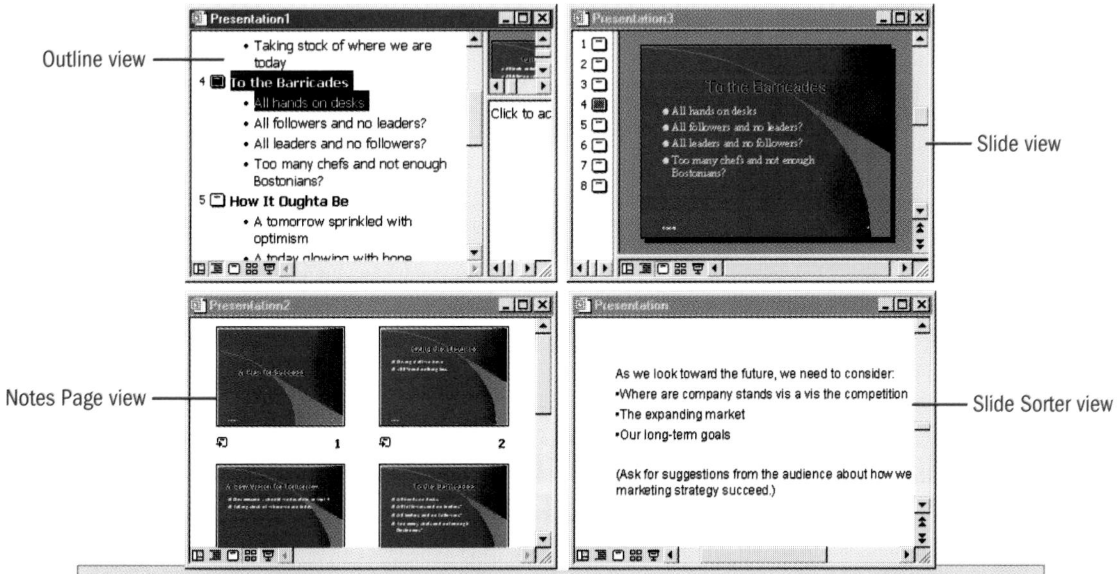

Figure 8.3: Four of the six ways of viewing slides

In Chapter 10, "Using Word Document Headings as PowerPoint Text" explains how you can save a lot of time and trouble by taking the headings from a Word document and turning them into the text of a PowerPoint presentation.

Entering the Text

The best place to enter the text for the presentation is Outline view. From there, it is easy to read the text on the slides, enter new text, or delete text. You can also call upon the Outlining toolbar as you enter text. The following table explains what the buttons on the toolbar do.

Outline Button	What It Does
←	Promotes text—a heading, subhead, or bulleted item—by one level.
→	Demotes text by one level.
↑	Moves text a line backward in the presentation.
↓	Moves text a line forward in the presentation.
−	Shows only the slide title.
+	Shows all slide text.
↑≡	Shows only the titles of all slides.
↓≣	Shows all text in the presentation.
▥	Creates a new slide from headings on slides you select.
ᴬ𝐴	Shows the font formatting of the text.

TIP

Don't forget, as you fool with the somewhat confusing Outline buttons, that you can always click the Undo button on the PowerPoint toolbar to reverse any error you make.

Writing and Printing What You Will Say in the Presentation

As I mentioned earlier, text on slides should be short and to the point. But that doesn't mean you can't write down what you want to say during a presentation. PowerPoint offers a special view, Notes Page view, for doing just that, and you can also write notes comfortably in Outline view in the window on the right side of the screen. As you write the text that will go on the slides, occasionally switch to Notes Pages view and write down what you want to say or what you want to ask the audience during the presentation. To switch to Notes Page view, choose View | Notes Page. You see a small picture of a slide and a box for entering notes. Click in the box and type what you want to say while the slide is onscreen.

When you print the notes, you get one page for each slide in the presentation. An image of the slide appears at the top of the page; the notes appear at the bottom. Follow these steps to print your notes:

1. Choose File | Print. You see the Print dialog box.

2. In the drop-down Print What menu, choose Notes Pages.

3. Click OK.

In Notes Page view, zooming in and out helps you see the notes that you write. "Learn to Zoom In and Zoom Out" in Chapter 1 gives you the scoop on zooming.

Moving and Deleting Slides

As a presentation takes shape, you sometimes have to move a slide forward or backward in the presentation. And sometimes you have to delete a slide. To perform these relatively simple tasks, switch to Slide Sorter view and do the following:

- **Moving a slide**   Click the slide you want to move and drag it to a new position. A vertical line shows where the slide will land when you release the mouse button. In this example, releasing the mouse button places the slide between what are now slides 1 and 2:

1   2   3

- **Deleting a slide**   Click the slide and then press the DELETE key.

Changing the Look of Slides

Earlier in this chapter, I explained that you can always choose a new design for your presentation by choosing Format | Apply Design Template, selecting a new template in the Apply Design Template dialog box, and clicking Apply. But suppose you want to fool with the slides' appearance on your own? I don't recommend straying from the design templates, because laying out slides and choosing colors on your own is a lot of work and requires a certain amount of expertise. Still, tweaking a slide's appearance is sometimes necessary. And you might be the adventurous kind who likes to experiment.

Read on to find out how to alter a design by making changes to the master slide, and how to choose new background colors.

Using the Master Slide for Consistent Text Formatting

SHORTCUT

A fast way to change fonts throughout a presentation is to choose Format | Replace Fonts. Then, in the Replace Font dialog box, choose a new font from the drop-down With menu, and click the Replace button. (Just be prepared to click the Undo button several times until you find a suitable font.)

The secret to a good layout is to make sure that the text on the slides is consistent from one slide to the next. Throughout the presentation, the letters in titles should be the same size and font. So should the letters in headings and bulleted lists. To be certain that slides are consistent with one another, you can do the formatting in what is called the *master slide*. Formatting changes made to the master slide appear in slides throughout the document, ensuring consistency.

Figure 8.4 shows how to make changes to the master slide and, in so doing, change formats throughout your presentation.

PowerPoint also offers the View | Master | Title Master command for changing the appearance of title slides in a presentation. Most presentations have only one title slide, the first, but if yours has more than one and you want them to be consistent with one another, make your format changes to the *title master slide*.

Choosing New Background Colors for Slides

If you have an artistic bent, you may want to experiment with the Format | Background and Format | Slide Color Scheme commands.

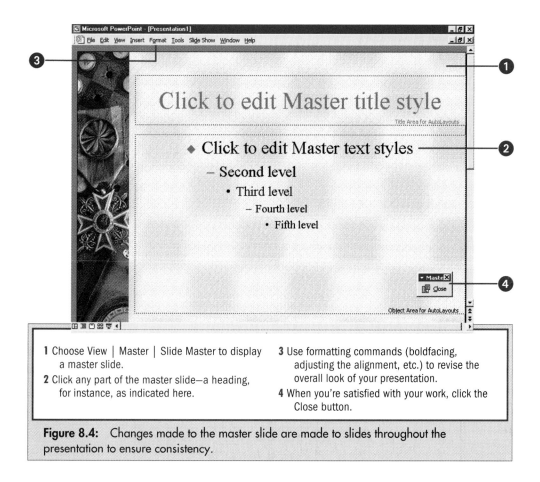

1 Choose View | Master | Slide Master to display a master slide.

2 Click any part of the master slide—a heading, for instance, as indicated here.

3 Use formatting commands (boldfacing, adjusting the alignment, etc.) to revise the overall look of your presentation.

4 When you're satisfied with your work, click the Close button.

Figure 8.4: Changes made to the master slide are made to slides throughout the presentation to ensure consistency.

The first changes the background color, and the second gives you the opportunity to choose a new color scheme for slide titles and bulleted lists as well as the background. Follow these steps to test-drive these commands:

1. Switch to Slide view and select the slide or slides whose appearance you want to change.

2. Choose Format | Background to choose a new background color or Format | Slide Color Scheme to change the color of various elements in the slides.

TIP

To change the color of a handful of slides in a presentation, switch to Slide Sorter view and select the slides. To do so, hold down the CTRL key and click each slide whose color scheme you want to change.

3. Make choices in the Background or Color Scheme dialog box:

- **Background**   Choose a new color from the drop-down menu, as shown in Figure 8.5. You can also choose an unorthodox color by clicking More Colors or a fill effect by choosing Fill Effects.

- **Color Scheme**   Select a new color scheme in the dialog box. You can click the Preview button to see what the slide or slides will look like after you choose a new scheme.

4. Click the Apply to All button to apply your changes to all of the slides in the presentation, or click the Apply button to apply your changes to the slide or slides you selected in step 1.

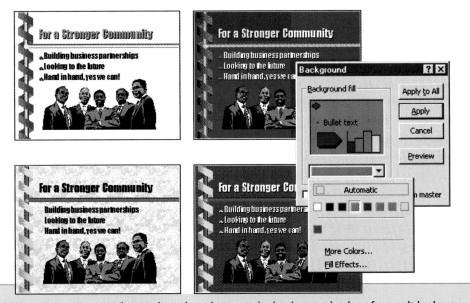

Figure 8.5:   You can change the color scheme or the background color of your slides by choosing Format | Slide Color Scheme or Format | Background.

Printing Handout Copies of a Presentation

One way to make a slide presentation more memorable is to print copies of it and hand out the copies after the presentation is over. That way, audience members can refer to your presentation or even marvel at it later on. You can find almost everything you need to know about printing a presentation in "Printing Your Work" in Chapter 2. However, you will find the following amenities at the bottom of the Print dialog box after you choose File | Print (or press CTRL-P):

- **Print What** Choose Handouts to print several slides on each page. Then, in the Slides per Page box, enter the number of slides to print on each page. The larger the number, the smaller the slides.
- **Grayscale** Prints your slides in white, black, and varying shades of gray.
- **Pure Black and White** Prints slides in black and white only, with no grays.
- **Scale to Fit Paper** Shrinks the slides, if necessary, to make them fit on the paper.
- **Frame Slides** Places a border around each slide.

Giving the Presentation

At last—the big day has arrived, and now you must give the presentation. "Break a leg," as actors say before they go on stage.

At the end of this chapter, "Seven Tricks for Making a Presentation Livelier" offers some advice for making your presentation a success.

EXPERT ADVICE

Be sure to rehearse the presentation one or two times. Take note of how long it takes for you to give the presentation. You might need to lengthen or shorten it. And before the presentation starts, make sure the machine on which you will give it is hooked up and in working order.

These pages explain how to give a standard slide show presentation as well as how to set up a kiosk-style presentation that shows itself.

Showing the Slides

Compared to the preliminary work, giving a presentation is a piece of cake. To get off to a good start, switch to Slide Sorter view or Outline view and select the first slide in the presentation. That way, you start at the beginning. Then do the following to show your slides:

- **Starting the show**   Choose View | Slide Show, press F5, or click the Slide Show button.
- **Going forward**   To go forward from slide to slide, click with the mouse, press N (for Next), press the PAGE DOWN key, right-click and choose Next, or click the button in the lower-left corner of the screen and choose Next.
- **Going backward**   To go backward through the slides, press P (for Previous), press the PAGE UP key, right-click and choose Previous from the shortcut menu, or click the button in the lower-left corner of the screen and choose Previous.
- **Going to a specific slide**   Right-click and choose Go | By Title and then the slide title, as shown in Figure 8.6. If the show includes many slides, choose Slide Navigator and then select the slide from the Slide Navigator dialog box.
- **Ending the show**   Press ESC, right-click and choose End Show from the shortcut menu, or click the button in the lower-left corner of the screen and choose End Show.

TIP

Get used to pressing keys or right-clicking to see the shortcut menu, because finding the button on a dark screen is almost impossible.

Figure 8.6: To select navigation options during a slide presentation, click the button in the lower-left corner, or simply right-click.

Giving a Self-Playing, Kiosk-Style Presentation

A *kiosk-style* presentation is one that plays on its own. You set the works in motion and it plays over and over on your computer until you or someone else comes along to press the ESC key. To give a kiosk-style presentation, you tell PowerPoint how long to leave each slide onscreen in the Slide Transition dialog box, as detailed in Figure 8.7.

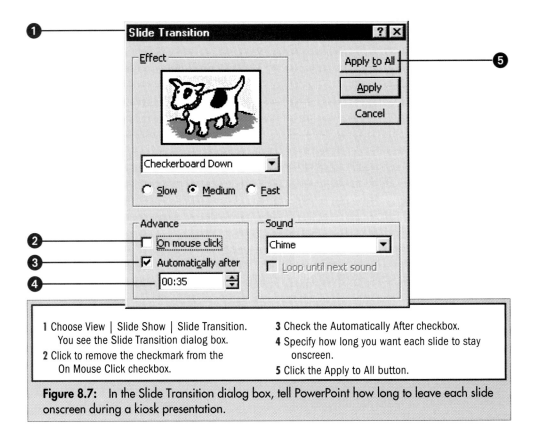

Figure 8.7:   In the Slide Transition dialog box, tell PowerPoint how long to leave each slide onscreen during a kiosk presentation.

Seven Tricks for Making a Presentation Livelier

Here are seven tricks for livening up your slide presentations. (You would do well to take advantage of some of these techniques. Time never passes as slowly as it does during a dull slide show.)

1. USE THE PEN FOR EMPHASIS   During the presentation, you can draw onscreen with the Pen, as someone has done in Figure 8.8. To use the Pen, right-click and choose Pointer Options | Pen from the shortcut menu. The pointer turns into a pen. Start drawing.

Press ESC when you are finished using the pen (but be careful not to press ESC twice, because the second press tells PowerPoint to end

Figure 8.8: Right-click and choose Pointer Options | Pen to draw onscreen during a presentation.

the slide show). Pen marks are not permanent. As soon as you move to the next slide, the pen marks are erased.

2. PUT THE SAME IMAGE ON EACH SLIDE Putting the same image on each slide—a corporate logo, for instance or a small clip art image—makes for a very elegant effect. The trick is to put the image on a master slide so that it appears on all the slides in the presentation. Choose View | Master | Slide Master to display the master slide. Then insert the clip art image or art file, shrink it, and tuck it into a corner of the master slide. "Decorating Files with Clip Art and WordArt" in Chapter 2 explains how to insert a clip art image. See "Handling 'Objects' in Files" in the same chapter to learn how to shrink and move a clip art image.

Earlier in this chapter, "Using the Master Slide for Consistent Text Formatting" explains what the master slide is.

EXPERT ADVICE

If you must remove pen marks right away, right-click and choose Screen | Erase Pen. You can choose different colors for the Pen by right-clicking, choosing Pointer Options | Pen Color, and choosing a color from the submenu.

---

3. CHOOSE INTERESTING SLIDE TRANSITIONS

If you created your slide presentation with the AutoContent Wizard, PowerPoint has already chosen a slide transition for you. A *slide transition* is PowerPoint's term for the way that a new slide arrives onscreen. The program offers 41 different transitions, including Dissolve, Wipe Right, and Fade Through Black. To choose your own slide transition:

1. Choose Slide Show | Slide Transition. The Slide Transition dialog box appears (see Figure 8.7).

2. Choose a transition from the drop-down Effect menu, and watch the dog or the key to see a preview of the transition you've chosen.

3. Click the Slow, Medium, or Fast option to choose a transition speed, and then click the Apply to All button.

4. USE SOUNDS TO MARK SLIDE TRANSITIONS

You can also mark the transition from one slide to another with a sound. To do so, choose Slide Show | Slide Transition and choose a sound from the drop-down Sound menu in the Slide Transition dialog box (see Figure 8.7).

5. CHOOSE UNUSUAL BULLET CHARACTERS

The standard round bullet is kind of dull. To specify a new style of bullet, select the bulleted text by dragging the mouse over it, and then choose Formats | Bullets and Numbering. In the Bullets and Numbering dialog box, click the Bulleted tab if necessary, and then choose a new bullet style. Besides the characters in the dialog box, you can choose a symbol by clicking the Character button. That takes you to the Bullet dialog box, where you can choose from many different symbols.

6. BLACK OUT THE SCREEN   Sometimes a slide show provokes an animated discussion among the members of the audience. When that happens, the audience's attention turns away from the screen and focuses upon itself. To keep stray members of the audience from staring at the screen and ignoring the discussion, black out the screen. To do so, right-click, choose Screen from the shortcut menu, and choose Black Screen. When you want to see a slide again, simply click on the screen.

7. PLACE A WORDART IMAGE ON A SLIDE OR TWO   WordArt looks especially good in PowerPoint presentations. "Decorating Files with Clip Art and WordArt" in Chapter 2 explains how to import a WordArt image into a file.

CHAPTER 9

Access 2000: Managing and Tracking Data

Includes

- Understanding how databases work
- Creating a database
- Finding your way around the Database window
- Creating database tables
- Filtering a database to gather information
- Querying a database
- Presenting database information in a report

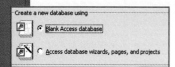

Create a New Database ➥ pp. 196–197

1. Start Access, click the Blank Access Database option button, and click OK. If you are already running Access, choose File | New, double-click the Database icon in the New dialog box, and click OK.
2. In the File New Database dialog box, choose a folder to store the database, enter a name in the File Name box, and click the Create button.

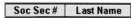

Soc Sec Number	Last
111-22-3434	Cranial
333-44-9898	Bellow
444-67-8769	Chin
555-987-2341	Hester
777-09-6754	Ruiz
999-876-1234	Zaks

Create a Database Table
for Storing Information ➥ pp. 198–199

1. Click the Database Window button to go to the Database window.
2. Click the Tables button and then double-click Create Table in Design View.
3. In the Design View window, click the Save button, enter a name for the table, and click OK.
4. Enter the fields for the table in the Design View window.

Soc Sec #	Last Name

Enter a Field ➥ p. 200

1. In th Design View window, enter a field name in the Field Names column.
2. Choose a data type to classify the field.
3. Enter a description, if you like, in the Description column.

How Often?
Never
Always
Sometimes

Make Sure Data
Will Be Entered Accurately ➥ pp. 202–203

- In the Design View window, click the Lookup tab, and then choose Combo Box from the Display Control menu. From the Row Source Type menu, choose Value List. In the Row Source text box, enter each option for the drop-down list.

- On the General tab of the Design View window, enter the maximum number of characters that can be entered in the field in the Field Size box.
- On the General tab, enter a default value for the field in the Default Value box.
- On the General tab, enter **Yes** in the Required box if you want to make sure that a value is entered in a particular field.

Establish the Relationships
Between Database Tables ➥ pp. 203–205

1. Choose Tools | Relationships, or click the Relationships button.
2. In the Show Tables dialog box, select the name of each table and click the Add button. Then click Close to see the Relationships window.
3. Click a field name in one table and drag it to the corresponding primary key field in another table to establish the relationship.
4. In the Edit Relationships dialog box, click the Create button to forge a relationship between the tables.

Sort the Records in a Database Table ➥ pp. 207–208

1. Switch to Datasheet view (choose View | Datasheet View) and click in the field that you want to sort the records on.
2. Click the Sort Ascending button for an ascending sort or the Sort Descending button for a descending sort.

Filter a Database to Get Information ➥ pp. 208–209

1. Click the Filter By Form button.
2. Click in each field you want to find information in, open the drop-down menu, and choose the value you want to search for.
3. Click the Apply Filter button.

Query a Database to Get Information ➡ pp. 210–212

1. In the Database window, click the Queries button, and then double-click the Create Query in Design View icon.
2. In the Show Table dialog box, select each database table you intend to query, click the Add button, and then click the Close button.
3. In the Select Query window, indicate which fields you want to query by choosing names from the drop-down lists.
4. Enter the search criteria in the Criteria boxes.
5. Click the Run button to see the results of the query.

Generate a Report from Query Results ➡ pp. 214–215

1. In the Database window, click the Reports button.
2. Double-click the Create Report by Using Wizard icon.
3. Follow the directions and answer the questions in the Report Wizard dialog boxes.

Most people feel kind of queasy when they hear the word "database." Who can blame them? Database terminology—*record, field, query, filter*—is ugly indeed. And databases can be intimidating. Even people with a considerable amount of experience with Word 2000 and Excel 2000 shy away from Access 2000, the Office 2000 database program. But Access can be invaluable for storing and organizing customer lists, inventories, addresses, payment histories, donor lists, and volunteer lists, to name only a few examples. What's more, you can get information from Access databases very, very quickly.

This chapter teaches you how to design and create a database with Access. You'll learn how to create database tables, how to enter the data, and techniques for making sure data is entered accurately. After you enter the data in a database, you can pester your database for information. This chapter explains how to do that by sorting, filtering, and querying a database. Finally, you'll discover how to generate a report from the data in a database.

What You Should Know Before You Begin

Whether they know it or not, no one is a stranger to databases. A telephone directory is a database. So is an address book. A recipe book is also a database. Any place where information is stored in a systematic way is a database. The difference between a computerized database and a conventional database such as an address book is that storing, finding, and manipulating data is much easier in a computerized database. Imagine how long it would take to find all of the California addresses in an address book with many entries. In Access, you can query a database and find all California addresses in a matter of seconds.

Information in databases is stored in tables like the one shown in Figure 9.1. In a database table, you include one *field* for each category of information you want to keep on hand. Fields are the equivalent of columns in a table. Your first duty when you create a database table is to name the fields and tell Access what kind of information you propose to store in each field. After you create the fields, you can start entering the records. A *record* describes all of the data concerning one person or thing. In Figure 9.1, six records have been entered in the database table.

A database can comprise one table or many different tables. If you are dealing with a lot of information, storing data in more than one table is to your advantage. To see why, consider Figure 9.2, which shows a database created to store information about employees. The database includes three tables: Retirement Plans, Departments, and Name and Address.

Suppose that all of the data were entered in one large table instead of three tables. You would have to enter complete retirement plan and department information for each employee as you entered his or her data. Under the arrangement shown in Figure 9.2, however, you need only enter a department number and retirement plan number in the Name and Address table to describe the employee's department and choice of retirement plan. Because the Name and Address table is related to the Retirement Plans and Departments tables (I'll show you how to relate tables later), the numbers you enter describe each

Fields

Soc Sec Number	Last Name	First Name	Phone Number
111-22-3434	Cranial	Dave	555-3431
333-44-9898	Bellow	Dirk	555-4321
444-67-8769	Chin	Susana	555-1289
555-987-2341	Hester	Juanita	555-9872
777-09-6754	Ruiz	Nigel	555-8787
999-876-1234	Zaks	Roscoe	555-0982

Records

Figure 9.1: Data is stored in database tables like this one. In a table, data about a person or thing is listed in a record, and each record is divided into fields.

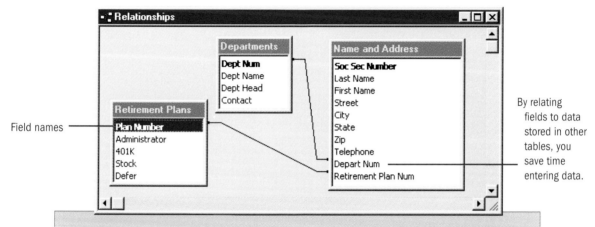

Field names ——

By relating
fields to data
stored in other
tables, you
save time
entering data.

Figure 9.2: The Relationships window shows how the tables that make up a database are related to one another.

employee's retirement plan and department. You don't have to enter the information time and time again. What's more, if the name of a retirement plan administrator or department head changes, you can simply enter new names in the Retirement Plans and Departments tables. If you kept all of the data in a single table, you would have to change the names in all of the records in the table.

Storing information in a database is only half the story. After you enter the data, you can query the database in different ways. A *query* is a question you ask of a database. In an address database, you can find all the people in a particular zip code or state. If information about contributions is stored in the database, you can find out who contributed more than $500 last year. Queries can get very complex. For example, you could find all the people in a particular city who

---

EXPERT ADVICE

Deciding how many tables to include in a database and how the tables relate to one another is probably the hardest task you can undertake in Access. Entire books have been written about database design, and this little book cannot do the subject justice. You can, however, store all your data in a single table if the data you want to store is not very complex. The time you lose by entering all the data in a single table will be made up by the time you save in not having to design a complex database with more than one table.

contributed between $50 and $500 and who volunteered more than eight hours in the past year. Next time you get a junk mail solicitation, study the letter and ask yourself, "How did I get in this database, and which database query produced my name?"

Creating a New Database File

TIP

You can also create a new database by means of a wizard. Click the Access Database Wizards, Pages, and Project option button in the Microsoft Access dialog box to create a database this way. The dialog boxes describe the choices you have to make to construct your database.

In Access 2000, you save and name a new database file the moment you create it. To create a new database, use either of these techniques:

- **If you have not started Access**   Start Access (click the Start button and choose Programs | Microsoft Access), double-click the Blank Access Database option button in the Microsoft Access dialog box, and click OK. In the File New Database dialog box, choose a folder to store the database, enter a name in the File Name box, and click the Create button.

- **If Access is running**   Choose File | New, click the Database icon in the New dialog box, and click OK. You see the File New Database dialog box. Choose a folder for storing your database, enter a name in the File Name box, and click Create.

As soon as you create your database, you see the Database window, as shown in Figure 9.3. The Database window is the starting point for working with a database, whether it is a new one or one you created long ago. The next section explains how to find your way around the Database window.

Finding Your Way Around the Database Window

As I mentioned at the beginning of this chapter, a database can include many different tables. It can include different queries and reports as well. When you want to create a new database table, query, or report, start from the Database window (see Figure 9.3). Likewise, you can open a table, query, or report that you've already created by

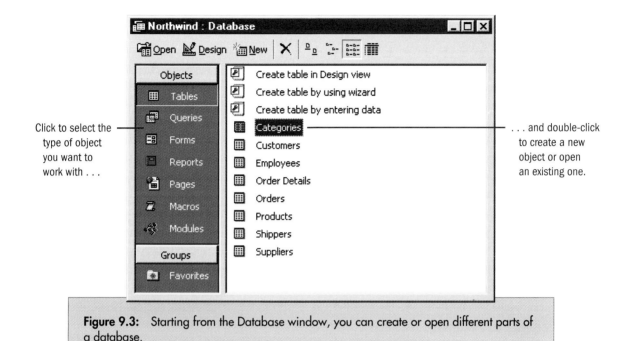

Click to select the type of object you want to work with . . .

. . . and double-click to create a new object or open an existing one.

Figure 9.3: Starting from the Database window, you can create or open different parts of a database.

choosing an object type in the Database window and double-clicking a name. Think of the Database window as the Grand Central Station of Access 2000.

Whatever you happen to be doing in Access, you can return to the Database window with either of these techniques:

- Click the Database Window button on the Table Database toolbar (or press F11).
- Click the Database Window button on the Taskbar.

Tables, queries, and reports appear in their own windows onscreen after you open them. Access places a new button on the Taskbar each time you open a new table, query, or whatnot. To go from window to window, click the buttons on the Taskbar. Click the Close button in a window to close a table, query, or report.

Creating a Database Table

Raw data is stored in database tables (or in a single table if you decide to keep all of the data in one place). After you have entered the data in the table or tables, you can query the database to gather information about the things and people that your database keeps track of. These pages explain how to create a database table, enter the data in the fields, and format the fields so that the data is entered accurately.

Creating the Table

Before you create a table, give a moment of serious thought to how many fields your table requires and whether you can save time by spreading the data across two or three tables. As you learned at the beginning of this chapter, a field, much like a column in a normal table, is a category of information. You need one field for each piece of information you want to store concerning the people or items your database table tracks. As for the number of database tables you need, see if you can save time by distributing the data across several tables.

When you are ready to get going, follow these steps:

1. From the Database window (see Figure 6.3), click the Tables button on the Objects list. The list of table options will appear on the right.

2. At the top of the options list, double-click Create Table in Design View. You see the Design View window, as shown in Figure 9.4.

3. Enter your field names.

4. For each field, choose a data type and, if you like, enter a description.

5. In the lower section of the Design View window, enter or choose field properties

6. Click the Save button (or choose File | Save).

7. Enter a name for your database table in the Save As dialog box.

8. Click OK. The name you've entered will appear in the Database window.

At the start of this chapter, "What You Should Know Before You Begin" explains the benefits and burdens of storing data in more than one database table.

Save button

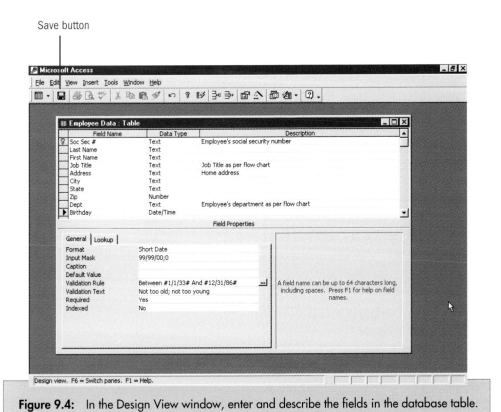

Figure 9.4: In the Design View window, enter and describe the fields in the database table.

After you create the database table, the next step is to enter the field names and choose a primary key field. (Keep reading.)

EXPERT ADVICE

If you intend to distribute the data across more than one table, make sure that one field in each table holds data whose entries will be different from record to record. Social Security numbers, invoice numbers, and check numbers make good choices for these kinds of fields, because those numbers are certain to be different from record to record. If you can't come up with a field that will be different in each record, you can tell Access to "autonumber" the records—that is, to assign each record a number. To do so, open the Data Type menu in the Design View window and choose AutoNumber (as explained later in this chapter).

Later in this chapter, "Making Sure Data Entries Are Accurate" offers tips for formatting fields in the Design View window to make it easier for data-entry clerks to enter the data.

CAUTION

Choose your data types carefully, because the way you classify the data that is entered in a field determines how you can query that field for information. Querying for a number range is impossible, for example, if the field you are querying has not been classified as a Number field on the Data Type menu.

Entering the Fields

In the Design View window (see Figure 9.4), enter field names in the Field Name column. Later, when you switch to Datasheet view and enter data in the table, the field names will appear along the top of the window, with the first name on the left side and each subsequent name to its right:

Soc Sec #	Last Name

Names cannot include periods, and they can be 64 characters long—but keep in mind that a very long name won't fit well along the top of the table.

After you enter a name in the Field Name column, choose a data type to classify the field, and enter a description in the Description column as well if you so desire. Table 9.1 lists the ten options on the Data Type menu.

Suppose you need to move, rename, or delete a field. To do so, switch to Design View if necessary (choose View | Design View) and follow these instructions:

- **Moving a field**   Select the box to the left of the field you want to move, and drag the box up or down to a new location.
- **Renaming a field**   Click in the Field Name box where the name is, delete the name that is there, and enter a new name.
- **Deleting a field**   Right-click the field and choose Delete Rows from the shortcut menu.

You can always return to the Design View window and enter new fields or remove fields from a table. To do so, choose View | Design View, or click the down arrow beside the View button and choose Design View.

Designating the Primary Key

Before you can leave the Design View window, Access asks you to declare which field is the primary key. If you are storing all your data

Data Type	What It Stores
Text	Text and combinations of text and numbers (such as street addresses).
Memo	Descriptions. Choose Memo, for example, to describe an item in an inventory database table.
Number	Numbers to be used in calculations and data comparisons. To choose a format for numbers, go to the General tab in the bottom half of the Design View window, click the down arrow in the Format box, and choose a format.
Date/Time	Dates and times. To choose a format for displaying the date and time, click the down arrow in the Format box on the General tab and choose a format.
Currency	Monetary values to be used in calculations.
AutoNumber	Sequential numbers that are created automatically in order to provide unique, one-of-a-kind numbers for records.
Yes/No	Either-or data.
OLE Object	OLE objects to be used in database tables. "OLE for Sharing Data Between Programs" in Chapter 10 explains how OLE works.
Hyperlink	Hyperlinks to other files.
Lookup Wizard	Drop-down option lists that you create with the help of the Lookup Wizard. (Drop-down lists of controlled data options help you prevent the entry of incorrect information. See "Making Sure Data Entries Are Accurate" later in this chapter to learn about creating drop-down lists.)

Table 9.1: Options for Classifying Data on the Data Type Menu

DEFINITION

Primary key: The field in a database table whose entries will differ from record to record. The primary key identifies the field where unique, one-of-a-kind data is stored.

in one database table, it doesn't matter which field you choose for the primary key, but if you intend to distribute the data across more than one table, each table needs a primary key. To relate the tables in a database to one another, you relate the field in one table to the primary key field in another. (See "Establishing the Relationships Between Database Tables" later in this chapter.)

To designate the primary key field, right-click the field in the Design View window and choose Primary Key from the shortcut menu. A key appears in the box beside the field's name:

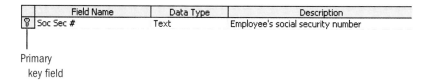

	Field Name	Data Type	Description
🔑	Soc Sec #	Text	Employee's social security number

Primary
key field

Making Sure Data Entries Are Accurate

Unfortunately, entering the data in a database table is one of the most tedious activities known to humankind. And because it is so dull, people are prone to make mistakes. One way to cut down on data entry mistakes is to take advantage of a handful of options on the General tab in the Design View window.

Later in this chapter, "Entering the Data in a Database Table" explains how to input your data.

- **Field Size**   The Field Size option controls the maximum number of characters that can be entered in a field. Suppose that the field you are dealing with is called "State," and you want to use it for storing two-letter state abbreviations. By entering **2** in the Field Size text box, you specify that only two characters can be entered in the field. This will prevent anyone from erroneously entering three or more characters.

- **Default Value**   When you know that the majority of records will require a certain value, number, or abbreviation, enter it in the Default Value box. That way, you can save yourself the trouble of entering the value, number, or abbreviation most of the time, because the default value will already appear in each record as you enter it. You can always override the default value by entering something different.

- **Required**   By default, no entry has to be made in a field, but if you enter **Yes** in the Required box instead of **No** and you fail to make an entry in the field, a message box tells you to be sure to make an entry. Enter **Yes** in the Required option box if you want to be certain that entries are made in a field.

The Lookup tab in the Design View window offers another means of making sure that data is entered correctly: a drop-down list. Instead of relying on your own—or someone else's—ability to enter data correctly, create a drop-down list whenever you know that only a handful of options can be entered in a particular field.

Follow these steps to create a drop-down list:

1. In the Design View window, click the name of the field that needs a list, and then click the Lookup tab.

2. From the Display Control menu, choose Combo Box.

3. From the Row Source Type menu, choose Value List.

4. In the Row Source text box, enter each option for the drop-down list. Enclose each option name in double quotation marks (").
Enter a semicolon (;) between the options. Here you see how entries on the Lookup tab translate into a drop-down list in a database table:

Establishing the Relationships Between Database Tables

If your database happens to include more than one table, you have to tell Access 2000 how the tables relate to one another. Unless Access understands the table relationships between your tables, you can't query more than one table or enter data in a field that refers to information that is stored in a different table.

Figure 9.5 shows how relationships between tables are mapped out in the Relationships window. To open the window, click the Relationships button. In the window, the name of each table you selected appears in its own window. The names of the fields in each table appear in the

TIP

If you mistakenly establish a relationship between the wrong fields, right-click the line between the fields, choose Delete from the shortcut menu, and click Yes in the confirmation box.

Relationships

windows as well. Primary key fields appear in boldface. You can move a table window to a new location in the Relationships window by dragging its title bar. To establish a relationship, you draw a line from a field name in one table to a primary key field name in another:

1. Choose Tools | Relationships or click the Relationships button to open the Show Table dialog box, shown in Figure 9.5.

2. Select the name of each table that you want to relate to another table.

3. Click the Add button. The Relationships window will appear.

4. Click a field name in one table and drag it to the corresponding primary key field in another table. In Figure 9.5, for example, I've linked the Dept Num field in the Employee Names table with the Dept Num field in the Departments table.

   When you release the mouse button, you see the Edit Relationships dialog box.

5. Make sure the correct field names—the names of the two related fields—appear in the dialog box.

6. Click the Create button to establish the relationship between the tables.

7. Repeat steps 4, 5, and 6 to establish more relationships, if necessary.

TIP

You can always click the Relationships button or choose Tools | Relationships to see how the tables in a database are related to one another.

Note that once the relationships are established between the tables in Figure 9.5, all I have to do to describe an employee's department is enter a department number in the Dept Num field of the Employee Names table.

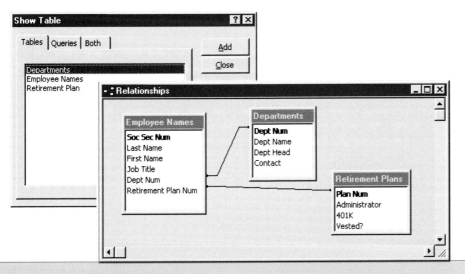

Figure 9.5: In the Relationships window, you establish the relationships between fields in different database tables.

Entering the Data in a Database Table

At last—you can start entering the data. You've set up your database table or tables, named the fields, and established relationships between the tables. Now you're ready to go.

To start entering data, switch to Datasheet view and start typing. You can switch to Datasheet view either by choosing View | Datasheet View or by clicking the down arrow beside the View button and choosing Datasheet View. Figure 9.6 shows what a database table looks like in Datasheet view. The bottom of the Datasheet View

EXPERT ADVICE

In a database table with many fields, it is sometimes hard to tell what data to enter. When the cursor is in the sixth or seventh field, for example, you can lose sight of the first field, which usually identifies the person or item whose data you are entering. To "freeze" a field so that it appears onscreen no matter how far you travel to the right side of the datasheet, click the name of the field at the top of the datasheet and choose Format | Freeze Columns. If you want to "unfreeze" the field, choose Format | Unfreeze All Columns. You can freeze more than one field by dragging across field names at the top of the data sheet before choosing Format | Freeze Columns.

TIP

To change the width of a field column, move the pointer to the top of the table, to the right of the field name. When you see the double-headed arrow, click and drag toward the right.

window tells you how many records have been entered in the datasheet and which record the cursor is in. You can scroll from place to place to enter your data, or you can use the buttons on the Record toolbar at the bottom of the window.

If you make a mistake, press the BACKSPACE or DELETE key to erase the error, and then enter the data all over again. To delete an entire record, right-click the box to the left of the record, choose Delete Record from the shortcut menu, and click Yes when Access asks if you really want to delete the record.

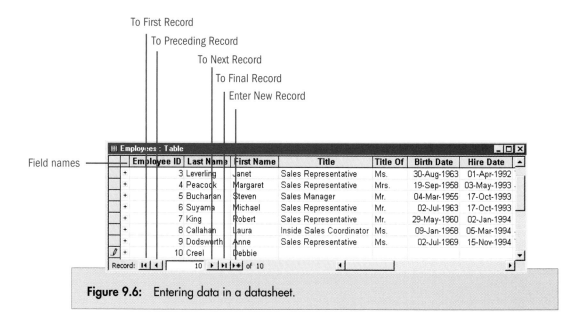

Figure 9.6: Entering data in a datasheet.

Getting the Data Out: Sorting, Filtering, and Querying

So much for entering the data in your database. Now that the raw data has been entered and safely stored away in database tables, you can start pestering your database for information. These pages explain how to sort records so that they appear in a particular order, filter records to dredge up records of a particular kind, and query a database to gather information about the people or things your database keeps track of.

Sorting Data to Make It Easier to Work With

By sorting your database, you can locate records faster. What's more, being able to sort data means that you don't have to bother about the order in which you enter records, because you can always sort them later to put them in a particular order.

Records can be sorted in ascending or descending order:

DEFINITION

Sort:
To rearrange records in a database table by one or more fields so that the records appear in alphabetical, numerical, or chronological order.

- **Ascending sort**   Arranges text in alphabetical order from A to Z, numbers from smallest to largest, and dates from earliest in time to latest.

- **Descending sort**   Arranges text from Z to A, numbers from largest to smallest, and dates from latest in time to earliest.

These database tables present the same information. In the table on the left, records have been sorted in ascending order in the Album Title field. In the table on the right, records have been sorted in descending order in the Year field:

Album Title	Year
Beggar's Banquet	1968
Between the Buttons	1966
Exile on Main Street	1972
Get Yer Ya-Ya's Out	1970
Goat's Head Soup	1973
His Satanic Majesty's Request	1967
Let It Bleed	1969

Album Title	Year
Goat's Head Soup	1973
Exile on Main Street	1972
Get Yer Ya-Ya's Out	1970
Let It Bleed	1969
Beggar's Banquet	1968
His Satanic Majesty's Request	1967
Between the Buttons	1966

Follow these steps to sort the records in a database table:

1. Switch to Datasheet view (choose View | Datasheet View), and click anywhere in the field that you want to sort the records on.

2. Click the Sort Ascending button for an ascending sort or the Sort Descending button for a descending sort.

Filtering a Database Table to Find Information

DEFINITION

Filter:
To isolate all the records in a database table that have the same— or nearly the same—field values.

Filtering a table is useful when you need to find records that contain specific information. For example, you could find all the people who live in New York, all the people under the age of 25, or all the people who live in New York who are under the age of 25. For that matter, you can filter by exclusion and see the records of all the people in a database table who do not live in New York and who are not under the age of 25.

Follow these steps to filter a database table:

1. Open the database table you want to filter. To do this, click the Tables button in the Database window and then double-click the name of a database table. You see the database table in Datasheet view.

2. Click the Filter By Form button, or choose Records | Filter | Filter By Form. Only field names appear at the top of the datasheet. (If you or someone else has filtered the database table already, the filtering criteria appear in the first row of the table. To remove the criteria, click the Clear Grid button. You will find it beside the Close button.)

3. Click in a field, open the drop-down menu, and choose the value you want to search for.

4. To search in more than one field, make selections from other drop-down menus. Here, I am searching for people who live in

New York who are 24 years old or younger, and whose income is higher than $25,000:

First Name	City	State	Zip	Age	Income
	▼			<="24"	>"25,000"

Albany
New York
Sleepy Hollow
Wye

SHORTCUT The fastest way to filter a database table is to click the field value that you want to find, and then choose Records | Filter | Filter By Selection. For example, to find only people who live in New York, click New York in the City field and choose Records | Filter | Filter By Selection.

You can enter *comparison operators* to look for values in numeric and monetary fields. Here is a list of the comparison operators you can use:

Comparison Operator	Name
<	Less than
<=	Less than or equal to
>	Greater than
>=	Greater than or equal to
=	Equal to
<>	Not equal to

Apply Filter

5. Click the Apply Filter button. The records whose values you described appear.

6. Click the Remove Filter button to return to the database table. (The button looks like the Apply Filter button, except that it is "pressed down.")

You can also filter a database table by excluding records of a certain kind. To do so, click the field value that you want to exclude and choose Records | Filter | Filter by Excluding Selection. For example, to see the records of everyone in a database except for people who live in New York, click New York in the City field and choose Records | Filter | Filter by Excluding Selection. Click the Remove Filter button if you want to see all the records again.

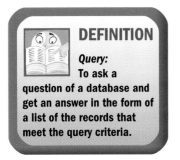

DEFINITION

Query:
To ask a question of a database and get an answer in the form of a list of the records that meet the query criteria.

TIP

You can drag to change the size of the Select Query window. Drag the boundary between the top and bottom halves of the window to see the tables and query grid better.

Querying a Database for Information

A query can search for information in more than one database table. "Who lives in Los Angeles and donated more than $500 last year?" is an example of a database query. In the results of the query you can show all the fields in a database table or only a few necessary fields.

Follow these basic steps to construct a query:

1. If necessary, click the Database Window button (or press F11) to go to the Database window (see Figure 9.3)

2. Under Objects, click the Queries button. The Database window lists the queries you've created, if you've created any. (To run a query, double-click its name in the Database window.)

3. Double-click the Create Query in Design View icon. You see the Show Table dialog box.

4. Select each database table you intend to query, and click the Add button.

5. Click the Close button when you are done selecting database tables.

You see the Select Query window shown in Figure 9.7. The top of the window lists the table or tables you selected, along with the names of the fields in each table. The bottom half of the window, called the *query grid,* is where you describe how to conduct the query.

The query in Figure 9.7 will find the names of people whose birthdays fall between January 1, 1944, and December 31, 1979, and whose Donation Category is 1 or 2. The query results will list the donors' names, the donors' telephone numbers, and the names of the people who administer Donor categories 1 and 2. The purpose of this query is to get a list of donors between the ages of 21 and 66 in categories 1 and 2 so that they can be called and solicited for more donations.

Tables to be queried

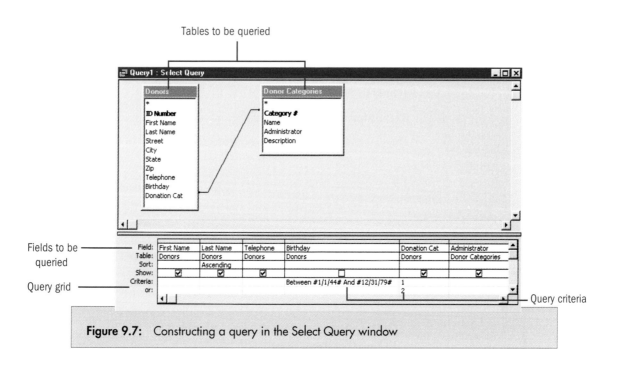

Fields to be queried

Query grid

Query criteria

Figure 9.7: Constructing a query in the Select Query window

6. Specify each field that you want to query by clicking in the Field box and choosing a field name from the drop-down list. If you are querying more than one database table, open the Table drop-down menu and choose the table's name before you select a field from the Field drop-down list.

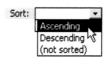

7. If you want to sort the query results on a certain field, open the Sort drop-down list in the field and choose Ascending or Descending. (The following section, "Sorting the Query Results," explains sorting.)

8. To keep a certain field from appearing in the query results, uncheck the Show checkbox in the field. In Figure 9.7, for example, the Birthday field is queried, but donors' birthdays will not be listed in the query results.

9. In the Criteria box of the field or fields you want to query, enter the criteria for the search. ("Entering the Query Criteria" later in this chapter describes this task in detail.)

10. Click the Save button.

11. Enter a descriptive name for the query in the Save As dialog box.

12. Click OK. Once you save your query, you can run it over and over again.

13. Click the Run button or choose Query | Run to see the results of the query. The results appear in a database table.

The final section of this chapter, "Presenting the Data in a Report," explains how to compile your data query results into an easy-to-read report.

Later, as you add records to the database table or tables that you queried, you can run the query again to get up-to-date results from the database. To run a query, click the Database Window button (or press F11) to go to the Database window, and then double-click the name of your query. To redesign a query, run the query and then choose View | Design View. You land in the Select Query window (see Figure 9.7), where you can change query criteria or do what you need to do to redesign the query.

Sorting the Query Results

Earlier in this chapter, "Sorting Data to Make It Easier to Work With" explains how sorting works.

To sort the results of a query on a particular field, open the Sort drop-down list while in the field, and choose Ascending or Descending. To sort the results on more than one field, make sure that the first field to be sorted appears to the left of the other fields. You can move fields in the query grid by clicking above the field name and dragging the field to the left or right.

Entering the Query Criteria

Enter criteria for the query in the Criteria boxes on the query grid. Query criteria fall into three categories: text, numeric, and date.

To enter text criteria, type the name of the item you are searching for in the Criteria box. You can search for more than one item in the same field by typing names in the boxes below the Criteria box. After you type a name, Access places quotation marks around it. The query

---

EXPERT ADVICE

For the purpose of entering two-digit years in dates, the digits 30 through 99 belong to the 20th Century (1930–1999), but the digits 00 through 29 belong to the 21st Century (2000–2029). For example, >4/1/24 refers to April 1, 2024, not April 1, 1924. To enter a date in 1929 or earlier, enter four digits instead of two to describe the year: >4/1/1929. To enter a date in 2030 or later, enter four digits instead of two: >4/1/2030.

---

shown here searches for people who live in four states: California, Nevada, Arizona, and New Mexico.

Criteria:	"CA"
or:	"NV"
	"AZ"
	"NM"

To enter numeric criteria (including monetary figures in currency fields), use numeric operators. Table 9.2 lists the numeric operators you can use in a query. When you enter numbers, do not enter commas—for example, enter **25000**, not **25,000**.

To enter date criteria, use the numeric operators listed in Table 9.2, but enter dates instead of numbers. Access places number signs (#) around dates after you enter them. Enter dates in *month/ day/ year* format. For example, entering >**4/1/00** in a field called Birthday finds the records of all people born after April 1, 2000. Entering **Between 1/1/34 And 12/31/1979** finds the records of people born between January 1, 1934, and December 31, 1979.

Operator	Name	Sample Query	Results of Sample Query
=	Equal to	=19.95	Items that cost exactly $19.95
<>	Not equal to	<>19.95	Items that don't cost $19.95
>	Greater than	>19.95	Items that cost more than $19.95
>=	Greater than or equal to	>=19.95	Items that cost $19.95 or more
<	Less than	<19.95	Items that cost less than $19.95
<=	Less than or equal to	<=19.95	Items that cost $19.95 or less
Between *value* and *value*	Between	Between 19.95 and 29.95	Items that cost between $19.95 and $29.95

Table 9.2: Operators for Use in Numeric and Date Fields

Presenting the Data in a Report

The preceding section of this chapter describes how to construct a query.

The prettiest way to present data in a database table or query is to create a report. Reports are easy to read. What's more, fashioning a report in Access is easy if you do so from a query. By querying first, you include only the fields you need in the report. You can save yourself a lot of time by creating a report from a query instead of from a database table.

After you have queried your database, follow these steps to create a report from the query results:

1. If necessary, click the Database Window button (or press F11) to go to the Database window.

2. Under Objects, click the Reports button. The right side of the window shows reports you've already created, if any. (You can regenerate a report you've created by double-clicking its name in the Database window.)

3. Double-click the Create Report by Using Wizard icon. You see the first Report Wizard dialog box.

4. From the Tables/Queries list, choose the query you want to present in the report. The fields in the query appear in the Available Fields list.

5. Select the name of each field you want to present in the report, and click the > button (or click the >> button to put all of the fields in the report). Then click the Next button.

6. Choose one field to define the *grouping level,* and then click the > button. A grouping level is like a report subheading. For example, if you make Last Name the grouping level, information in the report is presented under people's last names. Click Next to continue.

7. Click Next in the subsequent dialog box. It asks how to sort the field, but your fields are already sorted, since you are fashioning your report from a query.

8. Choose a Columnar, Tabular, or Justified report. The sample box in the Report Wizard dialog box shows what these choices mean. Click Next.

9. Choose a style for the report. Again, the sample box shows what the styles are. Click Next.

10. Enter a name for your report and click the Finish button. Your report appears onscreen in the Print Preview window.

11. Choose File | Save. The report is saved under the name you entered in step 10. You can print the report by clicking the Print button.

When you want to generate your report again, first run the query it is based on to make sure it is up to date. Then go to the Database window, click the Reports button, and double-click the name of the report.

Sharing Data Among Files and Programs

First Name	Street
Carlos	11 Guy St.
Hank	443 Oak St.
Shirley	441 Second St.

Use a Word Table as the Data Source for Form Letters and Labels ➡ p. 223

- Make sure a descriptive heading appears at the top of each column in the table.
- Save the table in its own file.

«First_Name» «Last_Name»
«Street»
«City», «State» «Zip_Code»

Hello «First_Name»,

Just want you to know that I'll be thinking about you come «Birthday» when your birthday rolls around. You're the most, baby! And I mean that, «Nickname».

Sincerely,

Generate Form Letters ➡ pp. 223–225

1. Open the document containing the text of the letter, and choose Tools | Mail Merge.
2. Under Main Document in the Mail Merge Helper dialog box, click the Create button and choose Form Letters, and then click the Active Window button.
3. Under Data Source in the Mail Merge Helper dialog box, click the Get Data button, choose Open Data Source, and choose the file where the names, addresses, and other information are stored.
4. Click the Edit Main Document button and insert the merge fields in the letter.
5. Save your document and click the Merge button on the Mail Merge toolbar.
6. Choose New Document or Printer from the Merge To menu in the Merge dialog box, and click the Merge button.

Insert Merge Field ▼

> Last_Name
> First_Name
> Street
> City
> State
> Zip_Code
> Birthday

Generate Labels for a Mass Mailing ➡ pp. 225–228

1. Choose Tools | Mail Merge, click the Create button in the Mail Merge Helper dialog box, and choose Mailing Labels.
2. Click the Active Window button and, under Data Source, click the Get Data button, choose Open Data Source, and select the file where the addresses are stored.
3. Click the Set Up Main Document button, and, in the Label Options dialog box, describe the labels that you will print your names and addresses on; click OK.
4. In the Create Labels dialog box, enter the fields for the labels, and click the Insert Postal Bar Code button to identify the field where the zip code or postal code is stored. Then click OK.
5. In the Mail Merge Helper dialog box, click the Merge button to open the Merge dialog box.
6. Choose New Document or Printer from the Merge To menu and then click the Merge button.

Merge the Main Document
and the Data Source ➥ p. 228

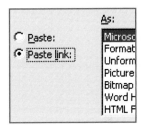

1. Click the Start Mail Merge button to open the Merge dialog box.
2. From the Merge To menu, choose either New Document (to save your letters or labels to disk) or Printer (to print them).
3. Click the Merge button.

Create an OLE Link
Between Two Files ➥ pp. 229–230

1. Open the file with the master data that you want to copy to the client file.
2. Select the data and copy it to the Clipboard.
3. Open the client file, click where you want to copy the data, and choose Edit | Paste Special.
4. In the Paste Special dialog box, click the Paste Link option button, choose the option in the As box that describes where you are copying the data from, and click OK.

Break, Lock, or Update an OLE Link ➥ p. 231–232

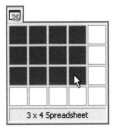

1. Choose Edit | Links.
2. In the Links dialog box, select a link and click the Update Now button to update it or the Break Link button to sever its relationship to the server file. You can also click the Locked checkbox to make the copied data stay the same, no matter how the data changes in the server file.

Create an Excel Worksheet
in a Word Document ➥ p. 232

1. Click the Insert Microsoft Excel Worksheet button.
2. On the grid that appears, click to indicate how many rows and columns you want in the worksheet.

Borrow Headings from a
Word Document for PowerPoint Text ➡ pp. 233–234

1. In PowerPoint, switch to Outline view and place the cursor in the outline where you want to start importing the headings from a Word document.
2. Choose Insert | Slide from Outline, and, in the Insert Outline dialog box, locate and select the Word document that you want to get the slide text from.
3. Click the Insert button.

Create a Hyperlink to Another File ➡ pp. 234–236

1. Select the words that will form the link, and choose Insert | Hyperlink.
2. In the Insert Hyperlink dialog box, click the Existing File or Web Page button.
3. To link to a different file, click the File button, locate the file in the Link to File dialog box, select the file, and click OK.
4. Click the ScreenTip button and describe the link, and then click OK to close the Insert Hyperlink dialog box.

The makers of Office 2000 have gone to great lengths to make sure that you have to enter data only once. That Excel 2000 worksheet you labored so hard to create can be turned into a Word 2000 table very quickly. The outline you prepared carefully in a Word document can be used again as the text in a PowerPoint 2000 presentation. You can get the addresses for mailing labels and form letters from the Outlook 2000 Contacts list or from an Access 2000 database table.

This chapter explains how to recycle your work by making use of it in different Office programs. To start, you'll learn how to generate form letters and labels for mass mailings. This chapter also explains how, thanks to Object Linking and Embedding, you can do the work in one program and make it appear in another. You'll learn how to insert an Excel worksheet in a Word document and use the headings in a Word document as the text in a PowerPoint presentation. The end of the chapter describes how to create hyperlinks between files and insert a hyperlink to a Web page on the Internet or to another file on your computer.

Generating Form Letters and Labels

This section describes *mail-merging*, Microsoft's term for generating form letters and mailing labels. No doubt you've received form letters in the mail and seen your name on mailing labels. Large companies generate form letters and mailing labels by taking names and addresses from databases. You can do the same in Word 2000. You can get the names and addresses from a Word table, an Access 2000 database table or query, or the Contacts list or Address Book in Outlook 2000. In your own small way, you too can be a junk mailer.

As the following pages explain in detail, mail-merging is a three-step process:

- **Create the main document in Word**   The *main document* is the document in which the merging takes place. In the case of form letters, you write the text of the letter. For mailing labels, you tell Office what size labels to use.

- **Get the data from the source**   Names and addresses come from the *data source.* The data source can be a Word table, an Access database table or query, or the Contacts list or Address Book in Outlook.

- **Merge the main document and data source**   Tell Word where to plug names and addresses from the data source into the main document, and then merge the main document and the data source to generate the form letters or mailing labels.

Figure 10.1 shows how the main document and data source are merged to create a form letter. In the figure, the data source is a Word

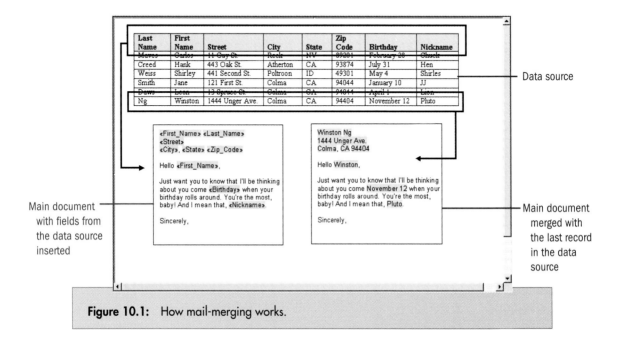

Figure 10.1:   How mail-merging works.

table. The following pages explain how to prepare a Word table to be the data source, generate form letters, and generate labels for mass mailings.

Preparing the Names and Addresses in a Word Table

In my experience, the easiest type of data source to manage is a Word table. Either create a name-and-address table from scratch or copy a table you are already using and save the table by itself as a document. You are ready to go if you plan to use the Outlook Contacts list, the Address Book, or an Access table or query as the data source for the names and addresses, but if you want to use a Word table, make sure it meets these standards:

In Chapter 4, "Constructing the Perfect Table" explains how to create a table in Word.

- A descriptive heading must appear by itself at the top of each column, as in Figure 10.1. When you merge the main document and the data source, you will choose column names from a drop-down list. So make sure each column is topped with a descriptive heading.
- No text can appear above the table in the document. To be on the safe side, save the name-and-address table in a document by itself.

By the way, a data source table can include other information besides names and addresses. In Figure 10.1, for example, the table includes nicknames and birthdays.

Generating Form Letters

In a set of form letters, only the particulars of each recipient are different—the recipient's name, the recipient's address, and perhaps one or two identifying facts about the recipient. Follow these steps to create and generate form letters:

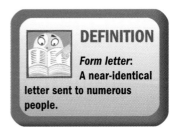

DEFINITION
Form letter: A near-identical letter sent to numerous people.

1. Open the document with the text of the letter, if you have already written the letter. If you're starting from scratch, create a new document.
2. Choose Tools | Mail Merge. The Mail Merge Helper dialog box appears.

3. Under Main Document, click the Create button and choose Form Letters from the drop-down menu. A dialog box asks if you want to use the document you are looking at as the form letter (Active Window) or create a new document for the form letter (New Main Document).

4. Click the Active Window button.

5. Under Data Source in the Mail Merge Helper dialog box, click the Get Data button and choose one of these options from the drop-down list:

• **Open Data Source**   Choose this option if the names and addresses are stored in a Word table, Access database table, or Access query. You see the Open Data Source dialog box. Find and select the Word document or Access database file where the names, addresses, and other information are kept. (In the case of Access databases, open the Files of Type drop-down menu and choose MS Access Databases.) Then click the Open button. (In the case of Access databases, click the Tables or Queries tab in the Microsoft Access dialog box, choose the name of the table or query where the addresses are kept, and click OK.)

• **Use Address Book**   Click this option to get the names and addresses from an address book or Outlook 2000 Contacts list. In the Use Address Book dialog box, choose which address book you want to get names and addresses from, and click OK. Then, in the Confirm Data Source dialog box, click OK again.

A message box informs you that the time has come to enter merge fields in the main document. A *merge field* is the equivalent of a column heading in a Word table or a field name in an Access table or query. By entering merge fields, you tell Word where to insert the data from the data source.

6. Click the Edit Main Document button in the message box to go into the main document and insert the merge fields. When you return to your document, the Mail Merge toolbar appears onscreen, as shown in Figure 10.2.

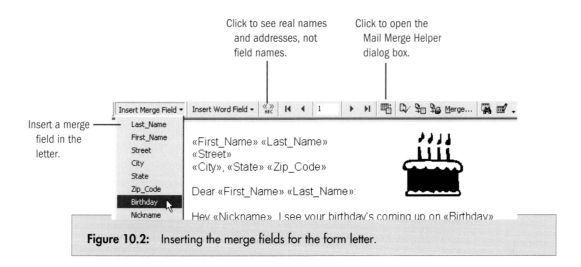

Figure 10.2: Inserting the merge fields for the form letter.

7. Compose the form letter if you haven't written it yet, and, as you do so, insert the merge fields by choosing their names from the Insert Merge Field list, as shown in Figure 10.2. Insert a merge field in the form letter wherever information about a recipient is required. In the main document, be careful when entering blank spaces and punctuation marks around merge fields. A blank space, for example, goes between the First_Name and Last_Name fields in the address. Enter a comma or colon after the Last_Name field in the salutation.

8. Save your document when you are done writing it and entering the merge fields.

9. Click the Merge button on the Mail Merge toolbar to start generating the form letters. See "Merging the Main Document and the Data Source," later in this chapter.

TIP

You can always click the View Merged Data button on the Mail Merge toolbar to see what the letters will look like when printed. Click the button a second time to see the merge fields again.

Generating Labels for Mass Mailings

Before you generate labels, take note of what brand of labels you have and what size your labels are. Word asks for that information when you generate labels. The program needs to know what size your labels are so that it can place the labels correctly on the label sheet you will print the names and addresses on. Follow these steps to generate labels for a mass mailing:

1. Create a new document in Word.

2. Choose Tools | Mail Merge to open the Mail Merge Helper dialog box.

3. Click the Create button and choose Mailing Labels from the drop-down menu. Word asks if you want to create a new document. That isn't necessary, since you just created one.

4. Click the Active Window button.

5. Under Data Source, click the Get Data button and choose one of the following options from the drop-down menu, to tell Word where to get the name and address information for the labels:

   • **Open Data Source** Choose this option if the names and addresses are kept in an Access database table, Access query, or Word table. In the Open Data Source dialog box, find and select the Access database file or Word document where the address information is kept. (To get the data from an Access database, open the Files of Type drop-down menu and choose MS Access Databases.) Then click the Open button. (In the case of Access databases, click the Tables or Queries tab in the Microsoft Access dialog box, choose the name of the table or query where the addresses are kept, and click OK.)

   • **Use Address Book** Click this option to print labels from an address book or Outlook 2000 Contacts list. In the Use Address Book dialog box, choose which address book you want to get addresses from, and click OK. In the Confirm Data Source dialog box, click OK again.

   A message box announces that you need to set up your main document.

6. Click the Set Up Main Document button. You see the Label Options dialog box, where you describe the labels you will print your names and addresses on.

7. Choose an option from the Label Products list and the Product Number list to describe the labels you will print on. The Label Information box clearly shows what size label you are choosing.

8. Click OK. You see the Create Labels dialog box shown in Figure 10.3.

9. As shown in Figure 10.3, click the Insert Merge Field button and insert each merge field that the labels require in the Sample Label box. Enter blank spaces and commas where they are needed. Press ENTER to move the cursor to the next line in the label. Here you can see how merge fields determine what is printed on a label:

10. Click the Insert Postal Bar Code button and, in the Insert Postal Bar Code dialog box (see Figure 10.3), open the drop-down menu and choose the field in the data source where postal codes or zip codes are kept. From the second drop-down menu, you can also choose the field where street addresses are stored if your labels are for a mailing in the United States. Postal codes help the Post

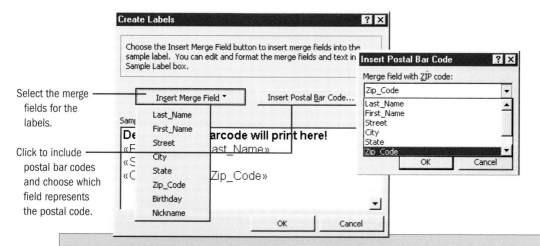

Figure 10.3: In the Create Labels dialog box, tell Word where in the data source to get the name and address information for the labels.

Office deliver letters faster. Click OK to return to the Create Labels dialog box.

11. Click OK. You return to the Mail Merge Helper dialog box.

To merge the main document and data source to generate the form letters, see the next section in this chapter.

Merging the Main Document and the Data Source

The final step in mail-merging is to merge the main document and the data source to generate the form letters or mailing labels. Follow these steps to complete the merge and emerge with a sheaf of form letters or a few sheets of mailing labels:

1. Open the Merge dialog box. To do so, click the Start Mail Merge button on the Mail Merge toolbar or, if the Mail Merge Helper dialog box is open, click the Merge button.

2. From the Merge To menu, choose either New Document or Printer:

- **Saving the form letters or labels in a new document**   Choose New Document to make all the form letters or labels appear in a new document. In the case of form letters, you can then scroll through the document and type a sentence or two in certain letters to give them the personal touch. Choose this option if you want to save your form letters or labels in a Word document so that you can print them at a later time.

- **Printing the form letters or labels**   Choose Printer to mail-merge and send the letters or labels straight to the printer. You save disk space with this option, as Word doesn't put everything in a new document before printing begins.

3. Click the Merge button. Your form letters or labels either print or appear in a new document, depending on which option you chose in step 2.

Whether you merge to a new document or merge to the printer, be sure to save the main document after the merge. That way, you can generate your mailing labels or form letters again by opening the main document, clicking the Merge button on the Mail Merge toolbar, and making selections in the Merge dialog box. As long as the data source is still intact, you can get up-to-date addresses from the data source.

OLE for Sharing Data Between Programs

Besides conventional ways of copying data, you can also link files so that changes made to the source are made automatically to the copy as well. The ability to update copies this way is called *Object Linking and Embedding* (OLE). A telephone list in Access 2000 that is updated regularly, for example, can be linked to a Word 2000 document so that changes made to the master telephone list in Access are made automatically to the Word document. These pages explain how to establish an OLE link so that copies can be made automatically, as well as how to update and alter a link.

In Chapter 2, "Copying and Moving Data" explains how you can copy data from one place to another or from one file to another by copying the data to the Clipboard or by using the drag-and-drop method.

Establishing the Link

For the purposes of linking files, the original file from which the copy is made is called the *server*. Its cousin, which gets updated when the copied data in the server file changes, is called the *client*. Follow these steps to establish an OLE link so that copied data in the client file is updated when data in the server file changes:

CAUTION

OLE links are broken when files are renamed or moved to different folders. If you are disciplined and can plan ahead, you can create OLE links safely—but linking files is more trouble than it's worth if you often move or rename your files.

1. Open the server file with the master data that you will copy to the client file.

2. Select and copy the data to the Clipboard (choose Edit | Copy or press CTRL-C).

3. Open or switch to the client file and click where you want the copy to go.

4. Choose Edit | Paste Special. You see the Paste Special dialog box, shown in Figure 10.4.

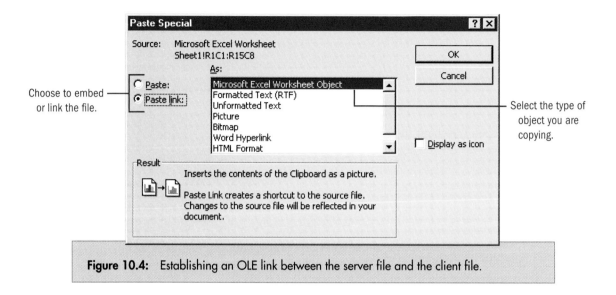

Choose to embed or link the file.

Select the type of object you are copying.

Figure 10.4: Establishing an OLE link between the server file and the client file.

5. Choose whether to link the server file to the client file or embed a copy of the server file in the client file:

- **Linking the file** Click the Paste Link option button. An OLE link is established between the server and client files.

- **Embedding the file** Click the Paste option button. A link is not established with the server file. However, you can double-click the data you copied into your file and in so doing open the program in which you created the data. With the program open, you can edit the data.

6. In the As box, choose the first option on the list. This option lists the name of the program in which the server file was created.

7. Click OK.

In Chapter 2, "Handling 'Objects' in Files" explains all the things you can do to move or change the size of an object.

The foreign data arrives in your file in the form of an object. As such, you can move it around onscreen by dragging it from place to place.

Managing OLE Links

OLE links are updated automatically, and the data in the client file is updated from the server file under these circumstances:

- When you make editorial changes in the server file and save the file
- When you open the client file

But you can decide for yourself how and when changes made in the server file show up in the client file. To do so, open the client file and choose Edit | Links. You see the Links dialog box, which lists all the links in the client file and gives you options for updating links and deciding how links should be updated. Select a link and do one of the following to update, break, lock, unlock, or reestablish it:

- **Updating a link**   Click the Update Now button to bring a link up to date.
- **Breaking a link**   Break a link when you want the copied material to stay the same no matter what happens to the source material in the server file. To break a link, click the Break Link button. After you break the link, you can't reestablish it.
- **Locking or unlocking a link**   Lock a link to make the copied material stay the same and not be updated from the server file. To lock a link, check the Locked checkbox. Unlike the Break Link option, however, a locked link keeps its relationship with the server file. You can still update the link by unchecking the Locked checkbox.
- **Reestablishing a link when the server file has changed locations**   Reestablish a link when you move the server file to a different folder, rendering its link to the client file invalid. To reestablish a link, click the Change Source button, find and

select the server file in the Change Source dialog box, and click the Open button.

- **Opening the server file**   Click the Open Source button to open the server file and perhaps edit the original data there. (You can also open the server file by right-clicking the link, choosing Linked File Object from the shortcut menu, and then choosing Open Link.)

Creating an Excel Worksheet in a Word Document

Word 2000 and Excel 2000 are joined at the hip. Merely by clicking the Insert Microsoft Excel Worksheet button on the Standard toolbar in Word, you can place an Excel worksheet in a Word document. The worksheet is embedded in your Word document. Whenever you click the worksheet, Excel buttons and tools appear onscreen instead of Word buttons and tools.

Follow these steps to place an Excel worksheet in a Word document:

Insert Microsoft Excel Worksheet

1. Click the Insert Microsoft Excel Worksheet button. A grid appears below the button so that you can choose the number of rows and columns you want.

2. Move the cursor onto the grid and click to specify a certain number of rows and columns. The bottom of the grid tells you how many rows and columns you'll get when you click.

After you click, an Excel worksheet appears onscreen. Look around and you will see that Excel menus, Excel buttons, and the Excel formula bar appear as well. Enter data in your worksheet and do all the things you love to do so much in Excel. You can call on all of the Excel commands as you work. When you click outside the worksheet, your Excel worksheet turns into a Word table and the Word menus reappear. Double-click the table to see the worksheet rows and columns again as well as the Excel menus and toolbars.

Using Word Document Headings as PowerPoint Text

In Chapter 4, "Styles for Consistent and Easy Formatting" explains how Word styles work.

Maybe the easiest way to enter the text in a PowerPoint 2000 presentation is to call on the Insert | Slides from Outline command and borrow the text from a Word 2000 document. Choose this command to use the headings in a Word document as the text in a PowerPoint presentation. If you think about it, headings serve the same purpose as slide text—they hit the high points and describe which topics are being discussed. To use headings from a Word document, however, you must have assigned heading styles to the heading text. As you can see in Figure 10.5, headings assigned the Heading 1 style become slide titles in the PowerPoint presentation. Heading 2 styles and beyond are put in bulleted lists on the slides.

Follow these steps to borrow headings from a Word document for the text in a PowerPoint presentation:

1. In PowerPoint, either create a new presentation or, in Outline view, place the cursor where you want to start importing the headings.

Figure 10.5:   You can borrow headings from a Word document (left) for the text in a PowerPoint presentation (right).

2. Choose Insert | Slide from Outline.

3. In the Insert Outline dialog box, locate and select the Word document you want to get the slide text from.

4. Click the Insert button.

Including Hyperlinks in Files

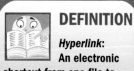

DEFINITION

Hyperlink:
An electronic shortcut from one file to another file, or from a file to a site on the Internet, or from one Internet site to another.

Clicking a hyperlink is the fastest way to go elsewhere. In Office files, text hyperlinks are usually blue and underlined. You can tell when you have encountered a hyperlink because the pointer changes into a gloved hand when it is moved over a link. What's more, a yellow box tells you where the link will take you. The Web toolbar appears after you click a hyperlink. Click the Back or Forward button on the Web toolbar to return to the Web sites or files you visited.

Follow these steps to insert a hyperlink to a different file or to a site on the Internet:

1. Select the word, phrase, data, graphic, or whatever that will form the hyperlink.

2. Choose Insert | Hyperlink, press CTRL-K, or right-click the word or graphic you selected and choose Hyperlink from the shortcut menu. You see the Insert Hyperlink dialog box shown in Figure 10.6.

3. Under Link To, click the Existing File or Web Page button.

4. Choose where you want the link to go:

   • **To a different file**   Click the File button (you will find it under Browse For on the right side of the dialog box). In the Link to File dialog box, find and select the name of the document you want to link to. Then click OK. You can also click the Recent Files button and select the file in the list of files you opened recently.

   • **To a site on the Internet**   Click the Web Page button to go on the Internet and find the page you want to link to. When you arrive at the page, its name appears in the Type the File or Web Page Name text box. You can also click the

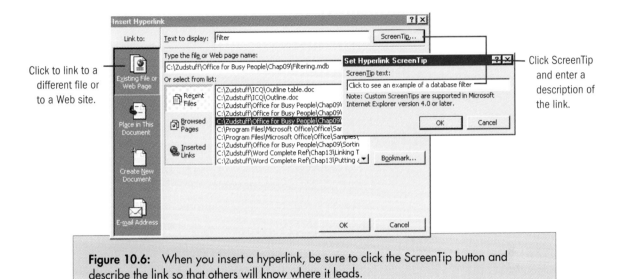

Click to link to a different file or to a Web site.

Click ScreenTip and enter a description of the link.

Figure 10.6: When you insert a hyperlink, be sure to click the ScreenTip button and describe the link so that others will know where it leads.

Browsed Pages button and try to find the page in the list of Web pages you visited lately, or type the address of the Web page into Type the File or Web Page Name text box.

5. Click the ScreenTip button and enter a brief description of the hyperlink. Anyone who points to the link will see the description you enter in a pop-up box. If you forget to provide a description, the pop-up box shows the path to the link, a series of folder names followed by a filename.

6. Click OK to insert the hyperlink.

Hyperlinks are kind of hard to edit and maintain. After all, if you click a hyperlink in order to, say, type a word in the middle of the link, you activate the hyperlink. And selecting hyperlinks is kind of hard, too, since you can't drag across the link without activating it. The trick to editing and maintaining hyperlinks is to right-click instead of click. When you right-click a hyperlink, you see a shortcut menu with the Hyperlink option at the bottom. Click the Hyperlink option and you get a bunch of commands for handling hyperlinks.

For you and you only, here are some techniques for editing and maintaining hyperlinks:

CAUTION
A hyperlink between files is rendered invalid if one of the files is moved or renamed.

- **Editing a hyperlink**   Right-click and choose Hyperlink | Edit Hyperlink. You see the Edit Hyperlink dialog box. Change the link destination, change the ScreenTip, or do what you will and click OK.

- **Removing a hyperlink**   Right-click and choose Hyperlink | Remove Hyperlink.

- **Deleting a hyperlink**   Right-click, choose Hyperlink | Select Hyperlink to select the link, and press the DELETE key.

- **Selecting a hyperlink so you can format it**   Right-click and choose Hyperlink | Select Hyperlink. The link is highlighted. Now you can change its font or font size, for example.

CHAPTER 11

Surfing the Internet with Internet Explorer 5

Includes

- **Fine-tuning your Internet connection**
- **Connecting to and disconnecting from the Internet**
- **Surfing the Internet quickly and productively**
- **Finding people's phone numbers and addresses on the Internet**
- **Subscribing to Web sites**
- **Copying photos, pictures, and text from the Web**

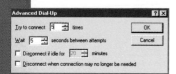

Disconnect from the Internet
Automatically If You Leave Your Desk ➡ pp. 240–242

1. Choose Tools | Internet Options, and click the Connections tab.
2. Click the Settings button and then the Advanced button.
3. Check the Disconnect If Idle For box, and enter the number of minutes you want to pass in inactivity before Internet Explorer disconnects you.

Start Internet Explorer ➡ pp. 242–243

- Double-click the Internet Explorer icon on the desktop or Quick Launch toolbar.
- Click the Start button and choose Favorites | Links and then the name of a Web site.
- Enter or choose a Web address on the Address toolbar and press ENTER.

Disconnect from the Internet ➡ p. 244

- Double-click the Internet icon and choose Disconnect in the Connected To dialog box.
- Right-click the Internet icon and choose Disconnect.

Go to a Web Site by
Entering Its Address ➡ pp. 244–245

1. Carefully type the address in the Address bar, or choose an address from the drop-down list.
2. Press the ENTER key.

Search for Data on the Web ➡ pp. 245–248

1. Click the Search button.
2. Enter keywords for the search in the text box in the Search bar, and then click the Search button.

Find Someone's Address
or Phone Number ➡ pp. 248–249

1. Click the Start button and choose Find | People.
2. Choose a search service from the Look In list, enter a name, and click the Find Now button.
3. Click the Web Site button and search for addresses at the service's Web site.

Go Back to Web Pages
You've Visited Before ➡ pp. 249–250

- Click the Back or Forward button—or open the drop-down Back or Forward menu and choose a Web page.
- Click the History button, click a day or week on the Explorer bar, click a Web site name, and then click a page to display it onscreen.

Visit a Web Site You've Bookmarked ➡ pp. 250–254

1. Click the Favorites button.
2. Click the Links folder in the Explorer bar and then click the name of the Web site.
3. Click the name of a Web page on the Web site.

Copy a Picture, Text, or a Web Page
from a Web Site to Your Computer ➡ pp. 257–258

- **Pictures and photos** Right-click the picture and choose Save Picture As. Then locate the folder in which you want to save the picture and click the Save button in the Save Picture dialog box.
- **Text** Drag over the text and choose Edit | Copy or press CTRL-C.
- **Web pages** Choose File | Save As, find a folder for storing the page in the Save Web Page dialog box, and click the Save button.

Office 2000 comes with a browser for surfing the Internet called Internet Explorer 5. Think of a browser as a kind of television set. Watching the nightly news or switching from channel to channel is impossible without a TV; without a browser, you can't locate information or skip merrily from Web site to Web site.

In this chapter, you'll learn how to explore cyberspace with Internet Explorer. Here you will find instructions for searching the Web, finding the addresses and phone numbers of people on the Internet, subscribing to Web sites, and scavenging pictures and text from the Web. Scattered throughout this chapter are tried-and-true techniques for surfing the Internet quickly and productively. I don't want you to waste any time staring at your computer as you wait for Web pages to appear.

DEFINITION

Browser: A computer program that connects to Web sites and displays Web pages.

Deciding How Many Times to Dial and When to Disconnect Automatically

Unfortunately, dialing and connecting to an ISP (*Internet service provider*) or online service sometimes takes more than one try. How many times do you want to try to connect? For that matter, how long do you want to maintain a connection to the Internet if you leave your desk and forget to disconnect on your own? Forgetting to disconnect ties up the phone line and prevents others from calling you. It can be expensive, too, if you are charged by the hour for being online.

Follow these steps to tell Internet Explorer how many times to dial and when to disconnect automatically:

1. Choose Tools | Internet Options.
2. Click the Connections tab in the Internet Options dialog box.
3. Click the Settings button. You see the Settings dialog box.

4. Click the Advanced button. The Advanced Dial-Up dialog box appears:

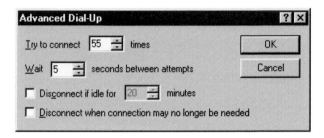

5. Enter the number of times you want your computer to redial before giving up.

6. Specify how long Explorer should pause before redialing.

7. Check the Disconnect If Idle For box if it is not already checked, and then enter the number of minutes you want Internet Explorer to pass in inactivity before you are disconnected. If later on you do nothing on the Web for the number of minutes you've allotted, you'll see the Auto Disconnect box:

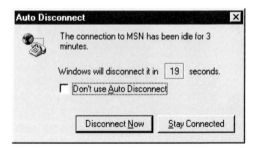

8. Click OK three times to close the dialog boxes.

The Basics: Connecting and Disconnecting

After you have told Internet Explorer how to dial the service and when to disconnect automatically, you are ready to blast off. The next few pages explain the basics of connecting to and disconnecting from

Internet
Explorer

the Internet. You'll also find out what to do if the connection doesn't work and how to shut down Internet Explorer.

Later in this chapter, "Surfing the Internet" explains how to search for information on the Internet.

The Eight Ways to Start Internet Explorer

Starting Internet Explorer is easy. Almost everywhere you go in your computer, you can find opportunities to start Internet Explorer and go on the Internet. Glance at Figure 11.1 to see the eight ways to open the program. (Some of the ways shown here are available only if you are running the Windows 98 or Windows NT 5 operating system.)

Which way of starting Internet Explorer is best? It's hard to beat double-clicking the Internet Explorer icon on the desktop, but typing

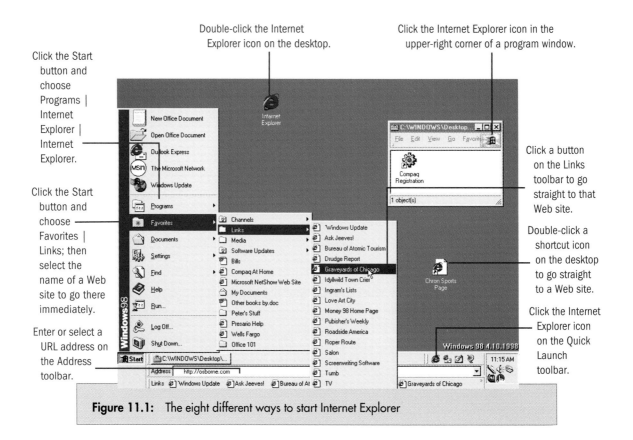

Figure 11.1: The eight different ways to start Internet Explorer

an address on the Address toolbar on the Taskbar is convenient as well if you are a good typist and you know exactly where you want to go.

As soon as you make the connection, either you go online or Internet Explorer appears onscreen and you see a password dialog box. Fill in the dialog box, if necessary, and click OK. Some chirping sounds come from your telephone and then Internet Explorer opens your home page. (See "Seven Ways to Surf the Internet Faster" later in this chapter if you don't like the home page you see.)

You can tell when you are truly online because the Internet icon—a pair of computer monitors, one blinking—appears in the lower-right corner of the screen next to the clock. Double-click the Internet icon and you see a dialog box that tells you how fast your modem is and how long you have been online:

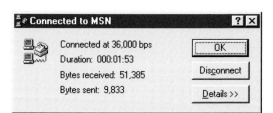

If You Can't Connect to the Internet...

A failed connection can occur for many reasons. The fault might lie not with you but elsewhere. There might be too much static on the phone line, or there might be a busy signal at the other end. To fix a missed connection from your side, try these techniques:

- Try to connect again. Your ISP might be overloaded with connections. Maybe you can squeeze in this time.

- See if the modem is connected correctly. Is the phone line plugged into the right place on both the computer and the modem?

- Make sure the address of your home page was entered correctly. Internet Explorer goes straight to the home page when you go online, but if the address is wrong it can't do that. If worst comes to worst, choose Tools | Internet Options, click the General tab in the Internet Options dialog box, and click

Later in this chapter, "Seven Ways to Search the Internet Faster" explains the home page in detail.

the Use Default button. Your default home page (probably **http://home.microsoft.com**) is sure to work.

- I hate to say it, and it would certainly be tragic to have to do the setup work again, but see if you set up the connection between your computer and your Internet service provider or online service incorrectly.

Disconnecting from the Internet

Disconnecting from the Internet is as easy as snapping your fingers. To disconnect from the Internet, do one of the following:

- Right-click the Internet icon in the lower-right corner of the screen and choose Disconnect.
- Double-click the Internet icon and click the Disconnect button in the Connected To dialog box.

Surfing the Internet

Surfing the Internet is a skill, and entire books have been written on the subject. To keep you from having to suffer through a long, tedious computer book, the following pages tell it in a hurry. These pages explain how to visit a Web site whose address you know, search the Internet for information and for addresses and phone numbers, and revisit sites you've been to before.

Visiting a Web Site Whose Address You Know

Every Web site and Web page has an address. While you are online, you can read the addresses of Web pages by glancing at the Address bar, the text box located directly below the standard buttons. (If you don't see the Address bar, right-click a toolbar or the menu bar and choose Address Bar.) To go to a Web site whose address you know, carefully type the address in the Address bar and press ENTER.

If you've entered the address before, you're in luck; you don't have to enter it again. Click the down arrow on the Address bar and, on the menu of addresses that appears, click the address of the Web page you want to visit:

Clicking Hyperlinks to Go Here and There

After you arrive at a Web site, you are sure to find many hyperlinks. Recall that a *hyperlink* is an electronic shortcut that takes you from one place to another. By clicking a hyperlink, you can go directly to another location on the Web. Hyperlinks come in the form of text, pictures, and images. You can tell when your pointer is over a hyperlink because it turns into a gloved hand.

Probably the most adventurous way to surf the Internet is to click hyperlinks and see where your search takes you. Fans of the World Wide Web are fond of saying that the Web is a three-dimensional world that brings together like-minded people from different places and different times. Click a few hyperlinks, see where your search leads, and decide for yourself whether the Web is a three-dimensional world or a mishmash of infomercials and unsound opinions. You can always backtrack by clicking the Back button (which you'll learn about in "Revisiting Web Sites You've Been to Before" later in this chapter).

n Chapter 10, "Including Hyperlinks in Files" explains in detail how hyperlinks work and how you can create hyperlinks of your own.

Searching for Information on the Web

To look for information on the Web, you choose a search service, declare what you are looking for, click the Search button, note how many Web pages your search yields, look through the list of Web pages, click a page that is worth a visit, and see the page onscreen. Sounds simple enough, but searching the Web can be frustrating because the Internet is crowded with all sorts of junk.

The secret to finding what you are looking for is to enter the right keyword or combination of keywords for the search. The more carefully you choose your keywords, the more fruitful your search will be. Choose keywords that pinpoint what you are looking for. For

ater in this chapter, "Finding Addresses and Phone Numbers on the Internet" explains how to look for people, not data, online.

DEFINITION

Keyword:
A word or phrase that tells your search service which words to look for on Web pages.

example, entering **giants** finds all Web pages with that word on it—a lot of Web pages, no doubt. But entering **giants san francisco baseball schedule**, depending on how you give the search command, yields only Web pages containing all five of those keywords—considerably fewer than you'd have to wade through after a search for **giants**.

Searching the Easy Way: Start from a Service's Home Page

The simplest way to search the Web is to start at the home page of a search service and use the search options that the service provides. You can use a search service without going to its home page, as I explain later in this chapter, but you can't take advantage of as many search options that way.

See "Bookmarking Sites So You Can Visit Them Quickly" later in this chapter to learn how to bookmark a site.

Figure 11.2 shows the advanced search options that are available from a service called Infoseek. Each service offers advanced search options like the ones shown here. Take advantage of options like these to search the Web.

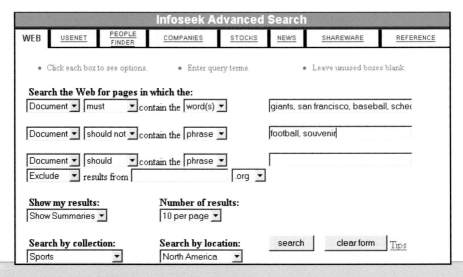

Figure 11.2: Maybe the easiest way to search the Web is to start at the home page of a search service and take advantage of the search options there.

EXPERT ADVICE

Click the Customize button in the Explorer bar to open the Customize Search Settings dialog box and choose the search service you are happiest with. The service you choose will appear automatically in the Explorer bar next time you click the Search button on the Standard buttons toolbar.

The home page addresses of the major search services are listed in Table 11.1. Pay a visit to these pages, click the Advanced Search hyperlink or button, experiment with the search options, and bookmark the service you like best so that you can use it whenever you search the Internet.

Searching the Clumsy Way: Using Internet Explorer's Search Commands

The clumsy way to search the Web is to use Internet Explorer's search commands. With this technique, you have to work in a cramped window onscreen, and you get fewer options for narrowing the search. But in the spirit of fair play, Figure 11.3 shows you how to search the Web with Explorer's search commands.

When you have found the Web page you are looking for, click the Search button to hide the Explorer bar so you can read the Web page better. To see the Explorer bar again, click the Search button once more.

TIP

When you're running a Web search, you can save a lot of time by learning a little bit about a Web page before you visit it. Once Explore has run your search, simply move your pointer over the hyperlink of any Web page and read the description that appears.

Search Service	Address
AltaVista	www.altavista.com
Excite	www.excite.com
HotBot	www.hotbot.com
Infoseek	www.infoseek.com
Lycos	www.lycos.com
WebCrawler	www.webcrawler.com
Yahoo	www.yahoo.com

Table 11.1: Search Services and Their Home Page Addresses

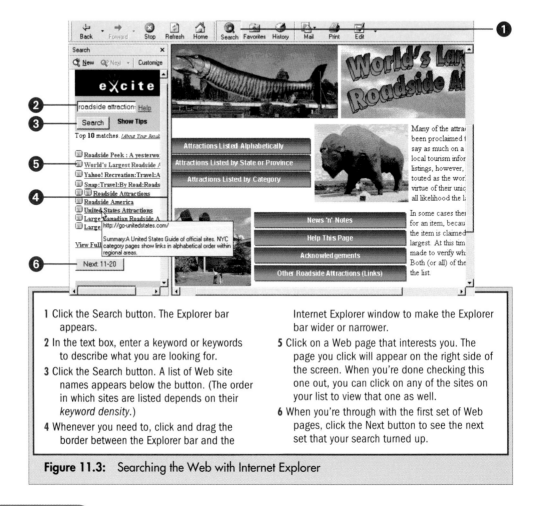

1 Click the Search button. The Explorer bar appears.

2 In the text box, enter a keyword or keywords to describe what you are looking for.

3 Click the Search button. A list of Web site names appears below the button. (The order in which sites are listed depends on their *keyword density*.)

4 Whenever you need to, click and drag the border between the Explorer bar and the Internet Explorer window to make the Explorer bar wider or narrower.

5 Click on a Web page that interests you. The page you click will appear on the right side of the screen. When you're done checking this one out, you can click on any of the sites on your list to view that one as well.

6 When you're through with the first set of Web pages, click the Next button to see the next set that your search turned up.

Figure 11.3: Searching the Web with Internet Explorer

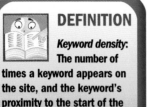

DEFINITION

Keyword density: The number of times a keyword appears on the site, and the keyword's proximity to the start of the Web page on which it is found.

Finding Addresses and Phone Numbers on the Internet

Data isn't the only thing you can search for on the Internet. You can also look for lost loves, long-lost friends, schoolyard bullies from days gone by, and bass players and drummers from obscure rock and roll bands. Figure 11.4 shows how to search for others' e-mail addresses, addresses, and phone numbers.

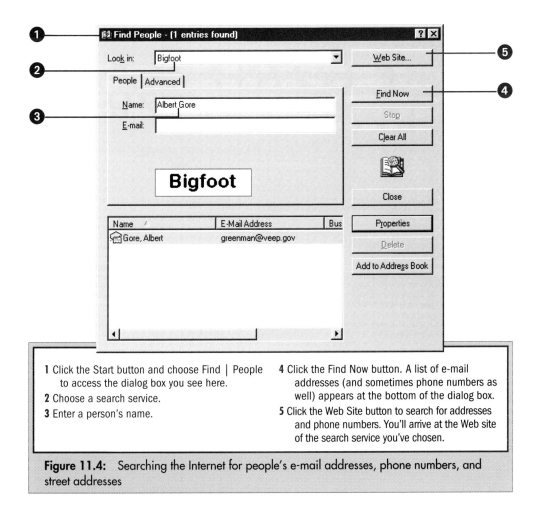

1 Click the Start button and choose Find | People to access the dialog box you see here.

2 Choose a search service.

3 Enter a person's name.

4 Click the Find Now button. A list of e-mail addresses (and sometimes phone numbers as well) appears at the bottom of the dialog box.

5 Click the Web Site button to search for addresses and phone numbers. You'll arrive at the Web site of the search service you've chosen.

Figure 11.4: Searching the Internet for people's e-mail addresses, phone numbers, and street addresses

Revisiting Web Sites You've Been To Before

Surfing is always an adventure, and many a Web surfer ventures too far and wishes to return to a page that he or she visited earlier. Fortunately, backtracking is pretty easy. By clicking the Back button or its drop-down menu, you can visit the pages you viewed since you started Internet Explorer. You can even view a Web page you visited in the past 20 days by clicking the History button. Following are the numerous ways to revisit sites with Internet Explorer.

THE BACK AND FORWARD BUTTONS   Click the Back button (or press BACKSPACE) to see the last page you saw; click the Forward button to move ahead to the page from which you retreated. Next to the Back button and Forward button is an arrow you can click to open a drop-down menu with the last several sites you visited. Don't be shy about using these drop-down menus. All you have to do to leap forward or backward is click the arrow and click a Web page name.

THE HISTORY BUTTON   Internet Explorer is watching you! The program keeps a record of the Web sites and Web pages you visited in the past 20 days. To return to one of those Web pages, you can click the History button and take it from there. Figure 11.5 demonstrates how to backtrack by clicking the History button.

THE FAVORITES BUTTON   The fastest way to revisit a site is to bookmark it, as explained just ahead. The names of sites you have bookmarked appear in the Favorites\Links folder, where you can get to them very quickly. Click the Favorites button, click the Links folder, and click the name of a site.

Bookmarking Sites So You Can Visit Them Quickly

Bookmarking a site means to mark it in such a way that you can revisit it quickly later on. When you bookmark a site in Internet Explorer, you place a shortcut to it in the Favorites\Links folder. From there,

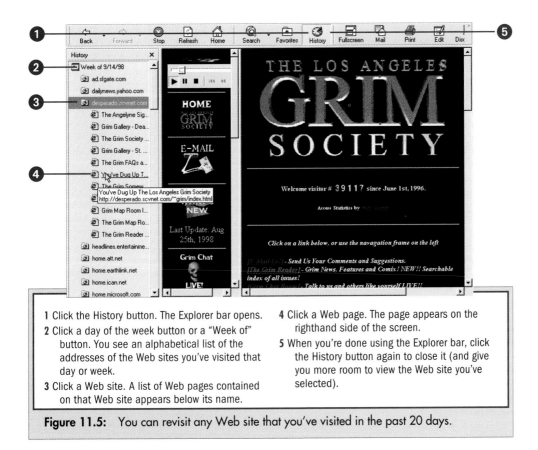

1 Click the History button. The Explorer bar opens.

2 Click a day of the week button or a "Week of" button. You see an alphabetical list of the addresses of the Web sites you've visited that day or week.

3 Click a Web site. A list of Web pages contained on that Web site appears below its name.

4 Click a Web page. The page appears on the righthand side of the screen.

5 When you're done using the Explorer bar, click the History button again to close it (and give you more room to view the Web site you've selected).

Figure 11.5: You can revisit any Web site that you've visited in the past 20 days.

opening it is easy. Don't be shy about bookmarking a site—you can "unbookmark" it very easily, as I'll explain shortly. These pages explain how to bookmark sites, visit the sites you have bookmarked, and manage your bookmarks.

Bookmarking Your Favorite Web Sites

Figure 11.6 shows how to bookmark a site and make it very, very easy to revisit. You are hereby encouraged to bookmark a site if you feel the least desire to return to it later. (Otherwise, finding it again could be like finding the proverbial needle in a haystack.)

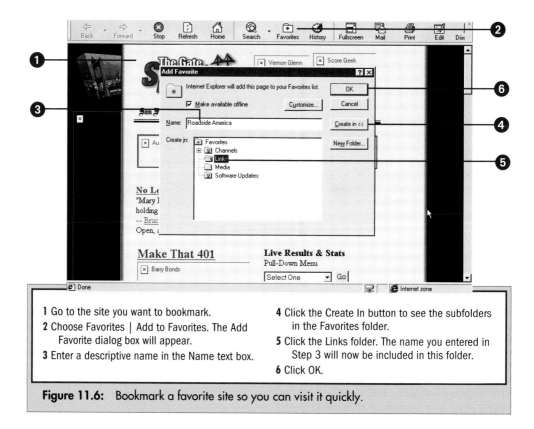

1 Go to the site you want to bookmark.

2 Choose Favorites | Add to Favorites. The Add Favorite dialog box will appear.

3 Enter a descriptive name in the Name text box.

4 Click the Create In button to see the subfolders in the Favorites folder.

5 Click the Links folder. The name you entered in Step 3 will now be included in this folder.

6 Click OK.

Figure 11.6:   Bookmark a favorite site so you can visit it quickly.

Going to a Site You've Bookmarked

After you have bookmarked a site, revisiting it is a lead-pipe cinch, as you can see in Figure 11.7.

Another way to quickly go to a Web site you have bookmarked is to choose Favorites | Links and the name of the site on the Links submenu. Come to think of it, you can also click the Start button and choose Favorites | Links there.

EXPERT ADVICE

Be sure to click the Links folder and place the shortcut to your Web site there. If you forget to do so and put the shortcut in the Favorites folder, your Favorites folder will soon fill up with shortcuts to Web sites. The fastest way to get to files you use most often is to place shortcuts to those files in the Favorites folder, as explained in Chapter 1. But if you crowd your Favorites folder with Web site shortcuts, you'll have trouble finding your files there.

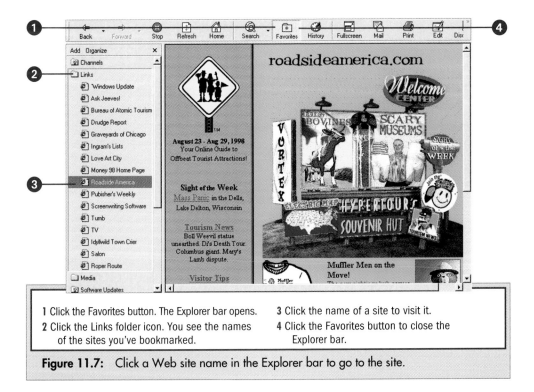

1 Click the Favorites button. The Explorer bar opens.

2 Click the Links folder icon. You see the names of the sites you've bookmarked.

3 Click the name of a site to visit it.

4 Click the Favorites button to close the Explorer bar.

Figure 11.7: Click a Web site name in the Explorer bar to go to the site.

Renaming, Deleting, and Managing Bookmarks

Follow these steps to rename a bookmarked site, "unbookmark" it, or change its position on the menu:

1. From the menu bar, choose Favorites | Organize Favorites. You see the Organize Favorites dialog box:

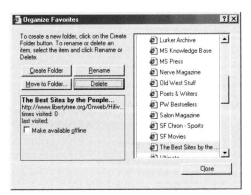

EXPERT ADVICE

It would be a sad day if your computer crashed and you lost the shortcuts to all the sites you bookmarked. To make a backup copy of your bookmarks, open the C:\Windows\Favorites\Links folder and copy all of the shortcuts in the folder to a floppy disk. If your computer fails, copy the backup shortcuts on the floppy disk to the C:\Windows\Favorites\Links folder.

---

2. Click the Links folder to see the names of Web sites you have bookmarked.

3. Click a Web site name.

4. Delete, Rename, or Move the bookmark:

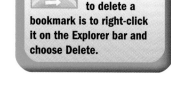

SHORTCUT
The fast way to delete a bookmark is to right-click it on the Explorer bar and choose Delete.

   • **Delete**   Click the Delete button and then click Yes when you are asked if you really want to delete it.

   • **Rename**   Click the Rename button and type a new name.

   • **Move to a different folder**   Click the Move to Folder button and select another folder in the Browse for Folder dialog box.

   • **Move up or down in the list**   Drag a Web site name up or down the dialog box to move it up or down on the Explorer bar and Favorites | Links menu.

Seven Ways to Surf the Internet Faster

In some circles, the World Wide Web is known as the "World Wide Wait." If you get impatient when you surf the Internet, try one of these eight techniques for surfing the Internet faster. Some of the techniques are described elsewhere in this chapter, but all are gathered here, because waiting for the Web is frustrating and I want you to be able to pick and choose quickly among speed techniques.

1. LEARN TO USE THE DROP-DOWN MENUS ON THE BACK AND FORWARD BUTTONS   Most people know that there is a Back button in Internet Explorer for revisiting pages and a Forward button for returning to pages you retreated from. But many people

don't realize that you can click the down arrow beside the Back or
Forward button and see a menu with all of the pages you've visited.
Instead of going forward or backward one page at a time, use the
drop-down Back or Forward menu to leap several ahead or behind.

2. CHANGE YOUR HOME PAGE   Your so-called home page is the
first thing you see when you access the Internet. And when you click
the Home button, you go straight to your home page. By a trick of
fate or computer programming, the Mighty Microsoft Corporation
makes **www.home.microsoft.com**, its own Web site, the home page
when you install Office 2000. Do you want that? I respectfully suggest
that you choose a home page that you like to visit. While you're at it,
choose a Web page that downloads fast so you can get on the Internet
more quickly.

   To choose a home page of your own, go to the page on the Web
that you want for a home page. Then choose Tools | Internet Options
and, on the General tab of the Internet Options dialog box, click the
Use Current button. If the button is grayed out, type in the address of
the Web site you want to see first when you go on the Internet.

3. BOOKMARK THE PAGES YOU VISIT OFTEN   By bookmarking
pages and putting them in the Links subfolder in the Favorites folder,
you can get to them quickly. All you have to do is click the Favorites
button, click the Links folder icon, and click the page. You can also
choose Favorites | Links and the name of the page. (See "Bookmarking
Sites So You Can Visit Them Quickly" earlier in this chapter.)

**4. CREATE SHORTCUT ICONS TO THE WEB PAGES YOU VISIT
OFTEN**   Why not create shortcuts to the Web pages you visit often?
Internet Explorer offers a special command for doing so. After you
have created a shortcut, all you have to do is double-click it on the
Windows desktop to go straight to your favorite Web site.

   To create a shortcut, go to the Web site you intend to visit often and
choose File | Send | Shortcut To Desktop. Then go to the Windows
desktop, right-click the shortcut icon you just created, choose Rename
on the shortcut menu, and enter a descriptive name.

EXPERT ADVICE

The desktop quickly gets crowded with shortcut icons. One way to practice crowd control is to create a desktop folder and keep shortcut icons inside it. To do so, right-click an empty place on the desktop, choose New | Folder, and enter a name such as "My Fave Sites." Then, one by one, drag the Web site shortcuts into the folder. When you want to visit a Web site, double-click your desktop folder to open it, and then double-click a shortcut icon.

---

5. CLICK THE STOP BUTTON EARLY AND OFTEN   Don't be afraid to click the Stop button. If you click a hyperlink and nothing happens for a moment or two, chances are nothing will happen. Click the Stop button to stop the search and turn it in another direction.

6. USE THE FIND COMMAND ON LARGE WEB PAGES   On large Web pages, finding what you are looking for can be difficult. Instead of endlessly scrolling down the screen to find what you are looking for, choose Edit | Find or press CTRL-F, enter a word or two in the Find dialog box, and click Find Next. The page scrolls to the word or words you entered.

7. DON'T DISPLAY FANCY STUFF ON WEB PAGES   A lot of time on the Web is wasted waiting for fancy pictures and animations to arrive on your computer. As a drastic measure to save time, you can tell Internet Explorer to download the fancy stuff only if you tell it to. Follow these steps:

1. Choose Tools | Internet Options.
2. Click the Advanced tab in the Internet Options dialog box.
3. Scroll to Multimedia in the list and uncheck Show Pictures, Play Animations, Play Videos, and/or Play Sounds.

You can still see pictures or play animations on Web pages after you have elected not to show them. To do so, right-click the picture or animation icon on the Web page and choose Show Picture on the shortcut menu.

Copying Pictures, Text, and Web Sites

To the delight of copyright lawyers and the displeasure of photographers and artists, you can copy any picture on the Internet. You can also copy text and entire Web pages.

1. Download your image, picture, or photograph.

2. Right-click the image and choose Save Picture As.

3. Use the tools in the Save Picture dialog box—the drop-down Save In menu and Up One Level button—to locate the folder in which you want to save the image.

4. Double-click the folder so its name appears in the Save In box.

5. Enter a descriptive name for the image in the File Name text box if you want to:

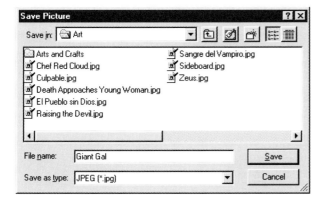

6. Click the Save button.

To copy text from a Web page, simply drag the mouse pointer over it (or press CTRL-A to copy the entire page). When the text is highlighted,

CAUTION

Copying text or art that you didn't create is okay, but be aware that using the material in your own work without obtaining the permission from the creator or owner is considered a violation of the copyright laws.

right-click it and choose Copy from the shortcut menu. The text is copied to the Clipboard. Click where you want to paste it, and choose File | Paste or click the Paste button.

To copy an entire Web page, choose File | Save As. In the Save Web Page dialog box, locate the folder where you want to save the Web page, and click the Save button.

To print an entire Web page, click the Print button. That's all there is to it. If you want to be choosy about how the page is printed, choose File | Print and choose from the options in the Print dialog box. Go this route, for example, if you want to print more than one copy or print the pages that are linked to the page you want to print.

CHAPTER 12

Publisher 2000: Creating Professional Publications

Create a Publication
from a Publication Design ➡ pp. 264–265

- Choose File | New, if necessary, to open the Microsoft Publisher Catalog.
- Choose a publication design, click the Start Wizard button, and answer the Wizard's questions.

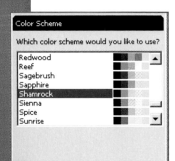

Change the Design of Your Publication ➡ pp. 265–266

1. Click the Show Wizard button.
2. Choose Design or Color Scheme in the Quick Publication Wizard box.
3. Select a new design or color scheme.

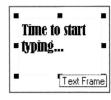

Insert a Frame for Text, a Table, WordArt,
a Picture, or a Clip Art Image ➡ pp. 269–270

1. Click the Text Frame Tool, Table Frame Tool, WordArt Frame Tool, Picture Frame Tool, or Clip Gallery Tool button.
2. Drag on the page to create the frame.
3. Enter the text, table, WordArt image, picture, or clip art image in the frame.

Change the Size or Position of a Frame ➡ p. 271

- Click to select the frame, and then drag a corner selection handle or side selection handle when you see the Resize pointer. Dragging a corner handle retains the frame's proportions.
- Click to select the frame, move the pointer onto the frame, and drag when you see the Move pointer.

Draw Layout Guides to Help You
Align Frames on the Page ➥ pp. 272–273

1. Choose Arrange | Layout Guides.
2. Enter the numbers of columns and rows you want in the Layout Guides dialog box and click OK.

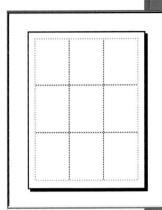

Make Objects and Frames Overlap ➥ pp. 273–274

1. Click a frame or object.
2. Click the Bring to Front or Send to Back button. If the object is in a stack and overlaps more than one other object, choose Arrange | Bring Forward or Arrange | Send Backward to move it backward or forward.

Wrap Text Around a
Clip Art Image or a Picture ➥ pp. 276–277

1. Select the text frame and click the Send to Back button to move it behind the clip art or picture frame.
2. Click the Wrap Text to Frame button to make the text conform to the frame, or the Wrap Text to Picture button to make the text follow the contours of the image.

Decorate Your Publication
with a Design Gallery Object ➥ pp. 278–279

1. Click the Design Gallery Object button.
2. Choose the kind of object you want in the Microsoft Publisher Design Gallery dialog box.
3. Click the object and then click the Insert Object button.

Welcome to Publisher 2000: the print shop in a can. Not so long ago, creating professional publications like the kind you can create with Publisher required sophisticated printing equipment and a background in graphic design. These days, however, even a novice can create a professional-looking publication with Publisher. As long as you rely on a publication design, which is a template that comes with Publisher, half the layout work is done for you. All you have to do is enter the text and the other particulars. Read on to find out how to create publications that stand out in the crowd.

What You Should Know Before You Start Working

DEFINITION

Frame: In an electronic document, a subsection that functions as a holder for text, a picture, a WordArt image, or a table. Frames do not appear in the finished product—they exist strictly to help with layout.

Publisher 2000 publications are composed of frames—either a handful if the publication is a simple one, or many dozens if the publication is a complicated newsletter or brochure. The publication in Figure 12.1 is made up of four frames that have been latched together to form a poster. On the left you can see the frame boundaries; on the right you see what the poster looks like after it is printed. Frames make laying out publications easier. When you want to move text, a picture, a table, or an image, you simply drag its frame to a new location.

To create a publication, you lay out frames on the page and fill the frames with text, images, or tables. Sounds complicated, I know, but here's some good news: You don't have to worry much about placing frames on the page if you start with one of the publication designs that Publisher provides. A *publication design,* similar to a template, is a prefabricated newsletter, brochure, catalog, flyer, letterhead, or whatever. Publisher offers many hundreds of publication designs. The frames have already been entered on the designs. Your job is to type your own words into the text frames and choose your own images for the picture frames.

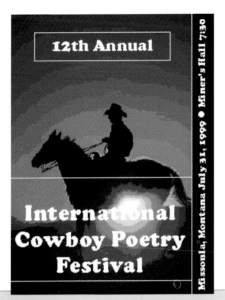
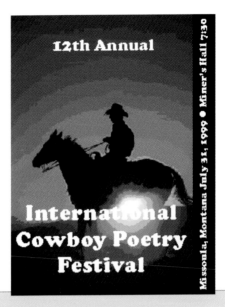

Figure 12.1: Publisher publications are laid out in frames (left), but the frames can't be seen when the publication is printed (right).

When you create a new publication, you state what kind of publication you want—a business form, flyer, or calendar, for example. After you choose a publication type, you can't go back on your decision, I'm afraid. If you ask for an advertisement, an advertisement is what you get. But you can change the color scheme of your publication or change its design. No matter how near completion your publication is, you can always remodel it with a new color scheme or design.

EXPERT ADVICE

If you're interested in publishing your document online, just select File | Save As | Web Page. Your document will be saved in HTML format—all ready for the Web—and *without* your having to fuss with any HTML code.

Creating a New Publication

TIP

To keep the Microsoft Publisher Catalog from appearing each time you start Publisher, choose Tools | Options, click the General tab in the Options dialog box, and uncheck the Use Catalog at Startup check box.

To create a new publication, you start from the Microsoft Publisher Catalog, choose the kind of publication you want, click the Start Wizard button, and answer all the questions that the Wizard asks. That's all there is to it. The important thing to remember as you create a publication is that, apart from deciding what kind of publication you want, you can always go back and reverse your decisions. No matter which design you choose, for example, you can always choose a different one later.

The Microsoft Publisher Catalog appears each time you start Publisher 2000, but if you have already started the program and you need to see the Catalog, choose File | New. As shown in Figure 12.2, start by choosing the publication you want in the Wizards list. Where

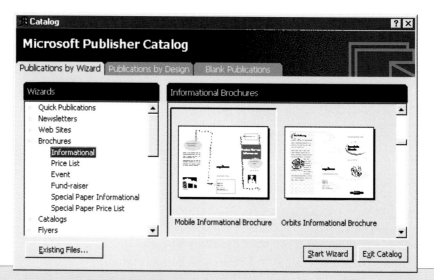

Figure 12.2: When you create a publication with the Microsoft Publisher Catalog, the layout work is done for you.

a triangle appears beside a name, you can click the name and choose from specific kinds of publications. Click a design on the right side of the dialog box and then click the Start Wizard button to proceed to the interrogation.

Which questions you have to answer depends on which kind of publication you chose. Usually, you choose a color scheme, decide whether to include information about yourself or your company, and say yes or no to including a placeholder graphic. Don't worry about getting it right the first time. As the next section of this chapter points out, you can always rethink your decisions. Keep clicking the Next button until you have fashioned a publication, and then click the Finish button.

EXPERT ADVICE

Be sure to check out the Web Site Wizard! With Publisher's prefab publication designs, you can set up your own Web site in a snap—complete with graphics, hyperlinks, sound, and even animation. (Be sure to preview your 21st-century masterpiece in Internet Explorer to make sure it looks and behaves just the way you want it to.)

Choosing a New Design or Color Scheme

When you created your publication, you chose a design and a color scheme and answered a series of questions. Suppose you made a mistake in the early going? What if you wish you had done it differently? No problem: You can click the Show Wizard button, if necessary, and start anew. Figure 12.3 shows you how to remodel a publication by revisiting the Wizard.

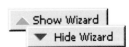

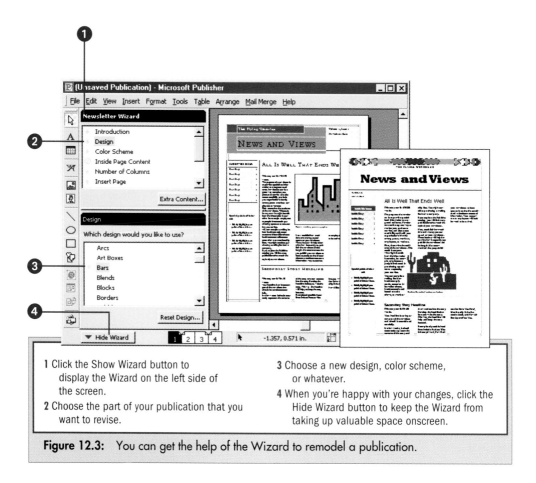

1 Click the Show Wizard button to display the Wizard on the left side of the screen.

2 Choose the part of your publication that you want to revise.

3 Choose a new design, color scheme, or whatever.

4 When you're happy with your changes, click the Hide Wizard button to keep the Wizard from taking up valuable space onscreen.

Figure 12.3:   You can get the help of the Wizard to remodel a publication.

Finding Your Way Around a Publication

The Publisher 2000 screen takes some getting used to. Looks kind of cluttered, doesn't it? And what are those blue and green lines for? To help you get acquainted with Publisher, these pages explain how to find your way around a publication and how to view the pages in different ways. Notice the buttons on the left side of the screen. They are for inserting frames and otherwise drawing on pages (you will learn about them shortly). If you have done any work in other Office 2000 programs, most of the buttons on the Standard toolbar along the top of the screen probably look familiar. You'll be glad to know that these buttons work the same way in Publisher as they do in other Office programs.

Getting a Better
View of Your Publication

As you can see in Figure 12.4, Publisher offers a bunch of different ways to get a better, or at least a different, view of your publication. Try these techniques to see precisely what your publication looks like as you work on it:

- **Zoom in and zoom out**   Because seeing the little details as well as the big picture matters so much in a publication, Publisher offers special Zoom In and Zoom Out buttons, as well as the Zoom menu. ("Learn to Zoom In and Zoom Out" in Chapter 1 explains the Zoom menu.) Click the Zoom

Zoom in and zoom out

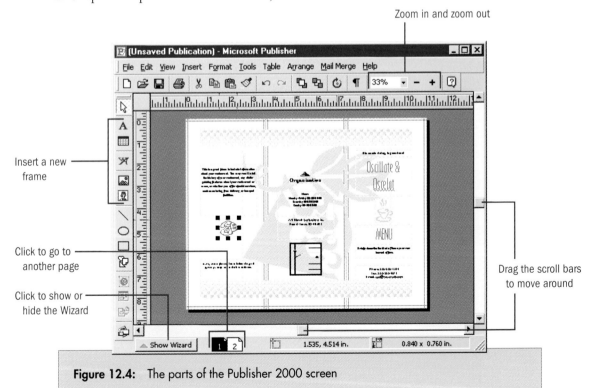

Insert a new frame

Click to go to another page

Click to show or hide the Wizard

Drag the scroll bars to move around

Figure 12.4:   The parts of the Publisher 2000 screen

buttons to quickly peer at or lean away from a document. You can also choose View | Zoom and choose one of the intriguing options on the submenu. For example, select an object and choose View | Zoom | Selected Objects when you want to focus on a single object.

- **Hide or display the rulers** Rulers are nice—they tell you precisely where you are on the page. But they also take up valuable space onscreen. To hide or display them, choose View | Rulers.

- **Hide or display the boundaries and guides** *Boundaries* (the blue lines) and *guides* (the green lines) show you where the page margins are and help you align frames on the page. But when you want to see what your publication will look like after it is printed, you have to hide the lines. To display or hide boundaries and guides, choose View | Show (or Hide) Boundaries and Guides. Here you see what the same page looks like when you can and can't see the boundaries and guides:

Going from Page to Page and Place to Place

As shown in Figure 12.4, you can go from place to place in a Publisher publication with these techniques:

- **Drag a scroll bar** Drag the horizontal scroll to go from side to side or the vertical scroll bar to go from page to page.

- **Click a Page Navigation button** In a publication with more than one page, click a Page Navigation button to go to a

different page. You can also choose View | Go to Page (or press
CTRL-G) and enter a page number in the Go to Page dialog box.

Frames for Laying Out the Pages

As "What You Should Know Before You Start Working" explained at
the beginning of this chapter, Publisher 2000 publications are made of
frames—text frames, table frames, WordArt frames, picture frames,
and clip art frames. In order to enter text or a publication in a
document, you have to enter it in the confines of a frame. These pages
explain everything you need to know about frames. You'll find out
how to insert a new frame, adjust the size of a frame, align frames, and
place borders around frames. You'll also learn how to make frames
and the words or images inside them overlap.

If you have any doubts where a frame is located in a document,
click. Square selection handles appear on the sides and corners of the
frame. As long as the selection handles appear, as shown here, you can
change a frame's size or adjust its position.

Inserting a New Frame

To insert a new frame, click one of the five frame tool buttons—Text
Frame Tool, Table Frame Tool, WordArt Frame Tool, Picture Frame
Tool, or Clip Gallery Tool—along the left side of the screen, click in
your publication, and drag. As you drag, you form a rectangle. Release
the mouse button when the frame is the right size. (The next section
in this chapter explains how to adjust the size and position of a frame.)

Do the following to create a text, table, WordArt, picture, or clip art frame:

In Chapter 2, "Entering and Formatting Text" explains the Formatting buttons in detail.

- **Text frame for articles and stories**   Click in the frame and start typing. You can call on the Font and Font Size menus to change the look and size of the text. You can call on the other buttons on the Formatting toolbar as well. (See "Entering the Text on the Page" later in this chapter to learn how you can enter the text in Word 2000.)

- **Table frame for tables**   You see the Create Table dialog box as soon as you create a table frame. Choose the number of rows and columns you want and, in the Table Format list, a layout for your table in the dialog box. Then click OK. After you have entered the text in the table grid, click outside the table to see what it will look like when you print it.

In Chapter 2, "Decorating a File with WordArt" explains what WordArt is.

- **WordArt frame for WordArt images**   The WordArt window opens when you create a WordArt frame. From the Shape drop-down menu on the left side of the toolbar, choose a shape. Then enter the text in the Enter Your Text Here box. As you experiment with fonts, font sizes, and the other commands, watch the text in the WordArt frame to see how its appearance changes. Click outside the WordArt frame when you are done. To return to the WordArt window, double-click the WordArt frame.

- **Picture frame for artwork you've stored on disk**   Double-click the frame after you create it. Then find the artwork you want to import in the Insert Picture dialog box and click the Insert button.

SHORTCUT
If you want to replace one clip art image with another, double-click a clip art frame to open the Clip Art dialog box.

- **Clip art frame for clip art images**   The Insert Clip Art dialog box appears as soon as you create a clip art frame. Find and insert a clip art image in the dialog box. (See "Inserting a Clip Art Image into a File" in Chapter 2.)

Adjusting the Size and Position of Frames

After you click a frame and can see the selection handles, you are ready to change the size of the frame or adjust its position on the page:

- **Changing the size of a frame** Move the pointer over a selection handle and start dragging when you see the Resize icon. If you are dealing with anything but a text frame, be careful about dragging a selection handle on the side of the frame. Dragging a side handle changes the frame's size as well as its proportions. Images can blur or become distorted when you change their proportions.

- **Changing the position of a frame** Move the pointer onto the frame, and click and drag when you see the moving van (cute touch, the moving van). Then release the mouse button when the frame is in the right position.

Putting Borders and Color Backgrounds on Frames

Select a frame and follow these instructions to give it background color or a border:

- **Background color** Click the Fill Color button and select a color on the drop-down menu. Choose No Fill to remove the background color or to create no background color so that frames below the frame you are dealing with can show through.

- **Color for the border** Click the Line Color button and choose a color from the drop-down menu. You must have chosen a line for the border in order to choose a color.

- **Line or dashed-line border** Click the Line Style button to open the drop-down menu and choose a line. Or choose More Styles to open the Border Style dialog box and choose from many different lines or put borders on one, two, or three sides of the frame.

Layout and Ruler Guides to Help with Precision Layouts

Choosing View | Show Boundaries and Guides (or pressing CTRL-SHIFT-O) displays blue *layout guides* and green *ruler guides* on the page. These guides are meant to help you line up frames. When you first display them, layout guides appear along the margins, but you can make them appear in a grid throughout the page if you are working on a catalog, for example, that requires precision layout work. As for ruler guides, you can draw them across the page wherever you please to help with lining up frames.

Figure 12.5 shows how to draw a series of layout guides on the page to make lining up frames easier. Follow these steps to draw a ruler guide across the page and get help with layouts that way:

1. Choose View | Go to Background (or press CTRL-M). All frames are stripped from the page and you see only the layout guides and ruler guides, if you already drew one or two of them.

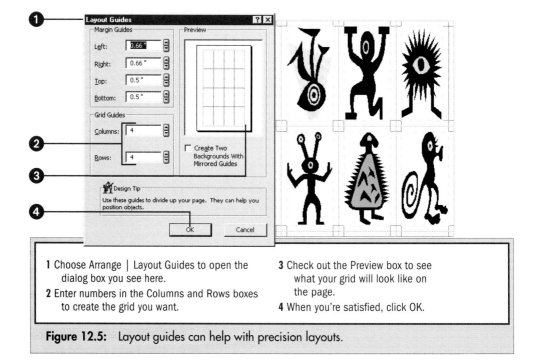

1 Choose Arrange | Layout Guides to open the dialog box you see here.
2 Enter numbers in the Columns and Rows boxes to create the grid you want.

3 Check out the Preview box to see what your grid will look like on the page.
4 When you're satisfied, click OK.

Figure 12.5: Layout guides can help with precision layouts.

2. Choose Arrange | Ruler Guides.

3. On the submenu, choose Add Horizontal Ruler Guide to draw a side-to-side line on the page, or choose Add Vertical Ruler Guide to draw a line that goes up and down the page. The ruler guide, a green line, appears on the page background.

4. Hold down the SHIFT key, move the pointer over the line, and click and drag when you see the Adjust pointer.

ADJUST

5. Release the mouse button when the guide is where you want it.

6. Choose View | Go to Foreground (or press CTRL-M).

There's your green ruler guide. Use it to help line up the frames. If you can't see it, choose View | Boundaries and Guides (or press CTRL-SHIFT-O). To remove the ruler guides, choose Arrange | Ruler Guides | Clear All Ruler Guides.

When Frames Overlap: Telling Publisher Which One to Put in the Foreground

When frames overlap, you have to tell Publisher which frame goes in front of the other. And you are hereby invited to overlap frames, since overlapping frames are artful and look good on the page. Figure 12.6

Figure 12.6: Detailed view of a newsletter. By overlapping text frames and other frames, you can create an artful presentation.

Later in this chapter, "Making Text Wrap Around a Picture or Other Kind of Frame" explains how to control what text does when it bumps against a frame.

shows a small portion of a newsletter. If you look closely, you can see seven different text frames in the figure. Overlapping frames like these make for a sophisticated layout.

Follow these steps to place one frame behind or in front of another:

1. Click to select the frame.

2. Choose a command to move it backward or forward in the stack:

   - **Put it on top**   Click the Bring to Front button or press F6. The frame appears above all others.

   - **Put it on the bottom**   Click the Send to Back button (or press SHIFT-F6). All frames that overlap the frame you clicked appear above the frame.

   - **Bring it toward the front**   Choose Arrange | Bring Forward. Choose this command when you are dealing with more than two frames and you want the frame you clicked to rise in the stack but not appear on top.

   - **Send it toward the back**   Choose Arrange | Send Backward. Choose this command when you are dealing with more than two frames and you want to send the frame into the background.

EXPERT ADVICE

Suppose you want a clip art image to appear behind text. In Figure 12.1, for example, the words "International Cowboy Poetry Festival" are superimposed on a picture of a cowboy and his horse. To perform that trick, place a text frame over a picture or clip art frame. Then select the text frame, click the Fill Color button, and choose No Fill. In effect, "no fill" means that no background color appears behind the text, which allows the image to show through.

Entering and Laying Out the Text

After you've created a new publication, the next step is to make it your own. In the case of a newsletter, you have a lot of writing to do. You need to replace the placeholder text with your own writing. If you are putting together a sign, you have but a handful of words to write.

These pages explain how to enter the text for your publication, make text jump from text frame to text frame, and make text wrap around a picture or other image.

In Chapter 2, "Entering and Formatting Text" explains how to choose a new font for text, change the size of text, and realign text.

Entering the Text on the Page

When you are dealing with a headline or other piece of prominent text, select the placeholder text that is already there and enter your own text. That's easy enough. But when you need to edit or write a long story in a brochure or newsletter, follow these steps to do the work in Word 2000:

1. Click in the text frame where the text is.
2. Choose Edit | Edit Story in Microsoft Word. Microsoft Word opens, and you see the placeholder text in its entirety.
3. Delete the text and enter your own text. You can call on all of the Word commands to edit the text. You can also copy text from elsewhere into the Word document.
4. When you are finished writing, choose File | Close & Return to (Publication).

EXPERT ADVICE

Many publications include addresses, phone numbers, and company names. In some cases, the address information appears in many different places. Suppose that your address and phone number change. You can laboriously find that information in your publication, delete it, and carefully enter it again, or you can choose Edit | Personal Information. Choosing that command opens the Personal Information dialog box, which offers convenient text boxes for entering addresses and phone numbers. The information you enter will be transcribed and put in the publication you are working on after you click the Update button.

Making Text Jump from Frame to Frame

One of the difficulties of working with newsletters and brochures is that text usually doesn't fit in the text frame (or the text frames if the article travels from text frame to text frame). When text doesn't fit, the Text in Overflow icon appears at the bottom of the text frame.

What to do? One way to handle the problem is to edit the text—in other words, to snip out a word or sentence here and there—to make it fit. You can also choose Format | AutoFit Text | Shrink Text on Overflow to make the text shrink just enough to fit in the frame or frames. Or you can solve the problem by creating a new text frame and making the overflow text travel there.

Create another text frame for the overflow text and follow these steps to make text flow into your new text frame:

1. Click the text frame in which the Text in Overflow icon appears.

2. Choose Tools | Connect Text Frame.

3. Click the Connect Text Frames button. The pointer turns into a pitcher.

4. Click in the text frame where the story is to be continued.

When text travels from frame to frame, the Go to Previous Frame and Go to Next Frame buttons appear above and below the frames. Click a button to go to the previous or next frame in the chain. To break the chain, click the text frame that is to be the last in the chain and then click the Disconnect Text Frames button.

Making Text Wrap Around a Picture or Other Kind of Frame

Wrap text around a clip art image, picture, or WordArt image, and you get a very elegant layout. Figure 12.7 shows text that has been wrapped around a clip art image. Looks nice, does it not? Wrapping text may be the easiest way to impress innocent bystanders with your layout prowess. Text can be wrapped to a frame or to a picture. As Figure 12.7 shows, text wrapped to a picture follows the contours of the picture, whereas text wrapped to a frame runs flush with the frame.

Follow these instructions to wrap text around a picture frame, clip art frame, or WordArt frame:

TIP

To make text come very close to a picture, wrap text to the picture and then click the Edit Irregular Wrap button. Many square selection handles appear around the image. Drag the handles to move the text closer to the image.

- **Wrap text to the frame** Move the text frame behind the other frame and click the Wrap Text to Frame button. Click the text frame and then click the Send to Back button to move the text frame behind the other frame.

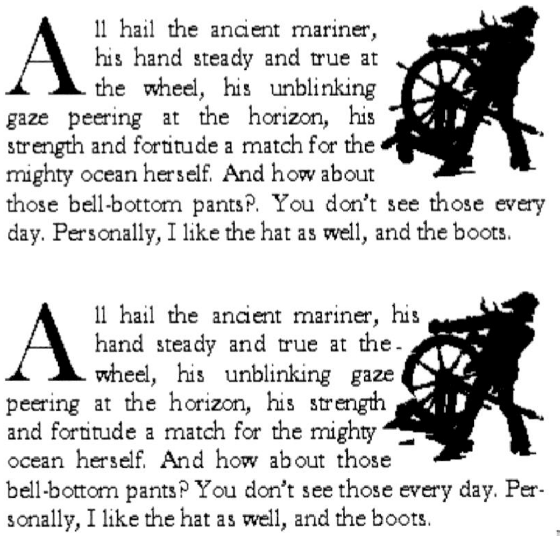

Figure 12.7: You can wrap your text to the frame (top) or to the picture (bottom).

- **Wrap text to the picture**   Move the text frame behind the other frame and click the Wrap Text to Picture button.

Inserting and Removing Pages

If you read "Going from Page to Page and Place to Place" earlier in this chapter, you know that you can click a Page Navigation button to go from page to page in a publication. But suppose you have too many pages or you need to add a page or two. Follow these instructions to insert or remove a page:

- **Inserting a new page**   Click a Page Navigation button to move to the place where you want to insert pages, and then choose Insert | Page (or press CTRL-SHIFT-N). In the Insert Page dialog box, enter the number of pages you want to add, and click an option button to put the new pages before or after the page you are on. Then, under Options, choose an option to tell Publisher 2000 what to put on the new page or pages, and click OK.

- **Removing a page**   Go to the page you want to remove, choose Edit | Delete Page, and click OK in the confirmation box.

Decorating Your Publication

The last part of this chapter is devoted to the Project to Beautify Publications, a joint effort of Osborne/McGraw-Hill and myself, aimed at making publications less bland and more original. I've noticed, on the bulletin boards and lampposts in my neighborhood, that the rummage sale and lost pet notices look a little rough around the edges. The neighbors are using sophisticated software to produce their notices, but they're not using it well. They are relying on templates, and as a result their documents tend to look very much alike. These pages explain a couple of simple tricks for making publications more sophisticated.

In Chapter 2, "Decorating Files with Clip Art and WordArt" explains how to place a clip art image or WordArt image in a file.

Getting Objects from the Design Gallery

The Design Gallery is a collection of objects—logos, pull quotes, accent boxes, and thingamajigs—that you can throw into your publications. Figure 12.8 shows how to put a Design Gallery object

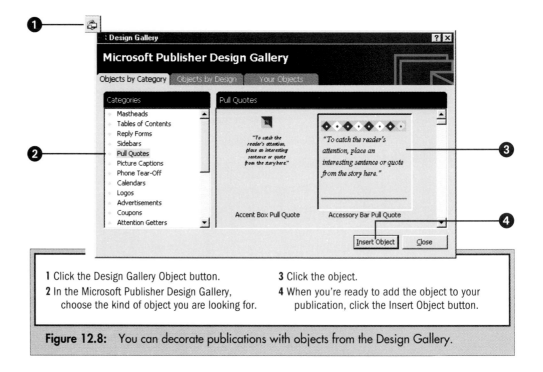

1 Click the Design Gallery Object button.
2 In the Microsoft Publisher Design Gallery, choose the kind of object you are looking for.

3 Click the object.
4 When you're ready to add the object to your publication, click the Insert Object button.

Figure 12.8: You can decorate publications with objects from the Design Gallery.

into a publication. After you've placed the object, you can change its size or shift its position by using the same techniques you use with other objects.

Rotating and Flipping Objects

Readers turn their heads when they see an object—a text box, clip art image, or other image—that has been rotated or flipped. In my opinion, being able to turn text on its ear is one of the neatest things going in Publisher. You can even turn text upside down. Select a frame and follow these instructions to turn it on its side:

- **Click the Rotate Right or Rotate Left button**   Each time you click one of these buttons, the frame rotates by 90 degrees.
- **Rotate the frame by dragging**   Hold down the ALT key and move the pointer over a corner selection handle. When you see the Rotate pointer, start dragging.

In Chapter 2, "Handling 'Objects' in Files" explains how to manipulate objects.

Installing Office 2000

INCLUDES

- **Installing Office**
- **Customizing the Installation to Suit Your Needs**
- **Reinstalling or Removing Office**

This appendix describes how to install and reinstall the different programs in Office 2000. Microsoft has adopted a new installation technique, as you will learn shortly. This appendix describes how to install the programs for the first time, how to pick and choose what you want to install, and how to reinstall one or a handful of the Office programs and features.

The New Installation Technique

With Office 2000, Microsoft has introduced a new technique for installing the different programs and Office tools. Instead of installing all of the programs, you can decide for yourself which ones to install. And instead of installing a program in its entirety, you can install only the essential parts (I explain how in this appendix). The same goes for the Office tools—you can install as many as you want. Later, if you choose a menu command or Office tool that hasn't been installed on your computer, you see a message box like the ones shown in Figure A.1. The message box tells you in so many words that the command you chose has not been installed on your computer, but

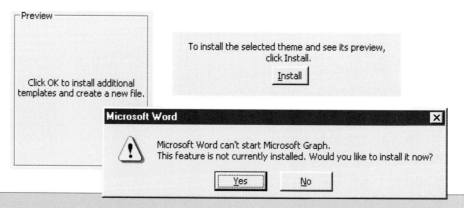

Figure A.1: Instead of installing an Office program all at once, you can install the essential parts first, and then install other parts as you need them.

that you can install it by clicking the OK button, the Install button, the Yes button, or whatever the button's name happens to be.

What the message box doesn't mention is that you need the Office 2000 CD to install the command. Before clicking the OK, Install, or Yes button, put the Office 2000 CD in your CD-ROM drive. When you click the button, Office copies program codes from the CD to your computer so that you can execute the command. The installation procedure takes only a few seconds. Without the CD, however, you can't install the program codes for the command you want.

Practically speaking, you need to keep the Office 2000 CD at your side when you use an Office program. You need the CD in case a program encounters a command that it can't carry out. How to put this delicately? The new installation technique has made it fairly impossible to borrow a copy of Office from someone else and install it on your computer. Since you need the installation CD at all times, you can't simply borrow Aunt Enid's copy of Office for a few days and load it on your computer. You can try your best to load all of the Office 2000 components you need on your computer from the start (see "Custom Installation: Choosing Which Features to Install," later in this appendix), but installing all the features requires a lot of disk space and is not practical for most people.

Before You Install Office 2000...

Before you install Office 2000, close all programs that are open. Microsoft also recommends backing up all important files and documents. While writing this book I installed and reinstalled Office many times and never lost a file or document, but I want you to know what Microsoft recommends.

Your computer must meet these requirements in order to install Office:

- An *x*86-compatible computer that meets minimum hardware requirements for Microsoft Windows 95, Windows 98, or Windows NT 4.0
- Windows or Windows NT

CAUTION

If you run the Windows NT operating system, you must have installed Service Pack 3 or Service Pack 4 before you can run an Office 2000 program. To find out which NT version you have and which Service Pack is installed, click the Start button, choose Tools | Windows NT Diagnostics, and click the Version tab of the Windows NT Diagnostics dialog box. The Version tab lists the Windows NT version you are running and the most recent Windows NT Service Pack on your system.

- A Pentium chip
- 32MB RAM or better (recommended)
- At least 280MB hard disk space
- A CD-ROM drive

Installing Office 2000

Follow these steps to install Office 2000:

1. Close all programs, if any are open.

2. Put the CD in the CD-ROM drive. In a moment, you see the Welcome to the Microsoft Office 2000 Installation Wizard dialog box. Twiddle your thumbs while you wait for the Wizard to prepare to install Office.

3. Enter your name and other personal information, as well as the CD key. (You will find this number in the Office 2000 package.) The User Name, Initial, and Organization information you enter here appears by default in many different places in the Office programs. For example, if you're working in Word later and choose Insert | AutoText | Signature, the name you've entered in the User Name box will be entered automatically.

4. Click Next.

5. Read the user agreement, and click the I Accept the Terms button.

6. Click Next. A dialog box offers three installation choices (or two if an earlier version of Office is not already installed on your computer):

   - **Upgrade Now** Removes previous versions of Office programs and replaces them with the newest versions. You get roughly the same installation you had before, except that newer editions of the Office programs are installed on your computer. If you click this button, the installation procedure begins right away.

TIP

If you don't see the Installation Wizard dialog box, follow these instructions to display it: Click the Start button and choose Settings | Control Panel. In the Control Panel window, double-click the Add/Remove Programs icon. In the Add/Remove Programs Properties dialog box, click the Install button. Click Next in the following dialog box, and then click the Finish button.

- **Typical**   The essential parts of the Office programs are installed on your computer. When you try to use a feature that hasn't been installed, you see a message box similar to the ones shown in Figure A.1 and you are given the chance to install the feature. I recommend choosing this option. As long as your Office 2000 CD is handy, you can simply install features as you need them.

- **Customize**   You pick and choose which parts of the Office programs to install. (For further information on this option, see the upcoming section, "Custom Installation: Choosing Which Features to Install.")

7. Click one of these three installation buttons.

8. A dialog box appears asking where on your computer to install the Office programs. By default, Office programs are installed in the C:\Program Files\Microsoft Office folder. Unless you know what you're doing or have an ulterior motive for installing Office in another folder, simply click Next. The Office programs will be installed in the default folder.

TIP

As you decide which features to install, be sure to take note of the Size figures at the bottom of the Installation dialog box. The figures tell you how much disk space is needed by the features you are installing, and how much free disk space is available on your computer.

The installation can take 20 to 30 minutes, depending on how many components are involved. If you decided to pick and choose which components to install, keep reading…

Custom Installation: Choosing Which Features to Install

In a custom installation, you decide for yourself which Office 2000 features to install on your computer. Figure A.2 shows you how:

- **Run from My Computer**   Loads the feature onto your computer.

- **Run All from My Computer**   Loads all the features in a set of features onto your computer. For example, if you click the icon

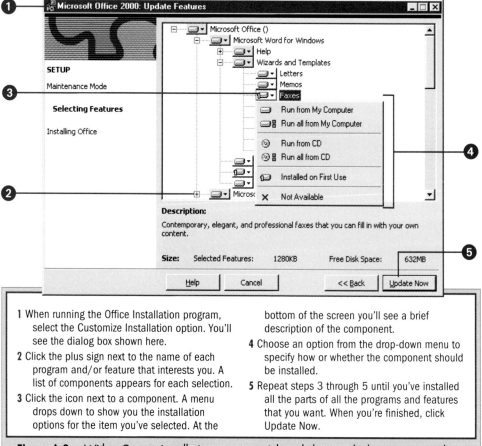

1. When running the Office Installation program, select the Customize Installation option. You'll see the dialog box shown here.

2. Click the plus sign next to the name of each program and/or feature that interests you. A list of components appears for each selection.

3. Click the icon next to a component. A menu drops down to show you the installation options for the item you've selected. At the bottom of the screen you'll see a brief description of the component.

4. Choose an option from the drop-down menu to specify how or whether the component should be installed.

5. Repeat steps 3 through 5 until you've installed all the parts of all the programs and features that you want. When you're finished, click Update Now.

Figure A.2: With a Custom installation, you can pick and choose which programs and components to install on your computer.

beside Microsoft Word for Windows and choose Run All from My Computer, all of the Word components are installed.

- **Run from CD** Runs the feature from the Office CD. This technique is not recommended, since running a program from a CD is markedly slower than running it from your hard drive. What's more, you then have to leave the CD in the drive to run an Office program.

- **Run All from CD**   Runs all the features in a set of features from the CD instead of from your hard drive. This technique is likewise not recommended.
- **Installed on First Use**   Does not install the feature on your computer but gives you the opportunity to install it when you choose it from a command menu or dialog box. When you try to activate the feature, you see a message box like the ones in Figure A.1.

Reinstalling (or Removing) Office 2000

Reinstall Office 2000 when you think the program files have been corrupted or you want to install or remove programs or features from your computer. To reinstall, insert the CD in your CD-ROM drive. In a moment, you see a dialog box for reinstalling Office. Choose one of these options in the dialog box:

- **Repair Office**   Click this button to repeat the last installation you made. All of the programs and features you chose the last time are reinstalled on your computer.
- **Add or Remove Features**   Click this button and you see the dialog box shown in Figure A.2, where you can pick and choose which programs and features to install. See the previous section in this appendix for information on the options in this dialog box.
- **Remove Office**   Click this button to remove Office from your computer.

Index

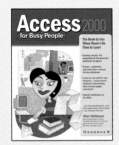